PCs
FOR
DUMMIES®
9TH EDITION

The Internet FOR DUMMIES
9th Edition

PCs FOR DUMMIES
9th Edition

Cheat Sheet

Getting Hooked Up

Plugging Things into Mr. PC

Want to know what plugs in where when setting up your computer? Check out the following figure.

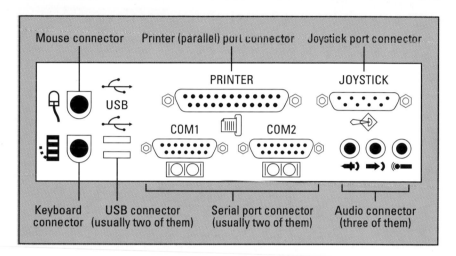

Choosing an Internet Service Provider

An important task in your quest for Internet access is picking an ISP (Internet Service Provider). You can find the names of ISPs by looking in your local Yellow Pages or newspaper ads, by asking friends or the public library's research librarian, or by checking the Web site net.gurus.com/isp.

When you're calling around to different providers, here are some good questions to ask:

- How much is unlimited dialup Internet access? (If that seems expensive, ask how much 100 hours per month costs.)
- Do you offer DSL accounts? (These faster connections are more expensive, but more fun.)
- Do you offer dialup access numbers that are local calls in my area?
- What technical support and extra help for beginners do you offer?
- How busy are the access lines? (If you have a dialup connection, getting online during peak hours can be difficult.)

- How many e-mail accounts will I get with my service? (All ISPs give you one mailbox; some offer five or more, so each member of your family can have a separate e-mail address.)
- Do you offer Web server space, and if so, how much space? (This is handy if you decide to create your own Web page. Server space of 5MB or 10MB is more than enough for a simple Web site.)

Knowing Your PC's Windows Desktop

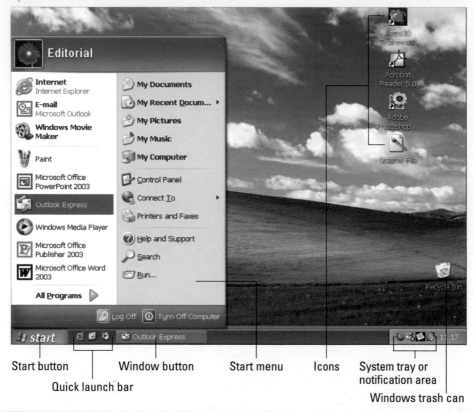

Start button

Quick launch bar

Window button

Start menu

Icons

System tray or notification area

Windows trash can

Navigating the Web

Click buttons to move between pages

Click buttons to see other pages

Click links to other spots online

Type a Web address here and click Go

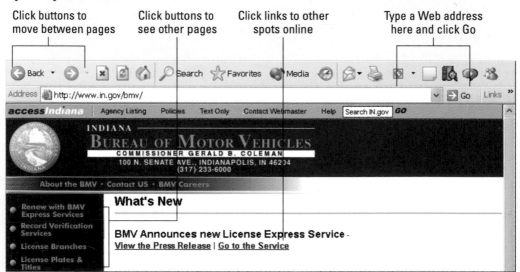

PCs

FOR

DUMMIES®

9TH EDITION

by Dan Gookin

WILEY

Wiley Publishing, Inc.

PCs For Dummies®, 9th Edition

Published by
Wiley Publishing, Inc.
111 River Street
Hoboken, NJ 07030

www.wiley.com

Copyright © 2003 by Wiley Publishing, Inc., Indianapolis, Indiana

Published by Wiley Publishing, Inc., Indianapolis, Indiana

Published simultaneously in Canada

No part of this publication may be reproduced, stored in a retrieval system or transmitted in any form or by any means, electronic, mechanical, photocopying, recording, scanning or otherwise, except as permitted under Sections 107 or 108 of the 1976 United States Copyright Act, without either the prior written permission of the Publisher, or authorization through payment of the appropriate per-copy fee to the Copyright Clearance Center, 222 Rosewood Drive, Danvers, MA 01923, (978) 750-8400, fax (978) 646-8700. Requests to the Publisher for permission should be addressed to the Legal Department, Wiley Publishing, Inc., 10475 Crosspoint Blvd., Indianapolis, IN 46256, (317) 572-3447, fax (317) 572-4447, e-mail: permcoordinator@wiley.com.

Trademarks: Wiley, the Wiley Publishing logo, For Dummies, the Dummies Man logo, A Reference for the Rest of Us!, The Dummies Way, Dummies Daily, The Fun and Easy Way, Dummies.com and related trade dress are trademarks or registered trademarks of John Wiley & Sons, Inc. and/or its affiliates in the United States and other countries, and may not be used without written permission. All other trademarks are the property of their respective owners. Wiley Publishing, Inc., is not associated with any product or vendor mentioned in this book.

For general information on our other products and services or to obtain technical support, please contact our Customer Care Department within the U.S. at 800-762-2974, outside the U.S. at 317-572-3993, or fax 317-572-4002.

Wiley also publishes its books in a variety of electronic formats. Some content that appears in print may not be available in electronic books.

Library of Congress Control Number: 2003105860

ISBN: 0-7645-4074-2

Manufactured in the United States of America

10 9 8 7 6 5 4 3 2 1

9B/RW/QZ/QT/IN

WILEY is a trademark of Wiley Publishing, Inc.

About the Author

Dan Gookin has been writing about technology for 20 years. He has contributed articles to numerous high-tech magazines and written more than 90 books about personal computing technology, many of them accurate.

He combines his love of writing with his interest in technology to create books that are informative and entertaining, but not boring. Having sold more than 14 million titles translated into more than 30 languages, Dan can attest that his method of crafting computer tomes does seem to work.

Perhaps Dan's most famous title is the original *DOS For Dummies,* published in 1991. It became the world's fastest-selling computer book, at one time moving more copies per week than the *New York Times* number-one best seller (although, because it's a reference book, it could not be listed on the *NYT* best seller list). That book spawned the entire line of *For Dummies* books, which remains a publishing phenomenon to this day.

Dan's most recent titles include *PCs For Dummies,* 9th Edition; *Buying a Computer For Dummies,* 2004 Edition; *Troubleshooting Your PC For Dummies; Dan Gookin's Naked Windows XP;* and *Dan Gookin's Naked Office.* He also publishes a free weekly computer newsletter, "Weekly Wambooli Salad," full of tips, how-tos, and computer news. He also maintains the vast and helpful Web page www.wambooli.com.

Dan holds a degree in communications and visual arts from the University of California, San Diego. He lives in the Pacific Northwest, where he enjoys spending time with his four boys in the gentle woods of Idaho.

Publisher's Acknowledgments

We're proud of this book; please send us your comments through our online registration form located at www.dummies.com/register/.

Some of the people who helped bring this book to market include the following:

Acquisitions, Editorial, and Media Development

Project Editor: Rebecca Whitney

Acquisitions Editor: Gregory Croy

Technical Editor: James F. Kelly

Editorial Manager: Carol Sheehan

Media Development Supervisor: Richard Graves

Editorial Assistant: Amanda M. Foxworth

Cartoons: Rich Tennant (www.the5thwave.com)

Production

Project Coordinator: Erin Smith

Layout and Graphics: Seth Conley, Carrie Foster, Joyce Haughey, LeAndra Hosier, Lynsey Osborn, Shae Wilson

Proofreaders: Laura Albert, David Faust, Nancy L. Reinhardt, Brian Walls

Indexer: TECHBOOKS Production Services

Publishing and Editorial for Technology Dummies

Richard Swadley, Vice President and Executive Group Publisher

Andy Cummings, Vice President and Publisher

Mary C. Corder, Editorial Director

Publishing for Consumer Dummies

Diane Graves Steele, Vice President and Publisher

Joyce Pepple, Acquisitions Director

Composition Services

Gerry Fahey, Vice President of Production Services

Debbie Stailey, Director of Composition Services

Contents at a Glance

Table of Contents

Introduction

● ●

*W*elcome to *PCs For Dummies,* the nearly all-new 9th Edition, fully updated for the twenty-first century. This is the book that answers the question "How does a computer turn a smart person like you into a dummy?"

Computers are useful, yes. And, a fair number of people — heaven help them — fall in love with computers. But the rest of us are left sitting dumb and numb in front of the box. It's not that using a computer is beyond the range of our intellect; it's that no one has ever bothered to sit down and explain things in human terms. Until now.

This book talks about using a computer in friendly and human — and often irreverent — terms. Nothing is sacred here. Electronics can be praised by others. This book focuses on you and your needs. In this book, you'll discover everything you need to know about your computer without painful jargon or the prerequisite master's degree in engineering. And, you'll have fun.

What's New in This Edition?

I'm pleased to announce that this book contains about 80 percent new material from the preceding edition. Yes, technology has leapt forward that much in the past two years.

This edition of *PCs For Dummies* is the first one in quite a while that concentrates on only one operating system — Windows XP, both Pro and Home editions. Aside from my updating the book to be specific to Windows XP, you'll find here the following information that has never been in a previous edition of *PCs For Dummies*:

- Full coverage of PC power options, including hibernation
- More information on key places to control Windows XP
- More detailed Zip disk information and information on organizing and manipulating files in Windows
- Full tutorials on burning CD-Rs and creating musical CDs
- New information on broadband technology and modems and their connections

✔ A networking chapter, complete with new home and wireless networking information (back after missing from two previous editions)

✔ Updated information on scanning and digital photography

✔ Advice about dealing with Internet woes, such as spyware, pop-up windows, and viruses

✔ Complete information on downloading files from the Internet

✔ General up-to-date and current information on all aspects of PC technology, hardware, and software

Gone from this edition is troubleshooting and problem-solving information, which is now in my new book, *Troubleshooting Your PC For Dummies* (Wiley Publishing, Inc.). That book is more involved with troubleshooting than I would ever have room here to explain. I recommend it as an ideal companion to *PCs For Dummies*.

As in years past, I present all the information in this book in a sane, soothing, and gentle tone that calms even the most panicked computerphobe.

Where to Start

This book is designed so that you can pick it up at any point and start reading — like a reference. It has 29 chapters. Each chapter covers a specific aspect of the computer — turning it on, using a printer, using software, and kicking it, for example. Each chapter is divided into self-contained nuggets of information — sections — all relating to the major theme of the chapter. Sample sections you may find include

✔ Turning the darn thing off

✔ What is virtual memory?

✔ Adjusting the monitor's display

✔ Using a network printer

✔ Really, really clearing the history list

✔ Look, Ma! It's an e-mail attachment!

You don't have to memorize anything in this book. Nothing about a computer is memorable. Each section is designed so that you can read the information quickly, digest what you have read, and then put down the book and get on with using the computer. If anything technical crops up, you'll be alerted to its presence so that you can cleanly avoid it.

Conventions Used in This Book

This book is a reference. Start with the topic you want more information about; look for it in the table of contents or in the index. Turn to the area of interest and read the information you need. Then, with the information in your head, you can quickly close the book and freely perform whatever task you need — without reading anything else.

Whenever I describe a message or information on the screen, it looks like this:

```
This is a message onscreen.
```

If you have to type something, it looks like this:

> **Type me**

You type the text **Type me** as shown. You'll be told when and whether to press the Enter key.

Windows menu commands are shown like this:

> Choose File⇨Exit.

This line means to choose the File menu and then choose the Exit command. The underlined letters are shortcut keys, which I explain in Chapter 3.

Key combinations you may have to type are shown like this:

> Ctrl+S

This line means to press and hold the Ctrl (control) key, type an *S*, and then release the Ctrl key. It works just like the way pressing Shift+S on the keyboard produces an uppercase *S*. Same deal, different shift key.

What You Don't Need to Read

Lots of technical information is involved with using a computer. To better insulate you from it, I have enclosed this type of material in sidebars clearly marked as technical information. You don't have to read that stuff. Often, it's just a complex explanation of information already discussed in the chapter. Reading that information will only teach you something substantial about your computer, which is not the goal here.

Foolish Assumptions

I'm going to make some admittedly foolish assumptions about you: You have a computer, and you use it somehow to do something. You use a PC (or are planning on it) and will be using Windows XP, either the Home or Pro version, as your PC's operating system or main program.

This book refers to the menu that appears when you click or activate the Start button as the *Start panel*. The Programs menu on the Start panel is referred to as *Programs,* though it may say *All Programs* on your screen.

I prefer to use the Windows Control Panel in Classic view. Click the item Switch to Classic View if you're using the Control Panel in Category view. Otherwise, instructions later in the book will be confusing.

This book doesn't cover any previous versions of Windows. When I refer to *Windows* in this book, Windows XP is implied. This book covers only those items common to both Windows XP Home and Pro.

Other editions of this book cover previous operating systems. Refer to the 8th Edition for coverage of Windows 98, Windows Me, Windows 2000, and Windows XP. Windows 95 is covered in this book's 6th and 7th editions. For coverage of DOS or earlier editions of Windows, refer to *DOS For Dummies,* 3rd Edition (Wiley Publishing, Inc.).

Icons Used in This Book

This icon alerts you to needless technical information — drivel I added because I just felt like explaining something totally unnecessary (a hard habit to break). Feel free to skip over anything tagged with this little picture.

This icon usually indicates helpful advice or an insight that makes using the computer interesting. For example, when pouring acid over your computer, be sure to wear a protective apron and gloves and goggles.

Ummm, I forgot what this one means.

This icon indicates that you need to be careful with the information presented; usually, it's a reminder for you not to do something.

Getting in Touch with the Author

My e-mail address is listed here in case you want to write me on the Internet:

```
dgookin@wambooli.com
```

Yes, that is my address, and I personally respond to every e-mail message. I cannot, however, troubleshoot or fix your PC. Remember that you paid others for your technical support and you should use them.

You can also visit my Web site, which is chock-full of helpful support pages, bonus information, games, and fun, interactive forums:

```
http://www.wambooli.com/
```

This book's specific page is at this address:

```
http://www.wambooli.com/help/pc/
```

If you want more information, free tips, weekly news, and updates, I encourage you to subscribe to my free weekly newsletter, "Weekly Wambooli Salad." Read more about the Salad at this address:

```
http://www.wambooli.com/newsletter/weekly/
```

Where to Go from Here

With this book in hand, you're now ready to go out and conquer your PC. Start by looking through the table of contents or the index. Find a topic and turn to the page indicated, and you're ready to go. Also, feel free to write in this book, fill in the blanks, dog-ear the pages, and do anything that would make a librarian blanch. Enjoy.

Part I
The Basic Stuff You Need to Know

The 5th Wave   By Rich Tennant

Oh come on— how fatal can it be?

FATAL ERROR

In this part . . .

Chris walks up to the counter at the convenience store. Normally, Steve, the counter guy, can tell what a customer wants. But Chris is a puzzle: Chris has showered recently. Chris doesn't dress in a white lab coat. Chris doesn't request the 128-ounce vat of Jolt Cola. Yet, what Chris wants is a computer; "I'll take that PC and monitor and a raft of software." Surprised at not recognizing a computer customer, Steve hands over the goods.

Say hello to today: The computer is a commodity. It's no longer that special office equipment, scientists' tool, or hobbyists' toy. No, the computer is a gizmo you can pick up off the shelf at the department store, right next to the TV sets, washing machines, and football-size vacuum cleaners that break when you drop them. Yet, despite its ubiquity, the PC remains a mysterious device, full of intrigue and obscurity. Fortunately, with this book in your hands, the PC shall remain a mystery no more.

Chapter 1

Hello, Computer
(Please Don't Explode!)

*N*o, your computer will not explode. If it did, don't you think it would make the nightly news? The newsfolk would announce "Another random computer blast today," and they'd shake their perfectly coiffed hairdos. "I just don't know why people keep buying them, Jane." "Is e-mail really worth losing a limb, Frank?" Naturally, using a computer would be on the Discovery Channel's top ten list of most dangerous jobs. "Number three: Using a word processor. Note all the padding John has to wear as he starts up a new document in Word." But that just isn't the case.

Though computers don't blow up, they certainly could be much friendlier. I would love to say that the computer is really rather easy to understand, but it's not. Even folks who readily take to computers discover new and useful things every day. Of course, you already have taken a giant stride into making the computer more of a friend than a potential powder keg: You have this book, which starts off with this friendly chapter, a pleasant introduction to the PC.

✔ If you don't already own a PC, I can recommend a great book: *Buying a Computer For Dummies,* written by yours truly and available from Wiley Publishing, Inc. It covers the basics of the PC, how to select one just right for you, and how to set it up for the first time.

✔ This book tries its best to be jargon free or at least to explain terms before using them. Other books and magazines cannot make the same promise, so I can recommend a good computer dictionary: *The Illustrated Computer Dictionary For Dummies,* also written by yours truly and available from Wiley Publishing, Inc.

✔ I promise not to plug any of my other books for the remainder of this chapter — well, except for in the last sentence.

What Exactly Is a PC?

A *PC* is a personal computer, named after its earliest ancestor, the IBM PC. IBM (International Business Machines) created the PC (personal computer) after years of making larger, more impersonal computers (IPs).

Most computers are now known as PCs, whether you're buying them for the home or office. They don't have to be made by IBM. They don't even have to be personal. If you use it and it's a computer, it's a PC.

✔ It helps to think of a PC is being a large calculator with a better display and more buttons. Technologically, that's all it really is.

✔ PCs let you work with words, numbers, or graphics. PCs can work by themselves, in a group (known as a *network*), or across the globe on the Internet.

✔ There are variations on the typical PC. For example, most PC models are called *desktops*. Portable PCs are called *notebooks* or *laptops*. They have the same abilities as desktop PCs, but they're specially designed to be portable. I mention various unique laptoppy things throughout this book to keep various unique laptop owners happy.

✔ Computers aren't evil. They harbor no sinister intelligence. In fact, when you get to know them, they're rather dumb.

What does a PC do?

Computers defy description. Unlike other tools that have definite purposes — a saw saws, a screwdriver screws, and a hammer hams — a computer can do a number of different things, solving an infinite number of problems for an infinite number of people in an infinite number of ways. Just about anything that can be done with words, numbers, graphics, information, or communication can be done with a computer. Infinitely.

In a way, a computer is just another electronic gadget. Unlike the toaster and your car's fuel injection system, which are programmed to do only one thing each, a personal computer can be *programmed* to do a number of interesting tasks. It's up to you to tell the computer what you want it to do.

- ✔ The computer is the chameleon of electronic devices. You can watch movies on it, listen to the radio, shop, talk, draw, or even do nerdy things, like math. A computer's potential is limitless.

- ✔ Computers get the job done by using *software*. The software tells the computer what to do.

- ✔ No, you never have to learn about programming to use a computer. Someone else does the programming, and then you buy the program (the software) to get your work done.

- ✔ Your job, as the computer operator, is to tell the software what to do, which then tells the computer what to do.

- ✔ Only on cheesy sci-fi shows does the computer ever tell *you* what to do.

- ✔ You can always *verbally* tell the computer what to do with itself. This happens millions of times a day by computer users all over the world. Things you can tell the computer include, but are not limited to, "What!" "Stop!" "You slow pig," and the popular "@#$%&!?!"

What does a PC not do?

Sing. Dance. Yodel. Play the kazoo. Perform Kabuki theater. Scuba dive. Herd yak. Go jogging. Mow the lawn. Pick up questionable people from late-night drinking establishments. Join the Hair Club for Men. Rave over sushi. Inflate that above-ground pool for you. Get cosmetic surgery. Clean the attic. Wear dentures. Lube the car. Windows (with a little *w*).

Hardware and Software

Two separate things make up a computer: hardware and software. They go hand in hand. You cannot have one without the other. It would be like romance without the moon, lightning without thunder, macaroni without cheese, yin without yang, frankincense without myrrh.

Everyone say "hardware." Say it hard: *Hardware*.

Hardware is the physical part of a computer — anything you can touch and anything you can see. Yet, hardware is nothing unless it has software to control it. In a way, hardware is like a car without a driver, a saw without a carpenter, Shields without Yarnell; you need both to make something happen.

Everyone say "software." Whisper it: *Software*.

Software is the brains of the computer. It tells the hardware what to do. Without software, hardware just sits around bored and unappreciated—like Republicans in college. You must have software to make a computer go. In fact, software determines your computer's personality.

- ✔ If you can throw it out a window, it's hardware.

- ✔ If you can throw it out a window and it comes back, it's a cat.

- ✔ Computer software is nothing more than instructions that tell the hardware what to do, how to act, or when to lose your data.

- ✔ Computer software is more important than computer hardware. The software tells the hardware what to do.

- ✔ Without the proper software, your computer's hardware has nothing to do. That's when the computer magically transforms into a boat anchor.

Your Basic Hardware (A Nerd's-Eye View)

Figure 1-1 shows what a typical computer system looks like. I have flagged the major computer things you should identify and know about. These are the basics. The rest of this book goes into the details.

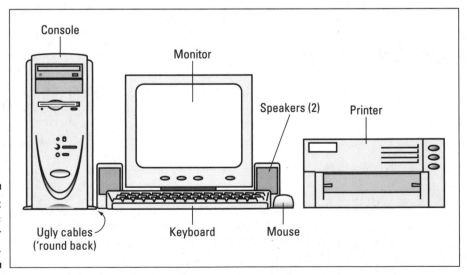

Figure 1-1:
Basic
computer
things.

Console — Monitor — Speakers (2) — Printer — Mouse — Keyboard — Ugly cables ('round back)

Console: The main computer box is the console, though it may also be called the *system unit* (geeky) or the *CPU* (incorrect). It's a box that contains your computer's guts plus various buttons, lights, and holes into which you plug the rest of the computer system.

Monitor: The monitor is the box where the computer displays information. It sits to the right or left of the console, or, if you put the console beneath a table, the monitor sits on top of the table. (Putting the monitor beneath the table is a silly thing to do.)

Keyboard: It's the thing you type on; it's the primary way you communicate with the computer. Clackity-clack-clack.

Mouse: Ah, the computer mouse. No rodent or pest, it's a helpful device that lets you work with graphical objects that the computer displays on the monitor.

Speakers: PCs bleep and squawk through a set of stereo speakers, either external jobbies you set up, as shown in Figure 1-1, or speakers built into the console or the monitor. Pay more money and you can even get a subwoofer to sit under your desk. Now, *that* will rattle your neighborhood's windows.

Printer: It's where you get the computer's output: the printed stuff, also called *hard copy.*

This list describes the basic computer system you see in Figure 1-1. You may find, in addition to these basic items, other things clustered around your computer, such as a scanner, digital camera, game pad (or joystick), external disk drive, high-speed modem, and many, many other toys — er, vital components.

One thing definitely not shown in Figure 1-1 — and something you will never see in a computer manual and especially not in advertisements — is the ganglia of cables that lives behind each and every computer. What a mess! These cables are required in order to plug things into the wall and into each other. No shampoo or conditioner on earth can clean up those tangles:

- ✔ These parts of the computer are all important. Make sure that you know where the console, keyboard, mouse, speakers, monitor, and printer are in your own system. If the printer isn't present, it's probably a network printer sitting in some other room.

- ✔ Chapters in Part III of this book go into more detail on the individual computer components just introduced and illustrated in Figure 1-1.

- ✔ CPU stands for *central processing unit*. It's another term for the computer's microprocessor. Even so, some folks refer to the console as the CPU. This term is incorrect, and those who confuse the CPU and console must be flogged.

Variations on the typical computer theme

Not all computers look like the image shown in Figure 1-1. The type of PC shown there is now the most popular, called the *mini-tower*. It can sit upright on top your desk or be tucked away out of sight, below the desk. And it's sleek and sexy.

PCs need not all be configured as mini-towers. For the first ten years or so of the PC's life, the larger *desktop* model was the most popular. Other models exist, each with an orientation, a size, and enough blinking lights to please any particular person.

This list describes the various types and models of PCs:

Mini-tower: The most popular PC configuration, where the computer sits upright on a desktop or beneath a desk (refer to Figure 1-1).

Desktop: Once the most popular PC configuration, with a slab-like console lying flat on the desktop with the monitor squatting on top. Desktops now exist as small-footprint systems, which earn their own paragraph:

Desktop (small footprint): A smaller version of the desktop, typically used in low-priced home systems. The *footprint* is the amount of desk space the computer uses. A small-footprint desktop model is just tinier than the full-size desktop model. Of course, in the end, it makes no difference: The amount of clutter you have always expands to fill the available desk space.

Notebook/laptop: A specialty type of computer that folds into a handy, light-weight package, ideal for slowing down the security checkpoints in airports. Laptop PCs work just like their desktop brethren; any exceptions are noted throughout this book.

Tower system: Essentially a full-size desktop standing on its side, making this PC tall, like a tower. Towers have lotsa room inside for expansion, making them the darlings of power-mad users. Towers typically sit on the floor, usually propping up one end of the table.

Stuff on the console (front)

The *console* is the most important part of your computer. It's the main thing, the Big Box, *el numero uno*. Every part of your computer system either lives inside the console or plugs into it.

Figure 1-2 shows what a typical PC console may look like. I have flagged the more interesting places to visit, although on your computer they may appear in a different location than what's shown in the figure.

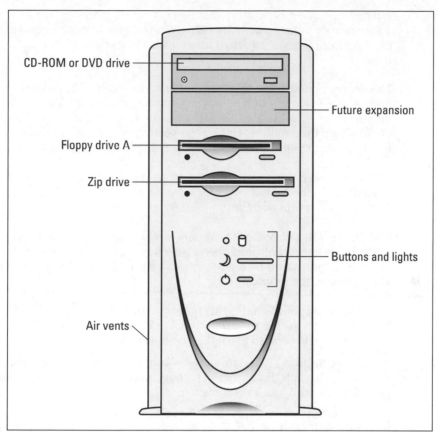

Figure 1-2:
Important
doodads on
the front of
the console.

CD-ROM or DVD drive: These high-capacity drives read discs that look exactly like musical CDs or video DVDs, although they contain computer information. See Chapters 4, 7, and 10 to see how these devices work.

 DVD drives have the "DVD" logo on them. If you don't see the DVD logo, your PC has a mere CD-ROM drive.

Future expansion: Ah, potential! You can add a whole grab bag of goodies to a mere mortal computer, and most consoles have plenty of room for it. Any blank spots or removable panels on the front of your computer indicate that you can add even more junk later. Such a space may already be taken, filled with such goodies as a tape backup unit, Zip drive, another CD-ROM or CD-R/RW drive, another hard drive, or an assortment of other computer things many folks eagerly spend their hard-earned money on.

Floppy drive: This slot eats floppy disks. Some software comes on floppy disks, and you can use these disks to move files from one PC to another.

Zip drive: A common option found on many PCs is the Zip drive, which is like a superduper floppy drive. On a Zip disk, you can store the equivalent of hundreds of floppy disks' worth of information! Not every PC has a Zip drive, however.

The secret panel: Some PCs, especially home models, have a secret panel or door that pops open. Behind it, you can find special connectors for joysticks, microphones, headphones, or other handy items you may need to plug and unplug from time to time. Having the secret panel is handier than having to reach around behind the computer and fumble for plugs and holes.

Air vents: Okay, this one isn't impressive, but most consoles sport some type of air vent on the front. Don't block the air vents with books or sticky notes! The thing has gotta breathe.

Buttons and lights: Most of a computer's buttons are on the keyboard. A few of the more important ones are on the console, and these buttons on fancier PCs are accompanied by many impressive tiny lights. These buttons and lights include the following:

 ✔ **Power button:** You use this button to turn the PC on or off, though it's more than just an on–off button. For example, on many PCs the button can also be used to place the computer to "sleep."

✔ **Reset button:** This button allows you to restart the computer without going through the bother of turning it off and then on again. Note that not every PC has a reset button.

 ✔ **Sleep button:** Pressing this button causes your PC to go into a coma, suspending all activity without turning the computer off. On some computers, this button and the on–off button are the same.

✔ **Disk drive lights:** These lights flash when the hard drive, floppy drive, CD-ROM drive, or Zip drive is working. For a hard drive, the light is your reassurance that it's alive, happy, and doing its job. For all other types of drives (with removable disks), the light indicates that the computer is using the drive.

Other fun and unusual things may live on the front of your console, most of which are particular to a certain computer brand.

✔ See Chapter 2 for more information about the power, reset, and sleep buttons and their purposes.

✔ Rarely, if ever, do you find a Panic button.

✔ Some newer computers have stickers that show the secret Windows installation number or proclaim such nonsense as "I was built to run Windows 3D" or "A Pentium Zillion lurks inside this box."

✔ Some PCs may not come with a floppy drive.

✔ Don't block the air vents on the front of the console. If you do, the computer may literally suffocate. (It gets too hot.)

✔ A hard drive light can be red or green or yellow, and it flickers when the hard drive is in use. Don't let it freak you out! It's not an alarm; the hard drive is just doing its job. (Personally, I find the green type of hard drive light most comforting — reminds me of Christmas.)

Stuff on the console (back)

The console's backside is its busy side. That's where you find various connectors for the many other devices in your computer system: a place to plug in the monitor, keyboard, mouse, speakers, and just about anything else that came in the box with the PC.

Figure 1-3 illustrates a typical PC's backside, showing you where and how the various goodies can connect. Your computer has most of the items shown in the figure, although they are probably in different locations on your PC's rump.

Power connector: This thing is where the PC plugs into a cord that plugs into the wall.

Keyboard connector: The keyboard plugs into this little hole. The wee li'l picture is supposed to be a keyboard. Note that some keyboard holes may be labeled *KBD* or even *Keyboard,* with all the vowels and the *R.*

Mouse connector: It's generally the same size and shape as the keyboard connector, although this hole has a mouse icon nearby to let you know that the mouse plugs in there.

USB port: Plug snazzy devices into these Certs-size Universal Serial Bus (USB) slots. If you have a USB mouse, keyboard, set of speakers, or printer, it plugs in here, not into the other ports (see Chapter 9).

Serial, or COM, ports: Most PCs have two of these ports, named COM1 and COM2, though often they're labeled with a series of *I*s and *O*s. This is where an external modem or serial mouse is plugged in. (Rare, but it happens.)

Printer port: The PC's printer plugs into this connector.

Joystick port: This port, used mainly for scientific applications, may be identified by an image (see the margin) or say Joystick or Game controller.

Monitor connector: Your PC's monitor plugs into this hole. Sometimes, the hole is on an expansion slot (refer to Figure 1-3) and is unlabeled. If so, you can tell what the monitor connector is because it has 15 little holes in it — more than the serial port, which is the same size but has only 9 holes.

Speaker/sound-out jack: It's where you plug in your PC's external speakers or where you hook up the PC to a sound system.

Line-in jack: This jack is where you plug in your stereo or VCR to the PC for capturing sound.

Microphone jack: The computer's microphone plugs into this hole.

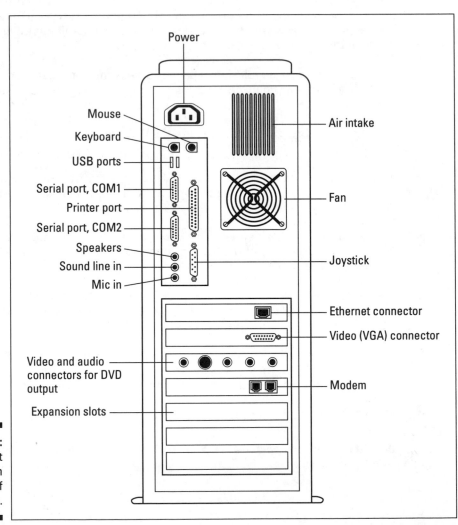

Figure 1-3:
Important
doodads on
the back of
the console.

Ethernet (network) connector: This is where you plug in a Local Area Network (LAN) connector, which looks like a huge phone connector. Not every computer has one of these connectors.

Dial-up modem: A dial-up modem can have up to two connectors, though some modems have only one. One of the two connectors, or the only connector, is where you plug in the modem to the phone jack in your wall. The other connector, if available, is used to connect a telephone to the computer so that you can answer the phone.

S-Video out: If your PC sports a DVD drive, it probably has several additional connectors for video and audio output. The S-Video connector allows you to connect an S-Video-happy TV to your PC. Other video connectors let you pump a DVD movie out to a TV set or VCR.

In addition to the ports, jacks, and holes on the back of the console are expansion slots. They're the backsides of various expansion cards you plug into your PC. Some expansion slots have connectors for other PC goodies as well.

The good news? You connect all this stuff only once. Then your PC's butt faces the wall for the rest of its life and you never have to look at it again (well, unless you add something in the future).

- ✔ If your computer has a DVD drive, use the sound jacks on the DVD expansion card, not the sound jacks shown earlier, in Figure 1-3. So, for example, if you plug your speakers into the plug shown in the figure and you get no sound, look for an identical hole on one of the expansion cards.

- ✔ The keyboard and mouse connector *are* different! Be certain that you plug the proper device into the proper hole, or else the keyboard and mouse don't work!

- ✔ See Chapter 9 for more information on these holes and what plugs into them.

- ✔ See Chapter 16 for more on modems.

"Oooh! It's color-coded!"

The current trend in computer hardware is to color-code the connectors on a PC's rump. So, in addition to the intergalactic icon for speaker or sound-out, you now have the color green. That's the good news.

The bad news is that each computer manufacturer tends to use its own color-coding for everything. So, what's red on one computer may be violet on another. This lack of logic is the hallmark of the computer industry.

Fortunately, the connectors still look different and are still tagged with the international symbol or text. Even so, I thought I should list in Table 1-1 the common colors used by most manufacturers.

Table 1-1	PC Connector Color Codes
Port/Connector	*Color*
Keyboard	Purple
Mouse	Green
Serial port(s)	Cyan
Printer	Violet
Monitor	Blue
Line out/speakers	Lime
Microphone	Pink
Audio line in	Grey
Joystick	Yellow

Your Basic Software

Computer software doesn't get the credit it deserves for running your computer, which is probably why it's overpriced. In any event, you need the software to make your hardware go.

The operating system (Or, "Who's in charge here?")

The most important piece of software is the *operating system*. It's the computer's number-one program — the head honcho, the big cheese, Mr. In Charge, Fearless Leader, *le roi*.

The operating system rules the computer's roost, controlling all the individual computer components and making sure that everything gets along well. It's the actual brains of the operation, telling the nitwitted hardware what to do next.

The operating system also controls applications software (see the next section). Each of those programs must bend a knee and take a loyalty oath to the operating system.

Finally, it's the operating system's job to communicate with you, dear human. On this level, it does a truly mediocre job, which is why you see so many books in the bookstores about using computer operating systems.

- ✔ The computer's most important piece of software is the operating system.

- ✔ The operating system typically comes with the computer when you buy it. You never need to add a second operating system, although operating systems do get updated and improved from time to time.

- ✔ For the PC, the operating system is Windows. It comes in various flavors: Windows 98, Windows Me, Windows 2000, and Windows XP. Chapter 3 chitty-chats about operating systems and Windows.

- ✔ When you buy software, you buy it for an operating system, not for your brand of PC. So, rather than buy "Dell software," you look in the Windows section of the software store.

Software that actually does something

The operating system is merely in charge of the computer. By itself, an operating system doesn't really do anything for you. Instead, to get work done, you need an application program. They are the minions, though the operating system is more of a sleepy supervisor.

Application programs are the programs that do the work.

Application programs include word processors, graphics editors, games, educational software, and so on. Whatever it is you do on your computer, you do it using an application program.

Other types of programs include utilities and programming software. And then there are all the Internet applications: Web browsers, e-mail programs, and software of that ilk. They are considered applications that do something, even when that something is the process of wasting time.

Some Consoling Words of Advice

At some point, something will go wrong with the computer. It's inevitable. Computers goof up. Programs have bugs. But no matter what happens, don't be so quick to blame yourself. Honestly: It's not your fault!

Most of the time, the problem is in the software you're using. This situation is quite common. Either the software was programmed incorrectly, or it's designed in a way that's confusing and not obvious. But, no matter — don't get down on yourself because the silly thing doesn't work. It happens to everyone.

- Don't assume that you have goofed up or somehow wrecked something. "Stuff happens," and most of the time it's just the computer acting dumb.

- For more information on troubleshooting your PC, refer to my book *Troubleshooting Your PC For Dummies* (Wiley Publishing, Inc.).

Chapter 2

The Big Red Switch

• •

In This Chapter

▶ Connecting all your devices to the power

▶ Turning the computer system on

▶ Logging on to Windows

▶ Turning the computer system off

▶ Placing your PC in suspended animation

▶ Hibernating the PC

▶ Knowing when to restart

▶ Deciding whether to leave your PC on all the time

• •

*I*t has been *years* since PCs had big red switches on them. With a satisfying CLUNK, they either turned the computer on or off. Life was simple then.

Today, the PC doesn't have an on–off switch. No, it has a *power button*. They call it that because sometimes it doesn't turn the computer on or off. No, the power button may "suspend" the computer or "wake" the system or "frustrate" the operator who merely wants the dang thing turned off!

This chapter covers the basics of turning on a computer. No, you don't woo the computer with sweets and love sonnets; you turn on a computer by simply punching its power switch. The delicacies of that operation, as well as what to do *after* that, are all covered here.

Too Many Power Switches, Too Little Time

Your computer system doesn't have a single power button, a switch that turns the entire system on at once. No, many buttons and switches and knobs require punching, throwing, and turning to get the whole thing going. Just be thankful that this isn't the old steam-powered days of computing, where you needed to crank-start the numerical coprocessor.

Surges, spikes, and lightning strikes

Like young Mary Jane Anyones walking down the aisle at her wedding, the power that comes from the wall socket into your computer is not always the purest thing. Occasionally, it may be corrupted by some of the various electrical nasties that do, every now and then, come uninvited into your home or office. Here's the rundown:

Line noise: Electrical interference on the power line, most commonly seen as static on the TV when someone uses the blender.

Surge: A gradual increase in power.

Serge: Some guy from Europe.

Spike: A sudden increase in the power, such as what happens when lightning strikes.

Brownout (or *dip*): The opposite of a surge, a decrease in power. Some electrical motors don't work, and room lights are dimmer than normal (brown).

Blackout: An absence of power coming through the line.

If possible, try to get a power strip with surge protection for your computer. You have a price to pay, but it's worth it. For an even better power strip, find one with both surge protection and noise filtering.

The most expensive form of protection is spike protection. That causes the power strip to lay down its life by taking the full brunt of the spike, saving your computer equipment.

Note that spikes come through not only the power lines, but also the phone lines. So, if lightning strikes are a common occurrence in your area, get a power strip with phone line protection.

For more information about nasty things that can walk into your house through your wall sockets, refer to your electrical company. It may offer its own solutions to help you keep your valuable electronics safe, such as power protection right at the breaker box.

Properly connecting all your devices

Just about every device on your computer has an on–off switch or power button. Rather than work yourself into some kind of computer startup ballet, where you bend, punch, flip, twist, flip, arch, flip-push, and eventually get everything going, may I offer a simple solution: The power strip, as shown in Figure 2-1. (Cue the angelic choir.)

The power-strip is the ideal way to manage your PC's various devices and also to turn everything on with one flip of a switch. Simply plug every one of your computer system's components into the power strip: the console, monitor, scanner, printer, and other devices. Then, plug the power strip into the wall. Flipping the switch on the power strip then turns on the console, monitor, printer — everything.

✔ Most power strips have six sockets, which is plenty for a typical computer system. If not, buy a second power strip, plug it into its own wall socket, and use it for the rest of your computer devices.

✔ I recommend the Kensington SmartSockets power strip. Unlike cheaper power strips, the SmartSockets lines up its sockets in a perpendicular arrangement, making it easier to plug in bulky transformers.

✔ Duh: Turn on all your computer's components before plugging them into the power strip. Otherwise, you lose the advantage of having the strip.

✔ Don't plug a laser printer into a power strip. The laser printer draws too much juice for that to be effective — or safe. Instead, you must plug the laser printer directly into the wall socket. (It says so in your laser printer's manual — if you ever get around to reading it.)

✔ With a power strip, you can turn on your computer system with your foot (if the power strip is on the floor). Or if you take off your shoes, use your big toe. And if you're really classy, use your big toe sticking out of a hole in your sock.

✔ The medical name for your big toe is *hallux*.

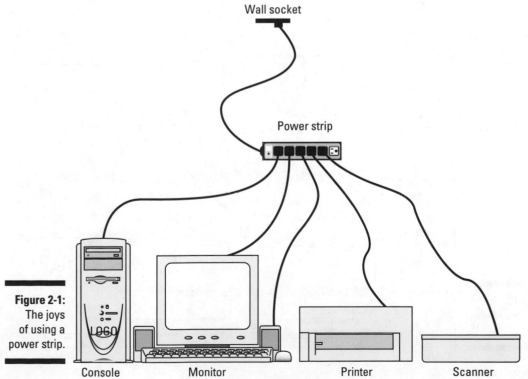

Figure 2-1:
The joys of using a power strip.

Wall socket

Power strip

Console   Monitor   Printer   Scanner

An even better power solution (the UPS)

Perhaps the best thing to plug your computer into is a UPS. Not the parcel company, *UPS* is an acronym for uninterruptible power supply. It's a power strip combined with a battery that keeps your computer running when the power goes out.

Depending on the number of outlets on the UPS, you can plug in your monitor and console, plus other items in your computer system. For example, I also plug my DSL modem (see Chapter 16) and external CD-R drive (see Chapter 10) into my UPS (it has four sockets). That setup keeps my computer system up and running during minor power outages.

Figure 2-2 illustrates one approach to how a UPS could work along with a power strip to power your computer system. Note that only the console and monitor are plugged into the UPS. Everything else goes into a power strip. The following dramatization illustrates my reasons for this arrangement:

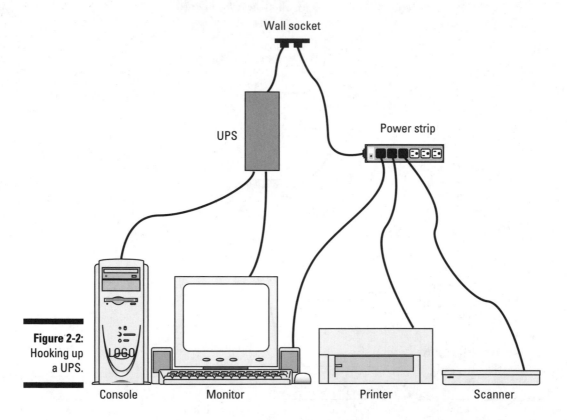

Figure 2-2:
Hooking up
a UPS.

Wall socket

UPS

Power strip

Console   Monitor   Printer   Scanner

A large boom is heard. The lights flicker and then go out. STAN is left sitting in the dark, but his computer is still on. GINGER rushes in.

> **GINGER:** The power is out! Those croissants I put in the toaster oven are ruined! Did you lose that lifesaving doodle you were creating in Paint?
>
> **STAN:** No, darling, I'm still working on it. See? Our UPS has kept the computer console and monitor on during this brief outage.
>
> **GINGER:** Well, hurry up and print it.
>
> **STAN:** Nay! I shan't print. Printing can wait, which is why I did not connect the printer to the UPS. It is as powerless as the toaster oven.
>
> **GINGER:** What can you do? Hurry! The UPS battery won't last forever!
>
> **STAN:** Relax, gentle spouse. I shall save to disk, thus. [Ctrl+S] Now I may shut down the computer, assured with the knowledge that my doodle file is safely stored on the internal hard drive. There. *(He turns off the computer and monitor.)* Now we can weather the storm with peace of mind.

Two hours later, after the power is back on, GINGER and STAN are sipping wine:

> **GINGER:** Honey, you sure are smart the way you used that UPS.
>
> **STAN:** Well, I'm just thankful I read Dan Gookin's book *PCs For Dummies*, published by Wiley Publishing, Inc. I think I shall buy more of his books.
>
> **GINGER:** Who knew that we could find such happiness, thanks to a computer book?

They canoodle.

Ignore what it says on the box: A UPS gives you *maybe* five minutes of computer power. So be like Stan and save your stuff to disk, and then shut down Windows and turn off the computer. You can print, scan, modem, or whatever when the power comes back on.

- ✔ A UPS works best for brief power outages. For example, those little power burps that may just flicker the lights can restart a computer. The UPS prevents that.
- ✔ Never plug a laser printer into a UPS.
- ✔ In addition to emergency power, a UPS provides higher levels of electrical protection for your equipment. Many models offer surge, spike, and dip protection, which keep your PC running smoothly despite any nasties the power company may throw your way.

Ignore these other terms for "starting a computer"

Any of the following terms are roughly equivalent to "starting the computer." Use them at your own risk, usually in the presence of a licensed, high-tech professional.

Boot	Cold start	Cycle power	Hard start	Power on	Power up
Reboot	Reset	Restart	Soft boot	Warm boot	

Time to Turn on the Computer

If you have plugged everything into a power strip or UPS, turn those devices on first. Next, if the computer and its components aren't on, turn them on; turn on the console last.

The sign of success here is that your computer system comes to life; you can hear the fan and disk drives whir and warble into action, and various lights on the console, keyboard, and other devices may flash at you or glow admirably. The scanner and printer may creak their weary bones into action. Get ready to start computing!

✔ By turning on the console last, you give the other devices in the computer system time to initialize and get ready for work. That way, the console sees that they exist, recognizes them, and lets you use those devices in your computer system.

✔ All computer devices have their own on–off switches.

✔ Some devices may not have a power switch. For example, some scanners, external disk (Zip) drives, or "USB-powered" devices lack an on–off switch.

✔ The largest button on the front of the monitor turns it on. Some older models may have the on–off switch in back. Indeed, many computer devices have their switches in the back, usually next to where the power cord attaches.

✔ If something doesn't turn on, check to see whether it's plugged in. Confirm that all the cables are properly connected.

Not turning certain things on

You don't always have to turn on *everything* when you start your computer. For example, if you're not going to use the scanner, why bother turning it on? And the printer needs to be switched on only before you plan on printing something.

Some things may, however, need to be kept on all the time. For example, you may want to keep your DSL or cable modem on all the time — your Internet Service Provider may even request that you do so. Some printers have a Power Save mode and use *less* power if you leave them on all the time than if you have to turn them on and off several times a day.

Recognize your PC's Startup program

At some point during the startup process, you see a message on the monitor about pressing a certain key, or keyboard combination, to enter the PC's Setup program. Pay attention to those keys!

You need to use the PC's Setup program to configure the computer's hardware, such as when you add more memory, a second hard drive, or other hardware options. Note now the keys required so that you can get into your computer's Setup program when needed.

Trouble in Startup Land!

Hopefully, Windows starts right up and you get on with your work. You may experience a few unwelcome detours along the way, such as:

Something was shut down improperly

If anything strange happens during the Windows shutdown process, you see this message when Windows starts up. Don't panic. Windows has merely recognized that something went wrong and is checking the system to ensure that everything is okay. See? This is a good thing.

Non-system disk

If you see this message, remove the floppy disk from drive A and press the Enter key. Your computer then starts up normally.

Don't mess with system passwords

Some PCs have the capability to have a system password. This sounds nifty: A prompt appears right after you turn on your computer, preventing unauthorized access. If you don't know the password — or you forget it — you can't use the computer. A password is great for security, but it's a serious risk if your brain suddenly forgets it.

My advice: Don't bother with system passwords.

Unwanted disk

Sometimes, your computer may try to start itself from a CD parked in your PC's CD-ROM drive. If so, wait until the computer pauses, and then remove the CD and restart your computer.

Safe mode

This is the worst of the lot. It looks like Windows, but with larger graphics and the words *Safe mode* plastered on all four corners of the screen. It means that Windows has detected some system problems. It's up to you to fix things, which may be obvious, thanks to an error message, or just plain mysterious, thanks to no error message.

My advice? Hey! Get my book *Troubleshooting Your PC For Dummies* (Wiley Publishing, Inc.) and learn how to fix these and other common startup woes.

Here Comes Windows!

After starting your computer (the hardware), the operating system (the software) takes over. Remember that the software controls the hardware and the main piece of software is the operating system. So the operating system is the first program your computer runs. That operating system is named *Windows.*

As Windows comes to life, you see various messages displayed on the screen. Whatever. Just sit and watch; most of it has low entertainment value, kind of like a long list of credits before a good film . . . or a mediocre film, in this case.

✔ Lots of chaos occurs as Windows loads. Don't fret over any of it.

✔ For everyone reading this book, the operating system is Windows XP, either the Home or Professional version. I just call it Windows.

✔ Earlier versions of Windows are covered in earlier editions of *PCs For Dummies*. For Windows 98, Windows Me, and Windows 2000, I recommend the 8th Edition.

✔ Before Windows, the PC's operating system was DOS. See *DOS For Dummies* (Wiley Publishing, Inc.) for more information.

✔ Some monitors may display text before Windows starts up. The text is basically telling you that the monitor isn't receiving a signal from the computer. Rather than just say "I'm not getting any signs of life from the computer," the monitor instead says `Invalid Sync` or `Error on input` or something even cruder. Ignore the message; it vanishes when the console comes to life.

Log in, mystery guest

No, you're still not using Windows yet. Like going into a bar or prison or anywhere else that's dangerous, the final phase of getting into Windows is to properly show ID. In this case, you need to click on the proper account name, as shown in Figure 2-3.

Follow these steps:

1. **Click on your account name or the cute picture by your account.**

   If you don't have an account name, you can use the Guest account, if it's present. (Refer to a book more specific to Windows for information on setting up accounts.)

2. **Enter your password into the box, if one appears.**

   Carefully type your password into the box.

3. **Click the green arrow or press the Enter key to have Windows check your password.**

Windows XP can be configured to have a less graphical logon screen than the one shown in Figure 2-3. In that variation, your name appears in a User Name box. You must type your password into a Password box and then click the OK button to log in. Such a thing is far too ugly for me to illustrate here.

If everything goes well, you next see Windows main location, its home plate, its lobby, which is called the *desktop*. Keep reading in the next section.

- ✔ Identifying yourself to Windows is known as *logging in* to your computer. Microsoft claims to detest the word *log,* but if you look carefully in Figure 2-2 (or on your screen), you see the phrase "After you log on," so get used to that term.

- ✔ If this is your first time running Windows XP, you're asked to create an account before you see the logon screen, as shown in Figure 2-3.

- ✔ Older versions of Windows have different methods of logging in. In Windows 500BC, for example, you needed two coconuts and had to recite portions of *The Iliad.*

Welcome to the desktop

Windows presents itself to you by showing you what's called the *desktop,* or the main starting place for doing anything in Windows. A typical desktop is shown in Figure 2-4. Believe it or not, that's your instinctive, intuitive, friendly, ready-to-use computer staring at you in the face. You've made it.

Figure 2-3: Let us in, the users beg.

Figure 2-4:
It's called
the desktop,
but it looks
more like a
windshield
after a long
car trip.

Getting Your Work Done

Between turning your computer on and off, you should do something. Get work done. Go. Do it now.

- ✔ Chapter 3 tells you more about your PC's operating system, Windows XP.
- ✔ See Part III of this book for more information on using software.
- ✔ Also see Part IV for information on using the Internet, which is like using software but also involves using a modem.

Turning the Computer Off (Shutdown)

Whatever you do, don't be logical and expect that punching the PC's power button turns the system off. It just doesn't work that way. Maybe 10 years ago, punching the power button turned off the computer, but, like trying to find inexpensive health insurance, it doesn't work that way now.

Is logging in necessary?

Yes, and you had better get used to it. In the old days, PCs lacked password-protected accounts or often had feeble password protection. But now, with the Internet and the privacy measures built into a modern operating system like Windows XP, passwords are a must.

Password-protected accounts are necessary for several darn good reasons:

✔ To identify you as one of several people who use the same computer

✔ To make it easier on you later so that you don't have to enter passwords to connect to the Internet or read your e-mail

✔ To connect you and your computer to a network (mostly at the office or, if you're *really* into computers, at your home)

✔ To give you one more reason to dislike the computer

Though you can configure Windows XP *not* to require a password, I recommend against it. That's because in the future, passwords will not be an option. Therefore, get used to it now.

No, when you want to turn off a computer, you must do it logically. In fact, unlike trying to make a left turn in Boston, there isn't just one way to turn off a computer.

"Oui, Monsier! Let me show you ze Shutdown menu!"

Before you even think about turning the computer off, know your options. Here they are:

Log Off: This option doesn't shut down Windows or turn off the computer. No, for network or multiple user systems, this option merely tells the computer (or network) that you're done. Windows doesn't quit, but instead displays the logon dialog box again, letting someone else use the PC.

Stand By: This option puts your computer into a special, power-saving Sleep mode. The monitor goes dark, the disk drives stop spinning, and the computer basically stands still. It's also known as Post Office mode.

Hibernate: This is a nifty option, but available only with certain swanky computers, bears, and adult male humans. The hibernation way of shutting down a computer quickly saves everything in memory and then turns off the PC.

When the computer is turned on again, it's instantly restored to its previous state — like an instant on, leaving you just where you last were. Hibernation is a quick way to turn the computer off without having to "lose your place."

Restart: This option gives you a way to turn the computer off and then on again, also known as a *reset*. You do this often after installing new software or sometimes to fix minor quirks — like slapping Windows upside its head.

Shut Down: Ah! The traditional option. Shutting down Windows stops the computer dead in its tracks. You're prompted to save any unsaved files, if any are lying about. Do so. Then Windows packs up its bags and leaves town. The computer then automatically turns itself off.

Now that you're familiar with the options, you can make your selection based on the following sections.

Why bother to log off?

If you're the only one using your computer, don't bother logging off. However, if several people use the computer, each with their own account, when you're done for the day you can merely log off, as opposed to turning the PC off. Here's how:

1. **Click the Start button.**

2. **Click the Log off button at the bottom of the Start panel.**

   You may see the Log Off Windows dialog box, as shown in Figure 2-5. If not, you're done, and someone else can log in and start using the computer. Otherwise, go to Step 3.

Figure 2-5: Get outta here, you bum!

3. **Click the Log Off button.**

   This step shuts down all your programs, prompting you to save any unsaved business to disk and closing you down for the day. Time for someone else to use the PC.

If you see the Switch User button (refer to Figure 2-5), you can use it to quickly log out and let someone else log in. Beyond speed, the advantage here is that you don't have to shut down your programs or really quit Windows. When the other user is done, you can switch back, and Windows looks just as you left it.

Another quick way to log out and *lock* the computer is to press the Win+L key combination. The Win key is the Windows key on your keyboard; L stands for Lock. To unlock the system and get back in, just log in to Windows as you normally would.

Making the PC snooze (Stand By mode)

As an alternative to turning the computer off and then on several times a day, consider giving it a coma instead. This advice doesn't imply giving the computer a concussion, and your PC won't have an out-of-body experience while it's down. Instead, you just tell your PC to take a nap. Zzzzz.

While it's sleeping, the computer shuts off power to the screen and disk drives, but maintains enough juice to remember what it was doing last. That way, you can instantly wake the computer up and get back to work.

To put your PC into Stand By (sleep) mode, obey these steps:

1. **Save your work!**

   This step is important: You must save your documents or files to disk before putting the PC into Stand By mode. If you want to be extra safe, close your programs. You may lose data if a power outage occurs while the computer is quiescent.

2. **Click the Start button.**

3. **Click the Shut Down button at the bottom of the Start panel.**

   The Turn Off Computer dialog box appears, as shown in Figure 2-6.

Figure 2-6: Various turning-off (or not) options.

4. Click the Stand By button.

The computer then appears to have turned itself off, but it's really just resting. Don't be fooled!

You wake the computer up by pressing a key on the keyboard or jiggling the mouse. The PC comes back to life, all refreshed and rested and resuming operations where you left off.

✔ If your PC has a sleep button on the console, you can use the button to instantly put the computer into Stand By mode.

✔ Also refer to the section "What good is the power button?" later in this chapter, for information on changing the power button into a sleep button.

✔ Sleep mode was invented for laptops, where battery power is as precious as leg room in coach. Most laptops have several methods for activating Sleep mode. The easiest way is simply to close the laptop's lid. It may also have a special button on the keyboard (a *function* button), and you can always follow the steps in this section to "sleep" your laptop.

✔ Sleep mode is controlled through the Power Options icon, in the Windows Control Panel. That's where you can set options to automatically put the PC into Sleep mode or to control which parts of the PC sleep and which don't.

✔ If Stand By mode doesn't work, ask your PC's manufacturer or dealer to get a system upgrade. Until then, avoid using Stand By mode.

Bears do it, PCs do it — why not hibernate?

Hibernating the computer is better than turning it off and is safer than resetting. To hibernate, follow these steps:

1. Click the Start button.

2. Click the Shut Down button at the bottom of the Start panel.

You see the famous Turn Off Computer dialog box (refer to Figure 2-6). But — what? No Hibernate button!

3. Press and hold the Shift key.

Either Shift key activates the Hibernate button, which is mysteriously in the same place as the Stand By button. Fine. Keep holding that Shift key!

4. Click the Hibernate button.

The computer's hard drive churns for a few seconds, and then it shuts off. Amazing.

Unlike Sleep mode, merely jiggling the mouse or tapping on the keyboard doesn't reawaken the computer. Remember: *The computer is off!* It's not snoozing!

To unhibernate the PC, punch the power button. Unlike a normal startup, the computer quickly jumps to life and returns to its former state — the condition it was in just before you left Windows.

If you have a PC that boots into multiple operating systems, you have to select Windows XP from that menu first. After that, Windows unhibernates and continues where it was.

The joy of restarting Windows

You need to reset or restart Windows in two instances. The first is when you install something new or make some change, in which case Windows tells you that you need to reset and presents some type of Reset or Restart button on the screen. Click that button with the mouse and the computer restarts.

The second time you need to restart is when Something Strange happens. For example, the mouse is gone! Or Windows just radically starts scrolling around, the monitor twists around 360 degrees, and green bile spews from the floppy drive! In that common instance, as well as others, restart by following these steps:

1. Click the Start button.

2. Click the Shut Down button at the bottom of the Start panel.

The Turn Off Computer dialog box appears (refer to Figure 2-6).

3. Click the Restart button.

Windows shuts itself down — almost as though it were turning the computer off. But just at the moment the system would have turned off, it starts back up again — a restart.

As with other shutdown options, you're asked to save any unsaved files before the PC restarts.

As the computer shuts down, you may encounter various End Now dialog boxes. These are stubborn programs that refuse to quit. If you see any, click the End Now button to expedite the restart process.

✔ Some PCs have a hardware reset button on the console. The button is there as a last resort; use it only in times of desperation. For example, Windows may be acting weird and you need to reset, but you can't use the mouse, the keyboard has turned into blue Jell-o, and the screen is showing Russ Meyer's *Faster, Pussycat! Kill! Kill!* In times of alarm such as those, feel free to wallop the hardware reset button.

✔ Some PCs let you use their power buttons as emergency resets. Refer to the section "What good is the power button?" later in this chapter. (Mind the suspense.)

✔ Remember to remove any floppy disks from drive A before resetting. If you leave a disk in there, the computer tries to start itself from that disk, which is dumb, but no one ever said that computers are smart.

Turning the darn thing off

To properly quit for the day:

1. **Click the Start button.**

2. **Click the Shut Down button at the bottom of the Start panel.**

   You see the Turn Off Computer dialog box, shown back in Figure 2-6.

3. **Click the Turn Off button.**

   After a spell and a fashion, the computer turns itself off.

If you had any unsaved documents or files, Windows asks you to save them before it fully shuts down.

When you need to turn the darn thing off and the mouse doesn't work, use these keys on your keyboard. Do this:

1. **Press the Windows key (Win) to pop up the Start panel.**

   If the keyboard lacks a Win key, press Ctrl+Esc instead.

2. **Press the U key to select the Turn Off Computer button.**

3. **Press R to select the Restart button.**

   The computer shuts down and starts up again — hopefully, fixing your mouse problem.

After turning off the console, go ahead and turn off the other components in your computer system: monitor, scanner, and other external devices. Or, if you have a power strip, simply flip its switch to turn everything off.

If you have a UPS, however, *do not* turn it off; you want to leave it on so that its battery remains charged.

> ✔ Some stubborn programs may require you to deliberately shut them down. That's fine. Do so properly; avoid using artillery, if possible.
>
> ✔ If the computer shuts down and then immediately restarts, you have a problem. Refer to your dealer or computer manufacturer for assistance.
>
> ✔ Try to avoid quickly turning the computer on again after turning it off. It's generally a good idea to wait at least 10 to 20 seconds before turning a PC on again. Otherwise, you may "shock" the system, and it could short out some of the electronics.

What good is the power button?

This chapter shows you five ways to ditch Windows, and not one of them involves the stinkin' power button! So, is the power button just for show? A mere decorative knob? A blemish? The PC equivalent of the human appendix? What?

No, unlike a heart in a lawyer or a brain in a politician, the power button isn't just for show. That button can, indeed, be used to turn off the computer. In fact, the power button's function is completely determined by software; *you* can tell the computer what happens when the power button is pressed. Here's how:

1. **Open the Windows Control Panel.**

   See Chapter 3 for information on opening the Control Panel, in case you need it.

Power Options

2. **Open the Power Options icon.**

   Point at that icon with your mouse, and then click twice to open it. This step displays the Power Options Properties dialog box.

3. **Click the Advanced tab.**

   Note that *Advanced* is often used in Windows to describe a miscellaneous category of things; it rarely means that the options shouldn't be messed with. In this case, the Advanced tab contains an option for setting the power button's function.

   Look for this text in the dialog box: "When I press the power button on my computer." A drop-down list below that text has options that tell the computer what to do when you press the power button.

For example, you can disable the power button while the computer is on by choosing the Do nothing option.

If you want the power button to be versatile, choose the Ask Me What to Do option. Then, pressing the PC's power button displays a list of choices on the screen.

Otherwise, you can choose from the options available.

4. **Select a function for the power button.**

Note the unfortunate lack of a Giggle option.

5. **Click OK.**

And now, the power button carries the function you have just assigned it.

Not all computers have programmable power buttons, and often the selection of power button functions is limited by the computer's design. Don't be disappointed if your PC lacks some of the abilities of others, or even lacks the ability to assign a function to the power button.

By the way, the power button has an override, one that truly gives it a purpose in life: If you press and hold the power button for about two or three seconds, it instantly turns the computer off. Remember this trick, but use it only in times of desperation. Otherwise, shut down the PC properly, as described in this chapter.

The Great Debate: Whether to Leave the Computer On All the Time

For years now, the great shutdown debate rages: Should you leave your computer on all the time? Does it waste electricity? Is it better for the PC to be on all the time — like the refrigerator or lava lamp? Will we ever know *the truth*? Of course not! But people have opinions.

"I want to leave my computer off all the time"

Hey, I'm with you.

TECHNICAL STUFF

In memory of the "three-finger salute" (Ctrl+Alt+Delete)

Since the early days, the Ctrl+Alt+Delete keystroke combination has held significance for the PC. When pressed simultaneously, this odd collection of keys has traditionally performed some shutdown function on the PC.

For example, in the days of DOS, the Ctrl+Alt+Delete keyboard shortcut forced the computer to immediately restart. It was known as the Vulcan nerve pinch. Like that subtle hand-on-the-shoulder maneuver Mr. Spock would make in the old *Star Trek* TV show, the Ctrl+Alt+Delete keyboard combination instantly rendered the PC unconscious.

In Windows, the Ctrl+Alt+Delete combo does different things, depending on the version of Windows. In Windows 98 and Windows Me, Ctrl+Alt+Delete brings up the Close Program window. In Windows 2000, it summons the Logon dialog box. And, in Windows XP, Ctrl+Alt+Delete summons the Windows Task Manager.

So, the old three-finger salute may not hold the shutdown significance it once did, but it still remains a valid Windows keyboard combination. In fact, if you press Ctrl+Alt+Delete in Windows XP, you find a Shutdown button in the Windows Task Manager dialog box. That Shutdown button contains all the commands covered in the latter part of this book.

"I want to leave my computer on all the time"

Anyone who knows anything will tell you "Yes, leave your computer on all the time, 24 hours a day, 7 days a week, and 14 days a week on the planet Mars." The only time you should turn a system off is when it will be unused for longer than a weekend. In that case, you can merely hibernate your PC rather than turn it off. (See the section "Bears do it, PCs do it — why not hibernate?" earlier in this chapter.)

Computers enjoy being on all the time. Even if you don't take advantage of Stand By (or Sleep) mode, having the PC run all the time doesn't increase your electrical bill much. And the true bonus is that any time you need to use the computer, it's there and it's on; you don't have to wait for it to start up.

✔ I leave my computer systems on all the time, mostly because I use them all the time. When I'm away from the computer for more than a few days, I hibernate it (if that option is available). Otherwise, I turn off my computers only when I take a vacation.

✔ Most businesses leave their computers on all the time.

✔ If you use your PC only once a day (during the evening for e-mail, chat, and the Internet, for example), turning it off for the rest of the day is fine.

✔ Whatever you do with your PC, it's always a good idea to turn the monitor off when you're away. Some monitors can *sleep* just like PCs, but if they don't, turning them off can save some electricity.

✔ If you do leave your computer on all the time, don't put it under a dust cover. The dust cover gives the computer its very own greenhouse effect and brings the temperatures inside the system way past the sweltering point, like in a sweaty Southern courtroom drama.

✔ Another good idea: Turn off the computer during an electrical storm. Even if you have spike protection or a UPS, *don't* let that nasty spike of voltage into your computer during a lightning storm. Unplug the computer. And remember to unplug the phone line. You can't be too careful.

Part II
Taming the Wild Information

The 5th Wave   By Rich Tennant

"They were selling contraband online. We broke through the door just as they were trying to flush the hard drive down the toilet."

In this part . . .

Computers are about storing information. This concept includes the things you create, things you collect, stuff you get from the Internet, plus endless programs and miles of data files. The job of storing, organizing, and maintaining that stuff is done by your computer's operating system, Windows.

Rather than be your pal, however, the operating system is more like a snotty little kid, the only one in the neighborhood who owns a bat and ball. It stands there and dictates rules to you when all you want to do is play. And, if the snotty little kid perceives even the most innocent slight, he grabs the bat and ball and heads home. Yes, you must play by his rules or else the game is over.

Welcome to Windows! No, it's not as terrible as the tyrannical tot on the baseball lot, but it's close! The chapters in this section help you deal with Windows and understand how best to work with your stuff on disk.

Chapter 3

Your PC's Operating System

*I*n the land of the computer, the operating system is the king. The PC began its monarchy with the DOS dynasty. You may still see some of its ruins on the PC landscape, and pagan circles still practice the strange and cryptic DOS religion. DOS was absorbed into the Empire of Windows, and for a while the two kingdoms existed peacefully. But then Windows threw DOS into the Dungeon of No Escape Key, where it has been left to rot for all eternity.

For nearly a decade now, Windows has reigned as The Supreme One on the PC. It's the main program that controls your computer's hardware, and, as such, knowing about Windows is a vital part of learning the basics of the PC.

This chapter is your general overview of Windows. Even if you feel that you know Windows well, review the sections that follow. They tell you what's important, what to ignore, and how to properly pay tribute to your computer's most powerful program.

Take Me To Your Leader

Computer operating systems have three basic duties:

➤ To control the computer hardware

➤ To control all the software

➤ To interact with you

Ideally (which means that it could never happen in real life), a computer's operating system should be quiet and efficient, never getting in the way and carrying out your instructions like a dutiful and grateful servant.

In reality, Windows is far from being dutiful or grateful. Yes, Window is your servant, but you must play the game by its own rules — and it often seems that Windows changes the rules in the middle of the game. The graphics, pictures, and mouse are supposed to make things easier on you. Even so, Windows can be devilishly frustrating.

Windows Déjà Vu

It's not that you don't know Windows — it's that you probably are unfamiliar with the various names given to those places in Windows you visit most often. As a refresher, I urge you to review the following sections.

The desktop

I cover this topic briefly in Chapter 2, but it's an important location and one most people know but don't recognize as the desktop.

Windows main screen is the *desktop*. It's the topmost location in the Windows computer system; everything else in the Windows system branches off from the desktop.

Figure 3-1 shows the desktop with the famous Windows XP background, or *wallpaper*. It's exactly like the one shown in Figure 2-4 (refer to Chapter 2), which shows the same desktop, but with a white background, or *wallpaper*.

- ✔ The *desktop* is merely the background on which Windows shows you its stuff — like an old sheet you hang from the wall to bore your neighbors with by showing your Cayman Islands vacation slide show.

- ✔ You can change the desktop wallpaper to any image. See Chapter 12.

- ✔ The desktop is called a desktop for traditional reasons. Several generations of computers ago, it really did look like a desktop, complete with paper pad, a clock, glue, scissors, and other desktop-y things.

The mouse pointer

To use Windows, you need to be able to control the computer's mouse. Moving the mouse around on your desktop moves a *mouse pointer* around on the Windows desktop. The typical mouse pointer is shown in Figure 3-2.

Figure 3-1:
The
Windows
desktop.

To make the mouse pointer even more useful, you must use the mouse's buttons. By pressing the left, or main, button (the one under your index finger), you perform a mouse *click.* This allows you to select things with the mouse, which is part of the basic computer operations.

✔ You need to know how to use a computer mouse to work Windows.

✔ If you're utterly clueless about your computer's mouse, please read Chapter 13, especially the section about basic mouse operation.

✔ Chapter 13 also contains useful information if you're an experienced mouse manipulator.

Figure 3-2:
The typical
mouse
pointer.

✔ Windows can also be manipulated with the keyboard, though it isn't as obvious as using the mouse. Various keyboard shortcuts do litter this book, similar to the way French fries and chicken nuggets find their way under a child's car seat.

Icons

The little pictures on the desktop are *icons*. In a church, icons depict pictures of saints and other famous holy people. In Windows, icons are little pictures that represent things in your computer, far from being holy. For example:

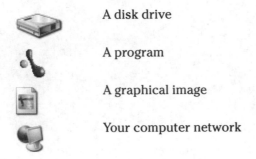

A disk drive

A program

A graphical image

Your computer network

Note that icons also have text, which further explains their content or meaning.

Icons are manipulated with the mouse and they can do all sorts of wondrous things. For now, know that they're called icons.

The taskbar

At the bottom of the desktop, you find the *taskbar,* which is a handy tool for controlling the Windows operating system. Note four important things on the taskbar, as shown in Figure 3-3: the Start button, the Quick Launch bar, window buttons, and the system tray.

Start button   Quick Launch bar   Window button   System tray

Figure 3-3:
The taskbar.

start   Wambooli - Microsoft ...   9:01 PM Wednesday

The Start button: This is where you start a number of activities in Windows. See the section "The Start Panel," later in this chapter.

The Quick Launch bar: This part of the taskbar contains buttons you can click to quickly start (or *launch*) various programs.

Window buttons: One window button appears on the taskbar for every open window or program in Windows. You switch between programs or windows by clicking its button on the taskbar.

System tray: This tiny bin on the opposite end of the taskbar from the Start button displays the current time and day, but also wee little icons that represent special programs running in Windows. You can see more information about the special programs by either double-clicking or right-clicking their wee tiny icons.

The taskbar can support other toolbars as well, such as the Sound bar from Microsoft Office, custom toolbars, and even an Address bar, where you can type Web pages or the names of commands to run. But mostly it's used to get at the Start button and click the various windows buttons that come and go as you plod through your computer day.

✔ Note that the icons on the Quick Launch bar lack text descriptions. To see a description of the button, point the mouse at the icon and hold it still for a second or two. A description then appears.

✔ Sometimes, Windows XP "stacks" window buttons on top of each other. For example, if you have three Internet Explorer windows open, you may see a button like this:

Clicking the button displays a pop-up menu from which you can choose a specific window.

✔ The system tray is also known as the *system notification area*. They were going to call it the *system notification observation tray*, but that acronym is SNOT, which Microsoft deemed unacceptable.

✔ The system tray in Windows XP routinely hides its little icons, especially if they don't do anything other than sit there. To see all the icons, click the Show More arrows (depicted in the margin).

✔ A supplemental Taskbar Tutorial is available on my Web page, www. wambooli.com. Look for the *E-Docs* link to find more information. Until then, the nearby sidebar, "Taming the taskbar," should sate some of your taskbar appetite.

Taming the taskbar

The taskbar is not welded to the bottom of your computer screen, nor is it of a fixed size. No, the taskbar is a bouncy, elastic little booger. It can live on any of the four edges of your computer screen, and it can be fatter than a club sandwich or thinner than a supermodel. Needless to say, these various and seemingly useless options can drive you batty.

You can move the taskbar with the mouse: Point the mouse at any blank area between the Quick Launch bar and system tray. Press and hold the mouse button and then *drag* the taskbar to any other edge of the screen.

To shrink or grow the taskbar: Point the mouse at the taskbar's top edge. The mouse pointer changes to a this-way-or-that-way arrow. Drag the taskbar to make it fatter or thinner.

If the taskbar appears to be missing, it was probably shrunk to a thin line. Look for that line. Then use the mouse to drag it out to a thicker size.

To prevent the taskbar from being molested: Right-click the mouse on any blank part of the taskbar. From the pop-up menu that appears, choose Lock the Taskbar. Clunk! The taskbar is now immobile and safe from corruption.

The Start Panel

Humans have a belly button; Windows has the Start button. The Start button is located on the left side of the taskbar, which isn't a navel-like center, like your belly button, yet it's not filled with disgusting lint either.

The Start button is handy because it summons the all-important Start panel, from which you start most of the programs you use in Windows, visit various important places, or make adjustments to the way your PC runs.

The Start panel is shown in Figure 3-4. Those icons on the left represent popular programs plus the last several programs you have run. Icons on the right show places to visit, plus a smattering of control and setting options.

To get at the full list of applications, you must click the More Programs button, found in the lower-left area of the Start panel. Clicking that button displays a cascading list of menus, which is where you find all your PC's programs listed.

    ✔ If you would rather use your keyboard to see the Start panel, press the Windows key or the Ctrl+Esc key combination. This works whether or not you can even see the Start button.

- Not all Start panels look alike. Figure 3-4 shows the standard view. A more limited, less graphical view can also be chosen. Also note that not all the options visible in Figure 3-4 may be present on your computer. The More Programs option may be titled All Programs or just Programs.

- The Programs submenus are rather slippery. They pop up and disappear as your mouse roves over them. So be careful! Accessing them can be aggravating if you're a sloppy mouse mover or your mouse is too sensitive.

- Refrain from beating your mouse into your table when it behaves erratically.

- The Start panel is controlled from the taskbar and Start Menu Properties dialog box, on the Start Menu tab. To visit that location, right-click the Start button and choose Properties from the pop-up menu. Use the Customize button on the Start Menu tab to control how the Start panel looks.

- The User Accounts icon in the Control Panel sits in the picture at the top of the Start panel. To change the image, just click the picture.

Figure 3-4:
The Start
panel.

Other, Fun Places to Visit

Windows is a graphical amusement park of fun things to play with, stuff to drive you crazy, interesting rides over which you waste colossal amounts of time, and enough junk food to unsettle even the most ironclad of stomachs.

The following are the amusement park's e-ticket rides. They're the ones you may have heard of or the places you may find yourself going to more often. Knowing these items, what they do, and how to get to them is important. Bone up:

 My Computer: This icon is on the desktop. Opening it reveals the contents of your computer, depicted as various icons. You see icons for each account's folders and for various hard drives and removable drives, and an icon for the Control Panel.

 My Documents: This icon is on the desktop. It represents a folder on the hard drive where most programs urge you to save your documents. Get it? You save *your documents* in the *My Documents* folder.

 My Network Places: This icon is on the desktop. It represents any network connections you may have, such as local networks, but also remote computers and the Internet.

 Recycle Bin: This icon is on the desktop. It represents File Hell — or that location where files are sent when you delete them. It's more like File Limbo in that it's possible to recover files from the Recycle Bin when you change your almighty mind.

 Control Panel: This icon isn't found on the desktop, but can be accessed through either the My Computer icon or, often, the Start panel. Opening the Control Panel displays zillions of icons used to control the PC's options and settings — an important place to note.

> ✔ You work with the Control Panel and its many icons throughout Part III of this book.
>
> ✔ Most activity in a computer is centered around the management of files, programs, and folders. These topics are covered over the next several chapters.

Here a Window, There a Window

Windows gets its name from the various windows displayed on the screen. That's why it's called Windows and not Doors or Casements or Transoms.

The windows displayed on the screen are used to show you information, presented in a manner that lets you see multiple things at one time. In a way, the windows work like multiple sheets of paper you can shuffle as you work through your day. But in another way, it doesn't work at all like that. Therefore, the following sections provide an introductory tutorial on basic window operation.

Moving a window around

Windows puts its windows wherever Windows wants. But you can be proudly disobedient and shuffle the window to wherever you desire. To do that, drag the window by its title bar, as shown in Figure 3-5.

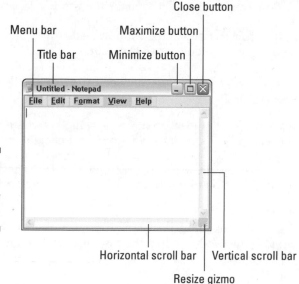

Close button

Menu bar

Maximize button

Title bar

Minimize button

Figure 3-5:
Basic
window
anatomy.

Horizontal scroll bar | Vertical scroll bar

Resize gizmo

If you cannot see the title bar, you can use your keyboard to move the window around. Obey these steps:

1. **Press Ctrl+Spacebar.**

   This step activates the window's Control menu, found in the window's upper-left corner.

2. **Press M (for Move).**

3. **Use the arrow keys on your keyboard to move the window.**

   Use the up-, down-, left-, or right-arrow key; press the key to inch the window in that direction.

4. **Press the Enter key when you're done.**

Note that you cannot move a window when it has been maximized. See the next section.

Changing a window's size

A window can be just about any size, from filling the entire screen to too small to be useful and everything in between.

To manually resize a window, point the mouse at the resize gizmo in the window's lower-right corner. Drag the mouse up and to the left to make the window smaller or down and to the right to make the window larger.

You can also point the mouse at any of the window's edges or corners and drag to make that part of the window move in or out.

To quickly change the window's size, you can use the resizing buttons on the window's title bar, on the right end:

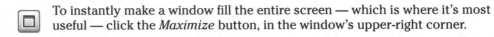 To instantly make a window fill the entire screen — which is where it's most useful — click the *Maximize* button, in the window's upper-right corner.

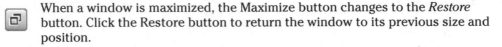 When a window is maximized, the Maximize button changes to the *Restore* button. Click the Restore button to return the window to its previous size and position.

The *Minimize* button is used to shrink the window into a button on the taskbar. That's useful for shoving the window out of the way and as a temporary alternative to closing the window.

Here's a slew of other window-resizing tips, advice, and nonsense:

✔ When you point the mouse at the edge of a window, the mouse pointer changes to a two-way arrow. It shows that you have found the sweet spot — for resizing the window, but also for directions in which to drag the mouse.

✔ To restore a minimized window, click its button on the taskbar. That restores the window from a button back to the way it looked before it was minimized.

✔ The keyboard commands for maximizing a window are Alt+spacebar (to display the window's Control menu) and then the X key.

✔ To restore a window with the keyboard, press Alt+spacebar and then press the R key.

✔ The keyboard commands to minimize a window are Alt+spacebar, N.

 ✔ To change a window's size with the keyboard, press Alt+spacebar and then S to choose the Size command from the Control menu. Use the arrow keys (up, down, right, or left) to select which edge of the window you want to move. Then press up, down, left, or right to move that edge of the window in that direction.

✔ Windows remembers the last location of your windows and tries to return them to that location when it opens the window again. Windows does not, however, remember when you maximized a window.

✔ Some windows can't be maximized. Some games, for example, have a fixed window size you can't change. Don't be greedy.

✔ To instantly minimize all windows on the screen, press the Win+M keyboard command. To restore the windows, press Win+Shift+M.

✔ If you're working with several programs, you may want to arrange their windows onscreen so that each is visible. To do that, right-click a blank part of the taskbar or right-click the time (on the right side of the taskbar). From the menu that pops up, select either Tile Horizontally, Tile Vertically, or Cascade Windows to arrange your windows onscreen.

Scrolling about

Often, what you're looking at in a window is larger than the window. To see everything, the window is equipped with *scroll bars* that let you slide the window's content up, down, left, or right. Figure 3-6 shows how you can manipulate a scroll bar.

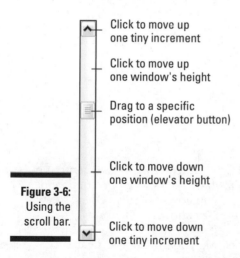

Click to move up
one tiny increment

Click to move up
one window's height

Drag to a specific
position (elevator button)

Click to move down
one window's height

Figure 3-6:
Using the
scroll bar.

Click to move down
one tiny increment

Figure 3-6 shows a vertical scroll bar. A horizontal scroll bar is used to help see items wider than the window's width.

Note that the elevator button's size changes relative to the amount of information visible in the window. If the button gets big enough, you can resize the window to see all the contents at one time. (When all the contents are visible, the scroll bars either vanish or "dim" and become unavailable.)

Using the menu commands

Commands in a graphical operating system like Windows are stored on menus, which appear on a menu bar inside a program's window, as shown in Figure 3-7.

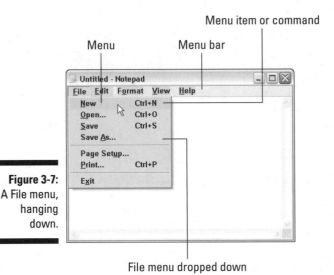

Menu item or command

Menu   Menu bar

Figure 3-7:
A File menu,
hanging
down.

File menu dropped down

Each word on the menu bar — File and Edit, for example — is a menu title. Each title represents a drop-down menu, which contains menu commands related to the title. For example, the File menu contains Save, Open, New, Close, and other commands related to files, as shown in Figure 3-7.

Menus are manipulated using the mouse or keyboard. To use the mouse, point and click at a menu name or command to choose it.

To use the keyboard, press the Alt key to activate the menus and then use the underlined letters in the names and commands to select items. For example, press Alt and note that the F on the File menu is activated. Press F to drop down the File menu, and then choose the command you want by pressing its underlined letter.

- ✓ Press the Esc (escape) key on the keyboard to cancel if you change your mind while perusing the menus.

- ✓ Some programs use *personalized* menus. These menus don't show all the commands and often rearrange commands as you use them. Though this sounds wonderful, in practice it can be frustrating. Refer to the program's Help file for information on disabling the personalized menus.

- ✓ In this book, I use the format File⇨Close to represent menu choices. You can use the mouse or, from the keyboard, use the underlined letters; press Alt, F, C.

Closing a window

Close a window by clicking the X button in the window's upper-right corner. This action removes the window from the desktop. If the window contained unsaved information, you're asked to save before the window closes.

- ✓ Some windows are really programs. In addition to clicking the Close button, you can choose the File⇨Exit command from the menu.

- ✓ The keyboard command to close a window is the utterly strange Alt+F4 combination. Who knows?

Struggling with a dialog box

When it comes to making choices, a specialized type of window, called a *dialog box* is displayed. The dialog box contains gadgets and gizmos you click, slide, and type, all of which control something or set certain optional options. Clicking an OK button sends off your choices to the program for proper digestion.

As with other parts of Windows, you should be familiar with the various parts of a dialog box, a typical example of which is shown in Figure 3-8. Each of the parts illustrated in the figure is manipulated by using the mouse — but that's not important. What is important is knowing the names:

Tabs: These display various panels or pages of a dialog box. Not every dialog box has tabs, but many do; some dialog boxes have up to 15 tabs! You click a tab to see the contents of its panel or sheet, or from the keyboard press Ctrl+Tab to *cycle* through the tabs.

Help button: Click this button and then point and click any gizmo in the dialog box to see a pop-up description of what that gizmo controls.

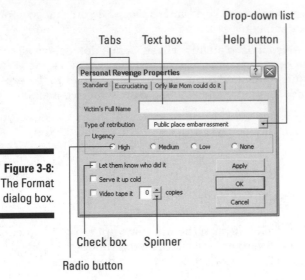

Tabs   Text box   Drop-down list   Help button

Figure 3-8:
The Format
dialog box.

Check box   Spinner

Radio button

Text box: This is where you can type information, also called an *input box*.

Drop-down list: Clicking the down-pointing arrow button to the right of the list displays a menu of choices. If the list is long, it has a scroll bar to one side, which you can use to scroll up or down.

Radio button: Click to select one of many options. Radio buttons are usually grouped together into families, such as the four that were shown in Figure 3-8. As with an old car radio, you can select only one button at a time.

Spinner: This device usually accompanies a text box with a value. You can enter a value directly into the box or use the spinner buttons and the mouse to increase or decrease the value.

Check box: When you click this box with the mouse, a check or X appears inside, indicating that you have selected that option. To remove the check mark and turn the option off, click the mouse in the box again. Unlike with radio buttons, you can click the mouse in as many check boxes as necessary.

After you have made your selections, you click the OK button to send those choices off to the program. Sometimes the OK button may be given a different name, such as Start, Next or Finish. It all depends on the nature of the dialog box.

Clicking the Cancel button disregards any changes and closes the dialog box. This action is the same as clicking the dialog box's X close button (in the upper-right corner).

Some dialog boxes sport an Apply button. You can click that button to apply changes without closing the dialog box. That way, you can preview things and continue to make changes in the dialog box without having to close.

- Pressing the Enter key in a dialog box is usually the same as clicking the OK button with your mouse.

- Pressing the Esc (escape) key on your keyboard is the same as clicking the Cancel button in a dialog box.

- If more than one input box appears in a dialog box, press the Tab key to move between them. Don't press the Enter key because that's the same as clicking the OK button and telling Windows that you're done with the dialog box.

- Many other types of gizmos can appear in a dialog box, from scrolling lists to pop-up menus to sliders and dials and you-name-it. These devices are all manipulated by using the mouse and are generally easy to figure out.

Begging Windows for Help

Help in Windows is always handy and occasionally useful. The key to remember is F1. Why they chose F1, I'll never know. F for "F anyone needs help?" or perhaps "Forget it, 1 needs help!" or even "Felp!" Anyone f'wonder f'what's going f'on? Oh, I give up. . . .

When you press F1 in Windows, you activate the Help and Support Center. In each individual program, pressing F1 offers help on whatever operation you're attempting — which is known as *contextual help* and can be rather handy.

Mostly, you work the help system by using the Search box to type a question and then see what kind of answers pop up. In Figure 3-9, you see the results for when I type **Close a window**. Item number 4 in the Full-text Search Matches is closest to what I want to know, so I can click that item to get more information. That's how it works.

- Click any text you see in the help system to get helpful information about that topic. Yes, the "helpful information" is essentially what would have been in the printed manual years ago. It's dry. Boring. And sometimes actually helpful.

- Note that often the help system tries to contact the Internet for some information. In fact, it's now the rage to put all the help files on the Internet.

- For troubleshooting help, search for the word *troubleshoot*.

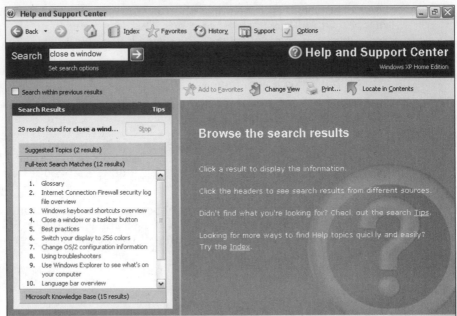

Figure 3-9:
Help?

The help engine is its own program. When you're done using help, remember to quit: Click the X Close button in the upper-left corner of the window.

Chapter 4

The Joys of Disk Storage

*A*s your number-one piece of software, Windows has many thankless jobs. One of its most underappreciated jobs is to manage your information inside the computer. Rather than whirl around like witches in a cyclone, information is carefully managed inside the PC. Windows stores information in the computer's memory while you're working on it, but otherwise it's kept safe and resting in your PC's disk drives.

Disk drives are your PC's closet, used for electronic storage. Your computer most likely has at least three different types of disk drives, possibly more, each of which stores information in a different way. This chapter tells you about those storage devices and to how to work with disk drives in Windows.

✔ Chapter 10 also covers disk drives, though from a purely hardware point of view.

✔ The terms *disk drive* and *disk* are often used interchangeably. Storing something *on disk* means to save it to a disk drive somewhere in your computer system.

✔ Watch out for the ugly term disk memory. Although technically correct, it's confusing. *Memory* (or *RAM*) is where your computer does its work. The *disk* is where your work is stored. *Disk memory* is just another term for disk or storage on a disk drive, so when you see *disk memory,* just think *disk drive.*

Why Use Disk Drives?

All your software, Windows, all those applications and programs, plus all that stuff you create has to be put someplace inside the computer. Those huge pictures your cousin e-mailed you of her new, ugly baby; the chart you keep of how much longer it will take to recover your 401K retirement investments; those four dozen attempts you have made at starting a novel; and the doodles you made when you phoned the Psychic Hot Tub Girls Network — they have to be stored somewhere.

Stow that data, sailor!

Disk drives provide the long-term storage solution for all your files, programs, and the stuff you create with your computer. They have been doing so for 40 years in the computer biz, though disk drives are now cheaper, weigh less, and cost much less than they did in psychedelic '60s.

- Think of the disk drive as a huge closet or garage. Don't worry about the mess; the operating system (Windows) helps you organize things and even find things when you're unable to organize them yourself.

- Before disk drives, there were many different and silly ways to store computer information. Most common was on those reel-to-reel tape machines, once the staple of old science fiction movies and TV shows. (Those machines were merely the storage unit, not "the computer," but they got face time on camera because they were visually interesting.)

The glories of long-term storage

A question you may have is "Why use disk drives when the computer comes with megabytes of memory?" That's a good question!

Computer memory, or RAM, is also a storage place inside the computer. But, unlike disk storage, RAM is *active*. When you run a program, work on a document, or edit an image, you're doing so in RAM. That's where the action is.

Alas, RAM is only short-term, temporary storage; when you turn off the computer, the contents of RAM go *poof!* This works like some guys I know: They're fine for limited tasks, which is like RAM. But for long-term stuff, they have to write things down — like storing files on disk. Just like those guys writing things down, your computer needs a more permanent form of storage, and that permanent storage comes in the form of disk drives.

✔ Your computer's disk drives provide long-term storage for the stuff you create, files, programs, and other information inside your computer.

✔ No, Bill. I don't mean you. Or Myles.

✔ See Chapter 11 for more information on computer memory (RAM).

Where Your PC's Disk Drives Lurk

Physically, your computer's disk drives are nestled inside the console, though your PC may also sport external drives. As far as Windows is concerned, the place to find your PC's hard drives is the My Computer window. Follow these steps:

1. **Locate the My Computer icon on the desktop.**

   Though you can configure Windows to hide this icon, it normally appears on the desktop.

2. **Double-click the My Computer icon to open it.**

   The My Computer window is displayed.

The My Computer window lists important files and locations inside your computer, plus lots of other unnecessary and immoral junk. Figure 4-1 illustrates the part of the My Computer window that displays the disk storage information. (What you see on your computer will be different.)

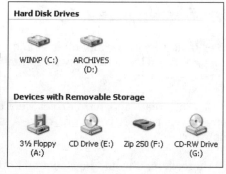

Figure 4-1: Disk drives lurking in the My Computer window.

Observe how each disk drive has an icon, a letter, and an optional name. For example, the first hard drive has the traditional hard drive icon, the letter designation *C,* and in Figure 4-1 it has the name WINXP.

Familiarize yourself with your PC's disk drives, their letters, and any names.

Disk drive icons

All disk drives have an icon. Quite a variety is shown in Figure 4-1, though your PC may not sport all of them. Even more icons are available. Here's a quick list:

 Floppy Drive icon: This represents your PC's floppy disk, which Windows describes as the $3^1/_2$ Floppy because the disks are 3½ inches square.

 Hard Drive icon: This represents the hard disk drive. Your computer may also have a second hard drive, in which case more than one icon is used, as shown earlier, in Figure 4-1. Each hard drive gets its own icon, letter, and name.

 CD-ROM or DVD icon: The same icon is used for CD-ROM, CD-R, CD-RW, DVD-ROM, and all drives of that ilk. It's the *shiny media icon*. This may seem confusing now, but it really isn't in practice.

 The CD-ROM or DVD drive icon changes when a disk is in the drive. For example, if a musical CD is in the drive, the icon changes to the music disc icon, as shown in the margin. Likewise, an icon for a DVD movie may appear, or the icon representing a program on the disk may also be used in place of the standard, boring CD-ROM/DVD drive icon.

 Zip drive icon: Other drives may exist in your system, such as the Zip drive shown in Figure 4-1. Each of these has its own, special icon.

Drive letters from A (skip B) to Z

Windows refers to its disk drives by letters of the alphabet — and note that it's the good old American alphabet, too. This is not only for alphabetical but also historical reasons. Here's how it works:

Drive A: The PC's floppy drive. Twenty years ago, hard drives were expensive, and the first IBM PC used floppy drives instead. Therefore, drive A is the PC's first drive and it's always a floppy drive.

Drive B: There is no drive B. If there were, it would be a second floppy drive. Yep: Twenty years ago, two floppy drives were more economical than one hard drive. Drive letter B is now reserved by Windows just in case — like nipples on men.

Drive C: The hard drive, which is the PC's main disk drive.

Drive D: If a second hard drive is available, drive D is that second hard drive. Otherwise it's the PC's CD-ROM or DVD drive.

Changing the letters of a removable drive (if you dare!)

In Windows XP, you can change the drive letters for any removable drives in your system. For example, make the DVD-ROM drive V and the CD-RW drive W, or the Zip drive can be drive Z. Follow these steps:

1. **Choose Run from the Start panel or press Win+R to display the Run dialog box.**

2. **Type COMPMGMT.MSC in the Open text box and then click OK.**

   This step runs the Computer Management console, an administrative tool in Windows XP.

3. **Under the Storage area (on the left), click to select Disk Management.**

   A scrolling list of your disk drives appears on the right side of the window. Removable drives are located in the lower part on the right; you may need to scroll down to see them.

4. **Right-click a removable drive on the scrolling list.**

5. **Choose the option Change Drive Letter and Paths from the pop-up menu.**

   Another dialog box appears.

6. **Click the Change button.**

7. **Select a new drive letter and click OK.**

   A warning appears, which applies to any programs that are run from the removable disk or that access files on that disk.

8. **Click Yes only if you're certain that programs won't be affected.**

9. **Close the Computer Management window.**

The change takes place immediately and can be seen in the My Computer window. If you need to change the letter back, simply repeat these steps and remove the new letter by clicking the Remove button in Step 6.

Honestly, after drive C, there is no tradition regarding disk drive letters. The pecking order goes like this:

- If the computer has any second or third hard drives, they're given drive letters D and up.

- After the last hard drive letter, the CD-ROM or DVD drive(s) get the next letter(s) of the alphabet.

- After the CD-ROM/DVD drives come any additional removable drives in whichever order the computer happens to find them when it first starts.

If you have a label maker, label your removable drives: Put *A* on drive A, and label your CD-ROM drive with its letter, as well as your Zip drive and other external drives.

Important drive D stuff

Drive D is important for many reasons. Let me make up a few:

First, if you have a hard drive D, *don't neglect it!* That's usable disk storage you have — so take advantage of drive D and store your stuff there. There's nothing wrong with installing software or saving your stuff to another hard drive.

Second, on many computers, drive D can be the CD-ROM or DVD drive — but note that this is not always the case. Never assume that drive D is a CD-ROM drive until you confirm it in the My Computer window.

- Sadly, drive D sits empty on most people's PCs.
- On my computers, I typically install games on hard drive D. I have no reason for this, other than that it forces me to use drive D.
- Don't depend on a PC's CD-ROM drive to have the same drive letter on every computer!

Don't forget your colon!

Disk drive names are not merely the letter that's given! A colon follows the letter. So, drive A is A: (A-colon) and C is C:. This is apparent if you study Figure 4-1 and note how each drive letter (in parentheses) has a colon next to it.

Note that it's proper to pronounce *A:* as "A-colon," as in:

Alex Trebek: People use this to digest food.

You: A colon.

Alex: I'm sorry, you must phrase that response in the form of a question.

Leering at Your Hard Drives

To peek at a disk drive's contents, open the drive! Double-click its icon in the My Computer window — though for a removable disk, there had better be a disk inside the drive or else Windows grumbles. For hard drives, however, it's always safe to open them and view their contents.

Disk drive letter examples

Disk drive letters are assigned differently, depending on the computer. The following table shows examples of how different computers use drive letters.

Mary's PC		Phil's PC	
Drive A, floppy		Drive A, floppy	
Drive C, hard drive		Drive C, hard drive	
Drive D, CD-ROM		Drive D, hard drive	
Drive E		Drive E, CD-ROM	
Drive F		Drive F, Zip	

Both Mary and Phil receive the instructions "Insert the installation disk into drive *D:*, where *D* is the letter of the CD-ROM drive." Each has unique tasks. Mary must insert the CD into drive D. Phil inserts the disc into drive E.

The point to all this is to know your disk drives. Remember that the drive letters for your PC are unique. That's why some instruction manuals are vague.

Opening a hard drive's icon displays the *root folder* for that drive. For this chapter, who cares? But you discover more about the root folder in Chapter 5, where it's more appropriate.

  For now, return to the My Computer window by clicking either the Back or Up button on the toolbar.

Official disk information

Windows knows more about your disk drives than what their icons, letters, or names are. Each disk drive in the My Computer window has a virtual beehive of information whirling about it. To see this stuff, follow these steps:

1. **Right-click a hard drive icon in the My Computer window.**

   A pop-up menu appears (which usually happens when you right-click something).

2. **Choose Properties from the shortcut menu.**

   The disk's Properties dialog box appears, as shown in Figure 4-2.

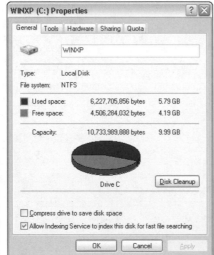

Figure 4-2:
Too much
information
about the
disk!

The information displayed in the disk's Properties dialog box is massive. Aside from the disk usage information (covered in the next section), most of the information displayed is trivial.

Note the disk File System type. That plays a role in how long the disk's name (in the upper text box in Figure 4-2) can be. For NTFS file systems, used primarily on hard drives, the disk's name can be up to 32 characters long. Disks using the older FAT file system type (floppies and Zip disks) can have a name only 11 characters long.

Other tabs in the dialog box offer other information or let you control certain aspects of the disk. The Tools tab, in particular, is used for everyday disk maintenance, as is the Disk Cleanup button on the General tab.

Click OK to close the Properties dialog box when you're done gawking.

- Ensure that a disk is in the drive before you attempt to view the Properties dialog box for a removable disk.

- To change the disk's name, type a new name to the text box shown in Figure 4-2.

- To remove the name, select the text and delete it. Disks don't need names, so this doesn't harm anything.

- The disk's name is also known as the *label,* or, if you want to be really la-di-da, it's the *volume label.*

- The NTFS and FAT acronyms describe the way information is written to a disk. The names appear in the disk drive's Properties dialog box (refer to Figure 4-2).

Is the disk drive half full or half empty?

Perhaps the most important thing shown in a disk drive's Properties dialog box is the disk usage information. In addition to the graphical pie chart, you should pay attention to three other values:

Capacity: The maximum amount of bytes the disk can store.

Used Space: The number of bytes occupied by programs, files, and other information storage on the disk.

Free Space: The difference between capacity and used space; the space still left on the drive for storing more stuff.

Obviously, you want to keep an eye on disk usage — specifically, the Free Space value. In most cases, you should have plenty of room on the disk for all your junk. But if you store things such as MP3 music files, videos, or lots of graphics, free disk space can dwindle rapidly.

- Disk storage is measured in *bytes* — mostly *megabytes* and *gigabytes.* See Table 10-1, in Chapter 10, for more information about what these terms measure.

- CD-ROM and DVD disks are always full! That's because those disks can only be read from, not written to.

Dealing with a rapidly filling hard drive

Will your hard drive run out of room? Hopefully not. When disk space gets tight, Windows automatically pops up a "You are low on disk space" warning.

Until that happens, you really don't need to worry about filling up a hard drive. In fact, I wouldn't become concerned about disk space until the disk pie (see Figure 4-2) is well beyond 80 percent full.

If you're really concerned, here are my thoughts for creating more disk space:

✔ Run the Disk Cleanup utility at least once a month. From the Start panel, choose Programs⇨Accessories⇨System Tools⇨Disk Cleanup. This removes unnecessary programs, deletes temporary files, cleans out Internet junk, and empties the Recycle Bin. It's amazing.

✔ Open the Control Panel's Internet Options icon. On the General tab of the Internet Properties dialog box, click the Settings button. Adjust the item labeled Amount of disk space to use to the lowest possible value. Click the OK button and close the various dialog boxes and the Control Panel. This trick saves a ton of space that Internet Explorer otherwise gobbles up.

✔ Consider archiving some graphics images, older document files, projects, and sound files to Zip disks or CD-Rs. For example, I archive each book I write after I finish writing it. Each one sits on a separate CD-R disc in my fire safe. I also have an archive on CD-R of all my favorite fonts. Graphics images, I save to Zip disks. This saves a ton of hard drive space.

If space gets really crunchy and you have tried everything, you have only one real choice: Buy your PC a second, larger hard drive. You can buy an internal drive, which can fit into most PCs. Or, if room is tight, get an external hard drive, a USB 2.0 or Firewire drive. This is a great way to expand your computer's storage system without having to sacrifice any files from the hard drive.

Finally, a warning: Please do not use disk compression to increase the space used on your disk drives. In Figure 4-2, at the bottom of a disk's Properties dialog box, on the General tab, is an option labeled Compress drive to save disk space. Don't click it! Disk compression programs often make a crowded disk situation worse, in my opinion. Installing a second hard drive is much better than putting up with the mental anguish of disk compression.

Using the CD-ROM and DVD Drives

If you have had any experience using a CD player at home or in your car, or if you have a DVD unit attached to your TV, you instantly know how to use the same device on your computer. What more can I say?

✔ See Chapter 7, which covers creating your own CD and DVD discs.

✔ Chapter 10 covers the mechanical side of using a CD/DVD drive.

Playing a music CD or DVD movie

This task is easy: To play a music CD or view a DVD movie, simply insert that disc into the drive. The music starts playing instantly, or the movie cues up and runs on your screen.

- ✔ DVD movies can be played only in DVD drives. Music CDs can be played in either CD-ROM or DVD drives.

- ✔ Unless you have another type of jukebox program, the Windows Media Player program plays music CDs. Use the various buttons on the Media Player as you would buttons on a standard CD player.

- ✔ When you put a music CD into your CD-ROM drive, the CD icon in the My Computer window changes to a musical CD icon, as shown in the margin.

- ✔ DVD movies are played in the Windows Media Player program, unless you have an alternative movie program installed.

- ✔ It's best to view a DVD movie in as large a window as possible.

- ✔ The DVD movie controls typically disappear a few moments after the movie starts. To see them again, just jiggle the mouse.

Running software from a CD-ROM

Pretty much all the new software you install on your PC comes on a CD-ROM disc. You insert the disk, the software is installed, or you see a menu from which you can install the software or tell the disk to go sit and spin.

Note that in most cases the software you install from a CD-ROM is fully copied from the CD to the hard drive. In other cases, such as games and various references, such as a collection of fonts or clipart graphics, most of the information stays on the CD. The good thing about this is that with the information still on the CD, it doesn't chew up precious hard drive space. The bad thing is that you have to remember to insert the CD disc into the drive whenever you play the game or use the software.

- ✔ In many cases, you're given the option of how much of a program to install when you first set it up. Use the Custom or Advanced option or whichever method allows you to copy everything from the CD to the hard drive.

- ✔ Note that some games require the CD to be inserted before you can play the game, no matter what; this is a form of piracy protection to ensure that you own the games you play.

> ✔ In addition to being supplied on a CD-ROM disc, new software may also come on floppies. More often, you *download* new software from the Internet. (See Part IV of this book.)

The Antique Floppy Drive

Floppy disk drives are holdovers from an older period in computers. Their main limitation is capacity: A floppy disk holds barely 1.5 *megabytes* of data. In 1988, when the average hard drive stored 20 *megabytes* of data, a 1.5MB floppy disk was a goodly size. But now, floppy disks just don't have the storage space needed to be useful on a modern PC.

> ✔ It's perfectly okay if you never use your PC's floppy drive.
>
> ✔ See Chapter 6 for information on moving files between a floppy disk and the hard drive.
>
> ✔ Floppy drives eat floppy disks. See Chapter 10 for more information.

Using a floppy disk

Though archaic, floppy disks can still be used, though I don't recommend doing so. If a file fits on a floppy disk, you can use it for mailing files (I do). Otherwise, creating a CD-R disc is almost as inexpensive, plus the CD-R disc holds 600 times more information.

If you must use a floppy disk, use it only for *copies* and not for original files. Create the file and store it on the hard drive. Then create a copy of the file on the floppy disk. See Chapter 6 for the details.

Never use the floppy disk to store files you're downloading from the Internet! A while back, some computer "guru" told people that it was safer to download files directly from the Internet on a floppy. This is hogwash. The hard drive is your first place to save files. Put only copies on floppies.

Floppy disk errors

If Windows tells you that a floppy disk is bad or unusable, has a read or write fault, or is otherwise indistinguishable from a slice of Velveeta inserted into the drive, *throw the damn disk away!*

The only other common floppy disk error you see is that it's unformatted. If so, format the disk. Keep reading.

Formatting floppy disks

A floppy disk must be formatted before it can be used. The best way to ensure that this happens is to buy floppy disks preformatted; it states right on the box that the disks are formatted or "IBM Formatted." If so, great. If not, you have to format your own disks. Here's how:

1. **Stick an unformatted disk in drive A.**

2. **Open the My Computer icon.**

3. **Right-click the floppy drive icon, Drive A.**

4. **Choose Format from the pop-up menu.**

   The Format dialog box appears, similar to what's shown in Figure 4-3.

Figure 4-3:
The Format
dialog box.

5. **Click the Start button.**

   A warning dialog box appears. Yeah, yeah: Click OK.

The formatting process takes between a cup of tea and a shave to complete, so occupy yourself until the computer has finished formatting.

If the disk cannot be formatted, click OK and then *throw the disk away*. Try again with a new disk.

If the disk survives the formatting process, click the OK button. Click the Close button to dismiss the Format dialog box. Then — most importantly — remove the disk from the drive. Apply a label to the disk. Now you're ready to use the floppy disk.

- ✔ Formatting any disk erases the contents of that disk. Reformat only older disks that contain information you don't want to keep.

- ✔ Always label your floppy disks.

- ✔ Don't use sticky notes as disk labels. They fall off when you're not looking and can sometimes get stuck inside your disk drives.

Using a Zip Drive

Zip drives are becoming popular alternatives and supplements to the traditional PC floppy disk. Zip drives eat Zip disks, which can store information in 100-, 250-, or 750-megabyte capacities, making them an ideal companion to a hard drive for saving, backing up, or transporting programs and all sorts of files.

- ✔ For technical operation of the Zip drive, see Chapter 10.

- ✔ Zip drives work like any other disk drive in your computer system. They're most similar to floppy disks, but, unlike floppies, they store massive amounts of information and are far more reliable.

Looking at the Zip menu

Zip disks have their own, special menu. After you insert a Zip disk into the drive, right-click the Zip disk icon in the My Computer window. You see a detailed menu pop up with special Zip menu items, as shown in Figure 4-4.

Note the special commands flagged by the *I* (for Iomega, Zip's manufacturer). These are Zip-drive-only commands:

Format: A customized format command specific to Zip drives. This command is the one you would use to reformat your Zip disks. (All Zip disks are preformatted, so this really should be the Reformat command.)

Protect: A nifty option that restricts access to the disk. This is one of the only ways you can password-protect your files in Windows. The single password applies to the whole disk.

Eject: Spits the disk out of the drive.

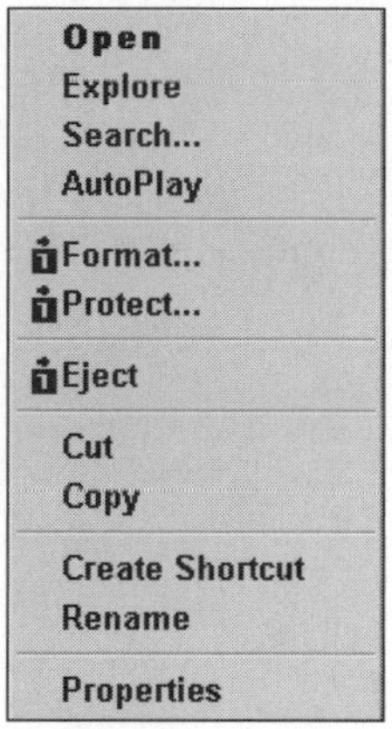

```
Open
Explore
Search...
AutoPlay

Format...
Protect...

Eject

Cut
Copy

Create Shortcut
Rename

Properties
```

Figure 4-4:
A Zip drive's
special
menu.

Different versions of the Zip software may display additional menu items. For the full details, you need to refer to the Zip disk manual.

Formatting the Zip disk

Zip disks fill up — even after you delete files from them. To fix this problem, you need to reformat the disk to get its space back. First, ensure that everything you want to keep is copied off the Zip disk and to the hard drive for safekeeping. Then, format the Zip disk using the special Format command on the Zip disk's pop-up menu; refer to the preceding section.

Putting a Zip drive shortcut on the desktop

I find my Zip drive so handy that I put a shortcut icon to the drive right on my desktop (refer to Figure 2-4, in Chapter 2). You can do this for any disk drive in your system. Here's how:

1. **Open the My Computer icon on the desktop.**

2. **Click the disk drive icon you want to copy from the My Computer window and to the desktop.**

3. **Choose File⇨Create Shortcut from the menu.**

   Windows doesn't let you create a shortcut in the My Computer window, so it recommends that you create the shortcut on the desktop instead — which is what you wanted in the first place!

4. **Click the Yes button.**

   The shortcut is created. To prove it:

5. **Close the My Computer window.**

You see the icon, right on the desktop.

To remove the icon, simply delete it. It's okay to delete shortcut icons, which doesn't delete the original. See Chapter 6 for more information on shortcut icons as well as how to delete things.

The "Deciding What to Do with the Disk" Window

Sometimes, inserting a removable disk (CD, DVD, or Zip) causes the What the Heck Do You Want Me to Do with This Disk? dialog box to be displayed (see Figure 4-5).

Figure 4-5: The "What the heck do you want me to do with this disk?" window.

Choose an option based on the disk's contents. For example, if the disk contains music, choose the Play option; if it contains images, choose the Copy pictures option; to work with files, choose the option to open the folder to view files; or click the Cancel button or choose the Take no action item to just ignore the disk and keep working.

On the bright side, you don't need to bother with the What the Heck (etc.) dialog box. You can preprogram Windows to deal with any inserted disk as you choose. Follow these steps:

1. **Open the My Computer icon.**

2. **Right-click the removable drive you want to configure.**

3. **Choose Properties from the pop-up shortcut menu.**

   The disk drive's Properties icon appears, as shown earlier, in Figure 4-2.

4. **Click the AutoPlay tab.**

   This tab appears on only certain types of removable disk drives. Figure 4-6 displays its contents.

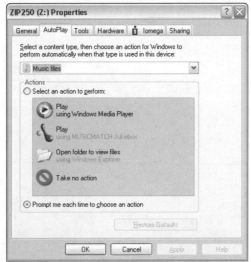

Figure 4-6:
Choose an
AutoPlay
option.

5. **If the disk will always contain files of a specific type, choose them from the drop-down list.**

   For example: Music files, Pictures (or photos), and so on.

6. **To always perform a specific action when the disk is inserted, click the button labeled Select an action to perform and then choose the action from the list.**

   For example, to have Windows not bother you whenever you insert a disk, choose the Take no action item. Or, to have Windows automatically play the music on the disc, choose a jukebox program from the disk.

7. **If you would rather be prompted with the dialog box shown in Figure 4-5, choose the item labeled Prompt Me Each Time to Choose an Action.**

8. **Click the OK button after making your choice.**

The next time a disk is inserted into the drive, Windows obeys whatever options you have selected.

Chapter 5

Keeping Track of Your Stuff without Going Insane

Stuff accumulates. If you don't have a garage, a drawer in your kitchen or in your office desk probably just contains *stuff*. Even organized people accumulate stuff. The difference there is that they're *organized*. They have all that same junk; they're just better at hiding it (and probably finding it).

As with real life, you're going to accumulate stuff inside your computer. It's going to happen. Don't try to avoid it. To handle the stuff, you must be *organized*. This is something you must do. Windows can help. But you must make a vigorous effort to use the tools Windows provides to help organize and keep track of your stuff.

This chapter is about organizing the stuff you create and eventually store on your computer's hard drives. It's the story of the *folder,* a handy tool used to keep similar files together and for putting all your files in order.

The Folder Story

The stuff you collect on your hard drive is put into containers called *files*. On your computer are zillions of them. Some files you create — documents, graphics, music, videos, and so on. The rest are programs and their support files, plus all the many (many!) files that come with the Windows operating system.

Windows uses *folders* to keep all those files organized. Yes, it works like a filing cabinet: Files are pieces of paper, and they can be stored inside folders to keep them handy and organized inside the filing cabinet (the disk drive).

Folders appear in Windows using the folder icon, as shown in the margin. To open the folder, double-click it with the mouse. This displays the folder's contents in a window — the folder window.

Without folders, what you would have are tens of thousands of files lounging around the hard drive, smoking, talking, being rude, and generally making it difficult for you to find things or keep related files together. But by organizing your files into folders, you avoid any perilous consequences and your computer life doesn't echo that of an ancient Greek tragedy.

- A folder is a storage place for files.

- All files stored on your computer's hard drive are kept in folders. The folders keep files together — like barbed wire keeps prisoners, vicious animals, and kindergartners from wandering off.

- Folders may also be referred to as *directories*. This term is merely a throwback to the old days of DOS (which is a throwback to the days of Unix, which King Herod used).

Famous Folders throughout History

You cannot use a PC without stumbling into a folder somewhere. All disk drives have one main folder, the *root* folder. Your hard drive has dozens of folders already created on it, some of them for you, others for Windows, and still others for the programs you run.

The following sections mull over the popular folders you use as you begin to understand how this computer thing works.

The root folder

Every disk — even the stupid floppy disk — has at least one folder. That one folder — the main folder on the disk — is the *root folder*. Like a tree (and this isn't a dog joke), all other folders on your hard drive branch out from that main, root folder.

The root folder doesn't have a specific icon. Instead, it uses the icon for the drive the root folder is on. So, the root folder on drive C has the same icon as drive C. (Refer to Chapter 4 for more information on drive icons.)

 ✔ The root folder is simply the main or only folder on a disk drive.

 ✔ The root folder is like the lobby of some grand building: It's merely a place you pass through to get to somewhere else. Where else? Why, other folders, of course!

 ✔ Had computer scientists been into construction rather than growing trees, they may have called it the *foundation folder* rather than the root folder. (There's no telling what would have happened had computer scientists been interested in ladies' garments.)

 ✔ The root folder may also be called the *root directory*.

The subfolder

Dive! Dive! Dive! Aaa-oooga! Aaa-ooga!

No! Not that kind of sub: *Subfolders* are merely folders inside of, or "beneath," another folder. For example, the Windows folder is a *subfolder* of the root folder. That means that if you open the root folder, you find the Windows folder nestled inside.

 ✔ In addition to holding files, folders can hold more folders.

 ✔ No limit exists on the number of subfolders you can create. You can have a folder inside a folder inside a folder, and so on. If you name the folders well, it all makes sense. Otherwise, it's just like a badly organized filing cabinet, though without the smell of booze.

 ✔ A subfolder can also be called a *child* folder.

 ✔ The *parent* folder is the folder that contains the subfolder. So, if Windows is a folder inside the root folder, the root folder is the parent folder and Windows is the child folder.

 ✔ Yes, parent folder and child folder are terms rarely used, Thank you, Jesus.

The My Documents folder

Though the root folder is the main folder on a hard drive, you don't save any of your stuff there. For your own stuff, you use the My Documents folder. It's your personal folder in Windows, where you can freely and wantonly store your stuff.

Because the My Documents folder is so important, you have many easy ways to get to the folder and display its contents.

The easiest way to find the My Documents folder is to look for it on the desktop. Double-click the folder's icon to open it and display its contents in the My Documents window. You may see files in that folder already, or perhaps even other folders — subfolders — ready to be filled with new files.

Here's a handy way to get to the My Documents folder in just about every part of Windows. The Start panel may even have a shortcut to the My Documents folder. (In Figure 3-4, over in Chapter 3, look at the upper-right area of the Start panel.)

The root folder on hard drive C is considered off limits, so you should use the My Documents folder on drive C for your stuff. On other drives, however, the root folder is fine for saving your stuff.

The My Pictures folder

One subfolder that may already appear in the My Documents folder is the My Pictures folder. That's the folder where many graphics applications yearn to save the images you create. See? It's organization in action, and you haven't even done anything yet!

The My Music folder

The My Music folder is used by many audio programs — specifically, the Windows Media Player — for storing the various music files you save on your PC.

The My Videos folder

Getting the hint? The My Videos folder is used to store video files on a computer. Already, you can smell the organization happening: If you want to save a video file, you choose the My Documents folder, open the My Videos folder, and then save the file there. Celebration organization!

Even more folders and subfolders!

During the course of your Windows travels, you may find other folders created in the My Documents folder, either by some program or by yourself. Use the folders for the specific documents they describe. And, if things don't go into folders, consider creating the popular Misc or Junk folder.

Famous Yet Forbidden Folders

In addition to needing folders for your stuff, your computer needs folders for the stuff Windows uses and folders for your applications. These are what I call the forbidden folders; don't mess with them!

- Though you may someday poke around inside a forbidden folder, don't mess with anything there.
- Use the My Documents folder, or any of its subfolders, to store your stuff. Don't store your stuff in a forbidden folder.
- Don't mess with any folders outside the My Documents folder or any folder you created yourself.
- Mess with a forbidden folder only if you are *specifically* directed to do so.
- The root folder of the hard drive is considered forbidden.

The Windows folder

Windows itself lives in the Windows folder, which may be named WINNT on some computers. This folder contains many files and a heck of a lot of subfolders, all of which comprise the Windows operating system and its support programs. *Touch ye not the files that lurketh there!*

You may occasionally hear the Windows folder (and its subfolders) referred to by their official, corporate name, the *System Folders*.

The Program Files folder

This folder is where your programs are installed. Each program sits inside its own folder inside the Program Files folder. Why not take a look?

1. **Open the My Computer icon on the desktop.**

2. **Open the drive C icon.**

   This step displays the root folder for drive C.

3. **Open the Program Files folder.**

   The Program Files window appears, showing you all the folders for all the software installed on your PC.

   Look, but don't touch.

4. **Close the Program Files window.**

See how each program lives in its own folder? Those folders may even have subfolders for further organization. For example, the Adobe folder may contain a subfolder for the Adobe Acrobat Reader program and then another folder for some other Adobe product you may have on your PC.

Other folders

Even more folders are on your hard drive C, some of which are specific to Windows and others that may have been installed by programs your dealer or computer manufacturer added.

Don't mess with any folder you didn't create yourself! You can look, but don't do anything else!

The Windows Explorer Program

To help you work with folders and generally manage your files and the junk stored on your disk drives, Windows provides you with the Windows Explorer program. In fact, you have probably used this program already; it's what displays the content's of a folder window. So, when you open a disk drive or folder icon, the window you see is the Windows Explorer program in action. Hello!

Windows Explorer is one of the easiest programs to run. My favorite way to start it is to press Win+E on the keyboard. You can also right-click the My Documents or My Computer icon on the desktop and choose Explore from the pop-up menu. The Windows Explorer program is shown in Figure 5-1.

Current folder   Toolbar

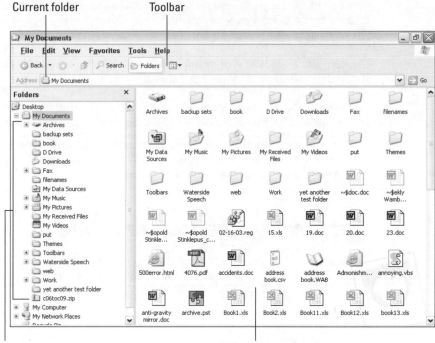

Figure 5-1:
Windows
Explorer
shows you
the tree
structure.

Folder tree   Folder contents

   ✔ The Windows Explorer program can also be found on the Start panel's Programs menu. Look for it on the Accessories submenu. The program's icon appears in the margin.

   ✔ The Windows Explorer program is similar to the Internet Explorer Web browser. See Part V of this book for more Internet information.

   ✔ Unlike other programs that display their name on the window's title bar, Windows Explorer displays the name of the folder you have opened.

   ✔ Be sure to close the Windows Explorer program when you're done playing.

Viewing the tree structure

The whole mess of folders on your hard drive is organized into something the computer nerds call the *tree structure*. It can be seen on the left side of the Windows Explorer window, titled Folders, as shown in Figure 5-1.

You can use the tree structure to quickly navigate to a specific folder in your computer system — if you know where to go. Just click a folder to display its contents on the right side of the window.

You can click the + (plus sign) by a folder to open it up and reveal any sub-folders there. Likewise, you can click the – (minus sign) by a folder to close that "branch" of the tree structure.

Clicking the + signs and opening folders allows you to quickly navigate through the folders on your hard drive.

✔ To display the Folders panel, click the Folders button on the Explorer toolbar. Or, you can choose View⇨Explorer Bar⇨Folders from the menu.

✔ If you don't see the toolbar in the Windows Explorer window, choose View⇨Toolbars⇨Standard Buttons. You may also want to choose Address Bar from the Toolbars submenu.

Not viewing the tree structure

When the Folders panel is hidden, the Windows Explorer program displays a list of tasks for your files and folders, as shown in Figure 5-2. These tasks provide links to things to do with the files in the folder, other places to go, and similar tasks.

Figure 5-2:
Folder tasks,
things to
do, places
to go.

The tasks displayed vary, depending on the type of folder viewed or whether a file is selected and what type of file it is.

  Note that each task panel can be displayed or hidden by clicking the up or down chevrons (see the margin).

Viewing the files in a folder

 The Views button, on the far right side of the Windows Explorer toolbar, displays a menu that lets you see files and icons displayed in various ways:

Filmstrip: Best for previewing graphics files.

Thumbnails: Also good for graphics files; previews the images inside the files in a tiny window instead of displaying the file icon.

Tiles: Displays large icons to represent the files stored in a folder.

Icons: Displays smaller icons to represent files.

List: Displays files in a list, with a very small icon and then the filename.

Details: Allows you to see detailed information about the files in a folder, displayed in columns.

If you have oodles of time to waste, click the button and choose a different view. (I like Large Icons view, but my friend Julia detests it.)

- These views can also be chosen from the View menu.

- Filmstrip view is available only if Windows has been told that the folder contains primarily graphics files. (The My Pictures folder is set up this way.)

Messing with Folders

As the wheel of time turns and stuff accumulates on your hard drive, you eventually need to create folders to help keep that stuff organized. Or, if you're like me, you create folders as you start new projects. Either way, you need to make some new folders and do things with them.

Generally speaking, folders are manipulated like files. After creating a folder, you can rename it, move it, copy it, delete it, or make a shortcut to the folder. See Chapter 6 for those details.

Creating a folder

Creating a folder is easy. Remembering to use the folder is the hard part. The following steps create a folder named Stuff in the My Documents folder on drive C:

1. **Double-click the My Documents icon on the Windows desktop.**

   If the folder appears messy, choose View⇨Arrange Icons⇨By Name from the menu. This step alphabetizes the folder's contents.

2. **Choose File⇨New⇨Folder.**

   The new folder appears. Its name is New Folder, but note that the name is *selected*. That means you can type a new folder name immediately.

3. **Type Stuff.**

   The folder is named Stuff, which is what you type at the keyboard. That name replaces the insipid New Folder as the folder's name.

4. **Press Enter to lock in the name.**

   The new folder is ready for use.

You can double-click the new folder's icon to open it. A blank window appears because it's a new folder and has no contents. See Chapter 6 for information on copying or moving files into the folder.

✔ Be clever with the name! Remember that this folder will contain files and possibly other folders, all of which should relate somehow to the folder's name.

✔ If you just created the Stuff folder and have no use for it, kill it off! See the section in Chapter 6 about deleting icons.

The miracle of compressed folders

A special type of folder is the *compressed* folder. It must be specially created and then can be used only in certain ways. The idea is simple, though: Compressed folders save disk space.

To create a compressed folder, use the File⇨New⇨Compressed (zipped) Folder command. This creates a compressed folder, similar to the way real folders are created (as shown in the preceding section). You can even immediately rename the compressed folder icon, just as you would for a real folder.

Compressed folders sport their own, unique icon, which has a zipper on it. That identifies the folder as compressed and not a regular folder.

Just as with regular folders, you can copy or move files and programs into a compressed folder. You can even create subfolders inside a compressed folder. Unlike regular folders, however, the stuff you create in a compressed folder occupies less disk space. For example, copying 400KB of text files into a compressed folder saves almost 380KB of disk space — which is impressive.

On the downside, compressed folders don't let you access their contents as readily as regular folders. For example, you cannot use the Open or Save As dialog boxes to access files in a compressed folder. Also, you cannot run programs saved inside a compressed folder. To make those things more accessible, they must be copied out of the compressed folder.

Here are some compressed folder words of wit and wisdom:

- Compressed folders are best used for *storage*. For example, you can store a bunch of images or text documents in a compressed folder. Storing stuff there helps conserve disk space.

- Compressed folders are *not* the same thing as compressed disks, which I recommend that you avoid.

- Many of the files you download from the Internet are stored in the Compressed folder file format. You can open the compressed folder to remove or examine the files. See Part IV of this book for more information.

- You can also create compressed folders, for example, to collect and send off files in a single e-mail attachment.

- Alas, there is no such thing as the Compressed Folder Diet.

- Refer to my Web page, www.wambooli.com, for an E-Doc tutorial on working with compressed folders. It goes into more detail than I can offer here, showing, for example, how compressed folders can be password-protected.

 - Compressed folders work by using complex and funky mathematical algorithms that allow files to take up less space. These files can be trash-compacted to a teensy size. But, unlike compacting trash, the files can be mathematically restored to their original size with no noticeable loss of information.

Using the Open Dialog Box

As you use your computer, you often find yourself digging through folders with the Open command, off to fetch a file somewhere on disk.

Figure 5-3 shows a typical Open dialog box, used by most programs in Windows. The following steps explain how this dialog box is used:

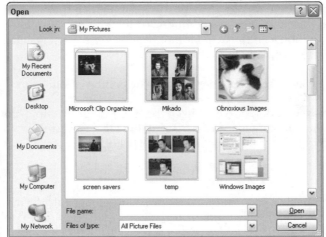

Figure 5-3:
The typical Open dialog box.

1. **Look for your file. If it's there, open it.**

   The center of the dialog box shows a buncha file icons. If you find your file there, double-click it to open it. That file then appears, ready for action in your favorite program.

   You may need to use the scroll bar at the bottom of the list to see more files.

    You can also click the Views button in the Open dialog box to show files in another arrangement. My favorite for dialog boxes is List view.

2. **If you can't find your file, look in another folder.**

   If you can't find your file on the list, you need to look in another folder. You have several ways to do this:

   - Click the My Documents button (on the left side of the Open dialog box), which displays the contents of the My Documents folder.

   - Double-click to open any folder displayed on the file list.

- If you want to go back up to the preceding folder, click the handy Up One Level button (as shown in the margin).

- Choose another folder from the Look in drop-down list, at the top of the dialog box.

If you find your file, open it!

3. **If you still can't find your file, switch disk drives.**

   Choose another drive from the Look In drop-down list, at the top of the Open dialog box. Then open folders in the larger part of the Open dialog box window until you find your file.

   If you find your file, open it!

After opening the file, you can view it, edit it, modify it, print it — whatever. But you must open the file (or *document,* which sounds much more lofty) before you can do anything with it.

- The Open dialog box is summoned by the File⇨Open command: by clicking the Open button on a toolbar or by using the Ctrl+O keyboard combination shortcut.

- At the bottom of the dialog box is a drop-down list titled Files of Type. It helps you narrow the kinds of files displayed on the Open dialog box's list. For example, in Figure 5-3, All Picture Files is selected, so any graphics file appears on the list. To narrow the list, a specific file type can be chosen.

- Note that not every program can open every type of file. Programs work best on the files they create themselves.

- The Browse dialog box is similar to the Open dialog box. It appears whenever you click a Browse button to hunt down a file for Windows.

- The Open button in the Open dialog box is used to open whichever file is selected in the dialog box.

- If you're nerdy, you can type the file's full pathname (if you know it) in the File name box. For example, to directly open a file named README.DOC on drive A, you type **A:\README.DOC** in the File Name box. As you can guess, few people bother to do this.

"What the heck is a pathname?"

A *pathname* pinpoints a file's location on a certain disk drive and in a certain folder. Long. Technical. Complex. It's a wonder that anyone has to deal with these things.

Suppose that a file named Check Please is in the My Music folder in the My Documents folder on drive C. The file's ugly pathname is

```
C:\My Documents\My Music\Check
    Please
```

It reads this way: C: means drive C; My Documents is the My Documents folder; My Music is the My Music folder; Check Please is the filename; and backslashes are used to separate things.

Occasionally, you find pathnames referenced in user manuals or in Windows itself. Suppose that you're told to go out and hunt down the file represented by this pathname:

```
C:\MyDocuments\Personal\Letters
    \Family\Zack.doc
```

You look on drive C, open the My Documents folder, open the Personal folder, open Letters, open Family, and then look for the file named Zack.doc.

Using the Save As Dialog Box

The Save As dialog box is the most important dialog box you ever use in Windows. It's the key to organizing your files in a sane manner. You feel almost as nifty as those people who buy that California Closet organizer or the Wonder Purse.

To use the Save As dialog box, you must first save something to disk. Any program that lets you create something has a File➪Save As command. It's used the first time you save your stuff to disk. Figure 5-4 shows the typical Save As dialog box.

Here's how you work the typical Save As dialog box:

1. **Hunt for the folder in which you want to save your stuff.**

   Start in the My Documents folder. If that folder isn't chosen — you don't see its name next to Save at the top of the dialog box — click the big My Document button (left side).

2. **To save on another hard drive, choose that drive from the Save in drop-down list.**

   For example, if you keep your graphics on drive D, use the Save in drop-down list to choose drive D.

3a. **If the current folder isn't the one you want, open a proper subfolder.**

   Keep opening subfolders until you find the one proper for your file. Or:

3b. Create a new folder for your stuff.

Click the New Folder button to create a new folder for your stuff. Refer to the section "Creating a folder," earlier in this chapter.

Name the folder properly! The folder's name should reflect its contents.

4. Type a name for the saved file.

The name goes into the box labeled File Name. Sometimes the program suggests a name, such as Document.rtf, as shown in Figure 5-4. You can use that name or make up a name on your own. (See Chapter 6 for more information about naming files.)

5. Optionally, choose a file type.

Normally, you leave alone the drop-down list labeled Save As Type; programs have a preferred file type for saving their stuff. Mess with it only when you know that you want to save the file as a different type. In that case, choose the new type from the drop-down list.

6. Click the Save button.

Click! This last, official act saves the file to disk, with a proper name and in a proper folder.

Figure 5-4:
The typical
Save As
dialog box.

After you save your stuff once, you can use the File⇨Save command to resave your file to disk or use the Ctrl+S keyboard shortcut. This command is a quick way to update the file on disk without having to work the Save As dialog box again.

✔ The Save As dialog box appears when you choose the File⇨Save As command from the menu or whenever you press Ctrl+S or click a Save button on a toolbar for the first time.

✔ The Save As dialog box appears only the first time you save your stuff to disk; from that point on, the Save command merely resaves a file to disk.

✔ If you want to save your file to disk in another spot, give it a new name, or save it as another type of file, you need to use the Save As dialog box again. In that case, choose File⇨Save As from the menu.

✔ If the Save button appears to be broken, you probably typed an improper filename. Try giving the file a new name (refer to Step 4).

✔ As with the Open dialog box, some Save As dialog boxes are more complex than the one shown earlier, in Figure 5-3. The same business goes on; they just have more things to get in the way.

✔ Both the Open and Save As dialog boxes work like mini–Windows Explorer windows. You can right-click files shown in these dialog boxes to manipulate them, just as you would in the Windows Explorer window. For example, to rename a file shown in the Save As dialog box, right-click its icon and choose Rename from the pop-up menu. Then you can rename the file. You can use this trick to rename, move, or copy files on the fly without having to leave the Open or Save As dialog boxes.

Chapter 6

Lording It Over Your Files

A t the end of the Data Storage Road, you find the File Village, where the information is stored. It's a long journey. The Data Storage Road starts with the disk drive forest, goes on down through the valley of the shadow of the folder, and ends up in File Village. To take the journey is to understand how information is stored in a computer. The benefits, aside from the healthy walk, are that you can quickly find information when you need it and you use your PC to the fullest of its abilities.

Though the operating system, Windows, may be in charge of most data storage aspects in the PC, you are the computer's File Lord. You're the one creating files, naming them, putting them on disk, and eventually moving them around or manipulating them in other ways. You also have tools for finding lost files, making you their gentle shepherd. And if a file gets out of line, you can rub it out of existence, sending it to its doom like a ruthless judge or gravel-voiced bad guy from a Saturday morning cartoon show. Such is the life of a File Lord, which I describe thoroughly in this chapter.

What the Heck Is a File?

The *file* is the basic knowledge nugget in Windows. It is information stored on disk. The information in a file can be a word-processing document, a picture, an e-mail message, or even a program or a piece of Windows itself. Whatever! All that stuff is stored as a file, a unique and separate thing inside a folder on a disk drive.

Files are identified primarily by their name. Each file is given a unique name, different from all other files in the same folder. Ideally, the name describes the file's contents or tells what the file is up to. In practice, sadly, filenames are often cryptic and mysterious. The moral is to properly name a file when it's created or use the file Rename command to give a file a better name. (More on that later in this chapter.)

The last part of a file's name is the extension. The *extension* tells Windows about the file's contents. For example, the TXT extension indicates a plain-text file, JPG indicates a type of graphics file, and EXE indicates that the file is a program.

Finally, in addition to the filename, Windows slaps each file with an *icon,* or a tiny picture, as shown in Figure 6-1. The icon clues you in to what type of file it is, and also provides a handy way to graphically manipulate the file in Windows.

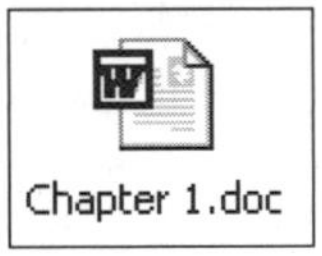

Figure 6-1:
A file with
an icon,
name, and
extension.

Chapter 1.doc

✔ Everything on disk is a *file.* Some files are *programs,* and some files are *documents,* or stuff you create.

✔ Windows may or may not display the filename extension. See the side-bar "What the heck is a filename extension?" later in this chapter.

✔ All files are stored in folders. Even if the file isn't in a subfolder, it's in the root folder on the disk. Refer to Chapter 5 for more information on folders.

Working with Groups of Files

Before you can mess with any file, you must select it. As in log rolling, you can select files individually or in groups.

To select a single file, click its icon once with the mouse. This step selects the file, which appears highlighted onscreen, similar to what's shown in Figure 6-2. The file is now ready for action.

Figure 6-2:
The icon
(file) on the
right is
selected.

- Clicking a file with the mouse *selects* that file.
- Selected files appear highlighted in the folder window.
- File manipulation commands — Copy, Move, Rename, Delete, and so on — affect only selected files.

Selecting all the files in a folder

To select all the files inside a folder, choose Edit⇨Select All from the menu. This command highlights all the files in the window — including any folders (and all the folders' contents), marking them ready for action.

You can also use the Ctrl+A keyboard shortcut to select all files in a folder.

Selecting a random smattering of files

Suppose that you need to select four icons in a folder all at once, similar to what's shown in Figure 6-3. Here's how to do that:

1. **Click to select the first file.**

   Point the mouse at the file's icon and click once.

2. **Press and hold the Ctrl key on the keyboard.**

   Either Ctrl (control) key works; press and hold it down.

Figure 6-3:
A random
smattering
of files is
selected.

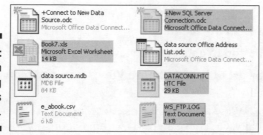

3. **Click to select the next file.**

   By holding the Ctrl key, you can select as many files as your clicking finger desires. (Otherwise, by clicking one file, you would unselect anything already selected.)

4. **Repeat Step 3 until you have selected all the files you want.**

   Or, until your clicking finger gets sore.

5. **Release the Ctrl key when you're done selecting files.**

Now you're ready to manipulate the selected files as a group.

To deselect a file from a group, just Ctrl+click it again.

Selecting a swath of files in a row

To select a queue of files, such as those shown in Figure 6-4, pursue these steps:

Name ▲	Size	Type	Artist
Bach's Brandenburg Concerto...	142 KB	MIDI Sequence	
Back to the Future.mid	39 KB	MIDI Sequence	
Beethoven's 5th Symphony.rmi	91 KB	MIDI Sequence	
Beethoven's Fur Elise.rmi	21 KB	MIDI Sequence	
bewitched.mid	9 KB	MIDI Sequence	
bigtop.mid	30 KB	MIDI Sequence	
bjs-ming.mid	6 KB	MIDI Sequence	
bohemian rhapsody.mid	51 KB	MIDI Sequence	
brunes.mid	47 KB	MIDI Sequence	
Bumble Bee.mid	14 KB	MIDI Sequence	
bumble.mid	21 KB	MIDI Sequence	
bwv538f.mid	25 KB	MIDI Sequence	
bwv538t.mid	36 KB	MIDI Sequence	
bwv948.mid	14 KB	MIDI Sequence	
Can't do that sum.mid	11 KB	MIDI Sequence	
CANYON.MID	21 KB	MIDI Sequence	
cartoons.mid	5 KB	MIDI Sequence	
Classical Gas.mid	8 KB	MIDI Sequence	
Dance of the Sugar-Plum Fair...	21 KB	MIDI Sequence	
Debussy's Claire de Lune.rmi	28 KB	MIDI Sequence	
doom1.mid	18 KB	MIDI Sequence	
elvis.mid	16 KB	MIDI Sequence	
EURYDICE.MID	90 KB	MIDI Sequence	
figaro.mid	38 KB	MIDI Sequence	

Figure 6-4:
A group of files in a row is selected.

1. **Choose <u>V</u>iew⇨List from the menu.**

   Or, use the Views button to choose List view.

2. **Optionally, sort the list of icons: Choose <u>V</u>iew⇨Arrange <u>I</u>cons By Submenu.**

   For example, choose <u>V</u>iew⇨Arrange <u>I</u>cons By⇨<u>M</u>odified to sort the list of files chronologically. Or, choose <u>V</u>iew⇨Arrange <u>I</u>cons By⇨<u>N</u>ame to sort them alphabetically — whatever helps you more easily select your files.

3. **Click to select the first file in your group.**

4. **Press and hold the Shift key.**

   Either Shift key on the keyboard works.

5. **Click to select the last file in your group.**

   By holding down the Shift key, you select all the files between the first click and second click, as shown in Figure 6-4.

6. **Release the Shift key.**

The files are now ready for action.

This file selection technique works best in List view. It works in other file views as well, though not as predictably.

Lassoing a group of files

Another way to select files as a group is to lasso them. Figure 6-5 illustrates how you do this by dragging over the files with the mouse.

To lasso the files, start by pointing the mouse above and to the left of the icon horde you want to rope. Holding down the mouse button, drag down and to the right to create a rectangle surrounding ("lassoing") the file icons, as shown in Figure 6-5. Release the mouse button, and all the files you have lassoed are selected as a group. A vocal "Yee-ha!" is considered appropriate in this circumstance.

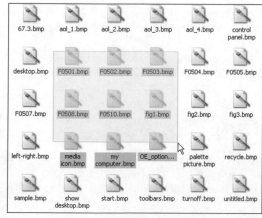

Figure 6-5: Lasso a group of files with the mouse.

Selecting all but a single file

This is a handy trick I use all the time. For example, if I want to select all files in a folder except for one file (or folder), here's what I do:

1. **Click to select the files you *don't* want selected.**

   I know, it seems weird, but bear with me. For example, if I want to copy all the files from a folder but not the subfolders, I click (or Ctrl+click) to select all the folders first.

2. **Choose Edit⇨Invert Selection from the menu.**

   Now all the selected files are unselected, and all the unselected files are selected — and ready for action!

This trick beats having to select all the files and try to hunt for those you didn't want selected in the first place.

Mixing selection techniques

Working with groups of files is something you do often, so hopefully one of the techniques in the previous sections can help you select files fast and easy. If not, keep in mind that you can mix and match techniques.

Suppose that you need to lasso two groups of files. If so, lasso the first group and then press and hold the Ctrl key to lasso and include the second collection.

You can Shift+click to select a swath of files in a row and then go back and Ctrl+click to remove specific files from that list.

Or, you can lasso a group of files you don't want to select and then choose Edit⇨Invert Selection to unselect those files and select everything else.

Finally, remember this: When you select a folder, you're selecting all the files and subfolders within that folder. Be careful!

Unselecting stuff

To unselect a file, simply click anywhere in the folder (but not on an icon). That unselects any and all selected files in the folder. Or, you can close the folder window, in which case Windows immediately forgets any selected files.

File-Naming Rules and Regulations

One thing mankind is good at is giving things names. Find a new bug, planet, beast, comet, or disease and you get to name it. Files are the same way, but without the fame and glory. Plus, there is an art to naming a file. Pay careful attention.

Choosing the best name

You name a file when saving the file to disk, which happens in the Save As dialog box (refer to Chapter 5). When naming a file, be brief and descriptive. Try using only letters, numbers, and spaces in the name. For example:

```
Vacation
Chapter 16
Industrial Espionage
Moby Dick Book Report
101 Reasons Why My Boss Is An Idiot
```

Each of these examples is a good filename, properly explaining the file's contents.

- ✔ Upper- or lowercase doesn't matter. Although capitalizing Smolensk is proper, for example, Windows recognizes that filename the same as smolensk, Smolensk, SMOLENSK, or any combination of upper- and lowercase letters.

- ✔ Though case doesn't matter in a filename, it *does* matter when typing a Web page address.

- ✔ The file's name reminds you of what's in the file, of what it's all about — just like naming the dog Sissydown tells everyone what the dog is all about.

- ✔ All the rules for naming files in this and the following sections also apply to naming folders.

Official file-naming rules

Here's the law when it comes to naming files in Windows. All this stuff is optional reading; as long as you stick with the simple rules in the preceding section, this stuff is merely trivia.

Length: Technically, you can give a file a name that's over 200 characters long. Don't. Long filenames may be *very* descriptive, but Windows displays them funny or not at all in many situations. Better to keep things short than to take advantage of a long filename.

What the heck is a filename extension?

The last part of a filename is typically a period followed by a handful of characters. Known as the *filename extension*, Windows uses it to identify the type of file. For example, a .bmp extension tags a bitmap graphics image (created by the Windows Paint program), and .DOC indicates a document created by Microsoft Word.

Windows can be told to hide or show the filename extension. If it's hidden, you have nothing to worry about. But, if the extension is visible, you must remember *not* to change it when you rename a file; rename anything but the extension. If you forget, Windows pops up a reminder dialog box; try again.

To show or hide the filename extension in Windows, follow these steps:

1. **Start Windows Explorer (press Win+E) or open the My Computer icon on the desktop.**

2. **Choose Tools⇨Folder Options.**

3. **Click the View tab in the Folder Options dialog box.**

4. **Locate the item on the list that says** Hide extensions for known file types.

5. **Put a check mark there to hide the extensions, or remove the check mark so that Windows displays the extensions.**

    Or, if the item is already set as you like, you're just dandy.

6. **Click OK to close the Folder Options dialog box.**

Forbidden characters: Windows gets angry if you use any of these characters to name a file:

```
*  /  :  <  >  ?  \  |  "
```

These symbols hold a special meaning to Windows. Nothing bad happens if you attempt to use these characters. Windows just refuses to save the file — or a warning dialog box growls at you.

Use periods sparingly: Although you can use any number of periods in a filename, you cannot name a file with all periods. I know that it's strange, and I'm probably the only one on the planet to have tried it, but it doesn't work.

Renaming a single icon

Windows lets you rename any file or folder at any time. You may want to do this to give the folder a better, more descriptive name, or you could have any number of reasons to give an icon a new name. Here's how it's done:

1. **Click the icon once to select it.**

2. **Choose File⇨Rename from the menu.**

    The file's current name is highlighted or selected — just like selected text in a word processor.

3. **Type a new name or edit the current name.**

4. **Press the Enter key to lock in the new name.**

Note that all files *must* have a name. If you don't give the file a name (you try to leave it blank), Windows complains. Other than that, here are some file-renaming points to ponder:

✔ In Step 3, you can edit the old name by using the Windows text-editing keys. (See Chapter 14 for information about common Windows editing keys.)

✔ Before pressing the Enter key (refer to Step 4), you can press the Esc key to undo the damage and return to the file's original name.

✔ Windows doesn't let you rename a file with the name of an existing file; no two items in the same folder can share the same name.

✔ If you have hidden the filename extensions, it may appear that two files share the same name. Note, however, that such files are of two different types and have two different icons.

✔ You can undo the name change by pressing the Ctrl+Z key combination or choosing Edit⇨Undo from the menu. You must do this *immediately* after the boo-boo for it to work.

✔ The keyboard shortcut for renaming files is F2. I prefer using this key to choosing the menu item because my hands need to be on the keyboard to type the new filename anyway.

Renaming a group of icons

Windows lets you rename a group of icons, if you have selected a group before you choose the File⇨Rename command or press the F2 key. The files are all given the same name, though with a number suffix. You cannot individually rename the files, but you can give the group sequential names. For example:

1. **Select a group of icons in a window.**

    Windows renames them from the top down or from left to right.

    Be sure to select the file you want renamed first as your last selection.

2. **Choose File⇨Rename or press the F2 key.**

   The last file you selected is chosen for renaming. Note that the other files in the group are all still selected.

3. **Rename the file.**

   Refer to the previous sections for the details.

4. **Press the Enter key.**

   All the files in the group are renamed. The original file (Step 3) gets its own name, and the rest in the group are given the same name followed by a number in parentheses.

For example, if you rename the first file Sam Birthday, the rest of the files are name Sam Birthday (1), Sam Birthday (2), Sam Birthday (3), and so on.

Files Hither, Thither, and Yon

Files don't stand still. You find yourself moving them, copying them, and killing them off. If you don't do those things, your hard drive gets all junky and, out of embarrassment, you're forced to turn off the computer when friends come over.

Moving or copying files to another folder (Move To, Copy To)

Suppose, in a fit of organization, that you desire to move some audio files that have been languishing in the My Computer folder to the Audio folder you just created. Here's one way to do that:

1. **Select the file(s) or folder(s) you want to move.**

2. **Choose Edit⇨Move to Folder from the menu.**

   The Move Items dialog box appears, as shown in Figure 6-6.

3. **Choose the destination folder from the scrolling list.**

4. **Click the Move button.**

   The files are moved from their current location to the folder you selected.

To copy the files instead, choose the Edit⇨Copy to Folder command in Step 2. This displays the Copy Items dialog box, similar to Figure 6-6, though its Copy button makes duplicates of the selected files or folders in the destination folder.

✔ If the destination folder doesn't exist, you can create it inside the Move Items or Copy Items dialog box: Click to select the parent folder and then click the Make New Folder button. Give the new folder a name and then choose it as the destination.

✔ To move or copy files or folders to another disk drive, simply choose that drive's letter from the list.

✔ Moving folders moves all the files and subfolders inside that folder. Be careful when you do this; Windows may lose track of the documents previously opened in those folders.

✔ The popular My Documents folder is at the top of the list of folders in the dialog box.

✔ Rather than copy a file, consider creating a shortcut instead. See the section "Creating shortcuts," later in this chapter.

Figure 6-6:
The Move
Items
dialog box.

Moving or copying files with cut-and-paste

In Windows, where everything is like kindergarten anyway, you cut and paste. You cut and paste to move a file, you copy and paste to copy a file. This technique comes in handy when you don't exactly know where the files need to be moved. Here's how it's done:

    1. Select the files you want to move or copy.

  2a. To move the files, choose Edit⇨Cut.

  2b. To copy the files, choose Edit⇨Copy.

If you cut, the files appear dimmed in the window, which means that they have been chosen for cutting. Nothing is wrong; keep moving on with the next step.

3. **Open the folder where you want the files moved or copied to.**

4. **Choose Edit⇨Paste.**

The files are moved or copied.

Windows remembers which files are selected for moving or copying until you select and cut or copy other files (or even select and cut or copy text or graphics). That makes this technique good for situations where time isn't pressing.

If you do select and copy or cut something else before pasting your files, you have to go back and start over with these steps.

✔ You can also use the handy keyboard shortcuts: Ctrl+C for Copy, Ctrl+X for Cut, and Ctrl+V for Paste.

✔ The Copy, Cut, and Paste commands are also available from the pop-up shortcut menu. To see that menu, right-click a selected file and then choose Copy or Cut. To paste, right-click in a folder's window and choose Paste from the pop-up menu.

✔ To cancel the operation, simply press the Esc (escape) key before you Paste the files. This restores the Cut files to a non-dimmed state.

✔ Don't eat the paste.

Moving or copying files can be such a drag

Perhaps the easiest way to move or copy a file is to have both the file's window and the destination window open on the desktop at the same time. To move, simply drag an icon from one window to the other. To move a group, select the icons and then drag them from one window to the other.

Copying files involves dragging their icons, but when you do, press and hold the Ctrl key on the keyboard. You notice a small + (plus sign) appear by the mouse pointer as you drag the icons. It's your clue that the files are being copied (duplicated).

When dragging between folders on different disk drives, Windows always elects to copy rather than move the files. To override this, press the Shift key as you drag the files; the Shift key enforces the Move operation, moving the files rather than copying them.

Duplicating a file

To make a duplicate, simply copy a file to its same folder. Use any of the techniques for copying files that I cover earlier in this chapter.

The duplicate is created with the prefix `Copy of` and then the rest of the filename. That's your clue that the file is a duplicate of the original stored in the same folder.

Copying a file to drive A (or a Zip disk)

For some reason people have a hang-up with copying files to a floppy disk, or to any external drive. It's quite simple to do. Here's how:

1. **Ensure that a disk is in the drive, ready to accept the file.**

2. **Select the file(s) to copy.**

   Remember that the floppy has only so much room. You cannot copy a file larger than 1.44MB to a floppy disk. (Zip disks can hold more than that; refer to the Zip disk's label for its capacity.)

3a. **Choose File⇨Send To⇨3½ Floppy (A:).**

3b. **Choose File⇨Send To⇨Iomega Zip 250 (Z:).**

   The files are copied to the drive.

Always make certain that a disk is in the drive and that the disk is ready to accept files before you copy.

> ✔ Note that the options on the Send To submenu may be subtly different on your computer; scan the menu carefully for your removable disk drive.

> ✔ To easily copy files from drive A, select the files and choose File⇨Send To⇨My Documents. That puts a copy of the file(s) in the My Documents folder. From there, you can move them to some place more appropriate.

Creating shortcuts

A file shortcut is a 99 percent fat-free copy of a file. It enables you to access the original file from anywhere on a computer's disk system, but without the extra baggage required to copy the file all over creation. For example, you can create a shortcut to Microsoft Word on the desktop, where you can always get to it — much quicker than using the Start panel.

Making a shortcut is done the same way as copying and pasting a file, as discussed in the section "Moving or copying files with cut-and-paste," earlier in this chapter. The difference is that, rather than use the Paste command, you choose Edit⇨Paste Shortcut.

Shortcut to the
old graveyard

- ✔ If no Edit⇨Paste Shortcut command is available, right-click the mouse on the destination. When a Paste Shortcut item appears on the pop-up menu, use it.

- ✔ To quickly create a shortcut on the desktop, right-click an icon and choose Send To⇨Desktop (create shortcut) from the pop-up menu.

- ✔ A shortcut icon has a little arrow in a white box nestled into its lower-left corner (see the figure in the margin). This icon tells you that the file is a shortcut and not the real McCoy.

- ✔ Shortcuts are often named `Shortcut to` followed by the original file's name. You can edit out the `Shortcut to` part, if you like. See the section "Renaming a single icon," earlier in this chapter.

- ✔ Have no fear when you're deleting shortcuts; removing a shortcut icon doesn't remove the original file.

Deleting icons

Part of maintaining the disk drive closet is the occasional cleaning binge or spring cleaning bustle. This involves not only organizing files and folders by moving and copying them, but also cleaning out the deadwood — removing files you no longer want or need.

To kill a file, select it and choose File⇨Delete. Or, you can press the Delete key on your keyboard to delete any selected file(s). Or, if you can see the Recycle Bin icon on the desktop, drag the file(s) with the mouse and drop it right on the Recycle Bin icon. Phew! The file is gone.

- ✔ Windows may warn you about deleting a file. Are you *really* sure? You probably are, so click Yes to delete the file. (Windows is just being utterly cautious.)

- ✔ You can delete folders just like files, but keep in mind that you delete the folder's contents — which can be dozens of icons, files, folders, jewelry, small children, widows, and refugees. Better be careful with that one.

- ✔ Never delete any file in the Windows folder or any of the folders in the Windows folder.

- ✔ Never delete any file in the root folder of a hard drive.

- ✔ In fact, never delete any file unless you created it yourself.

✔ Don't delete programs! Instead, you can use a special tool in the Windows Control Panel for removing old applications you no longer need. See Chapter 21 for more information.

✔ If you detest being warned every time you delete a file, right-click the Recycle Bin icon on the desktop. Choose Properties from the pop-up menu. On the Global tab of the Recycle Bin Properties dialog box, remove the check mark next to the item Display delete confirmation dialog. Click OK.

Deleting stuff for good!

The steps for deleting files in the preceding section don't truly remove the file, at least not in the same fashion as the Tsar's men tried to kill Rasputin. No, Windows merely tucks the file(s) away into the Recycle Bin for potential later recovery (see the next section).

If you really want a file dead, such as some sensitive file or something you don't want haunting you later, select the file and press Shift+Delete. Windows displays a warning dialog box, explaining that the file will be utterly crushed (or something to that effect). Click Yes to consign it to eternity.

Undeleting files (Files of the Undead!)

You probably want your file back in a hurry, so there's no wasting time with creepy coffin jokes.

If you just deleted the file — and I mean *just deleted* it — you can choose the Edit⇨Undo command (Ctrl+Z). That gets it back.

If Edit⇨Undo doesn't do it, or undo it (or whatever), take these steps:

1. **Open the Recycle Bin on the desktop.**

   Its window opens like any folder window, though the files appearing here have long since departed — and are also protected so that they cannot be messed with. *Do not play with the dead!* No, you must *restore* the file(s).

2. **Select the file you want recovered.**

   Choose View⇨Arrange Icons⇨by Date Deleted from the menu to display files in the order they departed (by date). That way, it's cinchy to find any recently deceased files you may want back.

3. **Choose File⇨Restore from the menu.**

   The file is magically removed from Recycle Bin limbo and restored afresh to the folder and disk from which it was so brutally seized.

4. **Close the Recycle Bin window.**

Windows has no definite time limit on how long you can restore files; they can be available in the Recycle Bin for months or even years. Even so, don't let the convenience of the Recycle Bin lull you into a false sense of security. Never delete a file unless you're certain that you want it gone, gone, gone.

Finding Wayward Files

Losing track of your files in Windows is no big deal. Unlike losing your glasses or car keys, Windows sports a nifty Search Companion. Lost files are found almost instantly. Even the Amazing Kreskin couldn't find things faster!

The key to finding a wayward file is information. The more you know about the file, the better your results. Knowing one or more of the following tidbits helps tremendously:

 ✔ The file's name or at least part of it

 ✔ Any text in the file, words, or part of sentences you remember

 ✔ The date the file was created, last saved to disk, or modified

 ✔ The file's type (or which program created it)

 ✔ The file's size

To find a file in Windows, use the Search Companion, which is part of any Windows Explorer window. To use the Search Companion, abide by these steps:

1. **Open any folder window.**

2. **Click the Search button.**

   Or, choose View⇨Explorer Bar⇨Search. The Search Companion appears on the left side of the window.

3. **Click to select all files and folders.**

   The other options sound good, but this choice gives you the most flexibility, as shown in Figure 6-7.

4. **Type all or part of the file's name.**

   If you know the exact filename, type it. Otherwise, you can be vague here. For example, if you remember that the file contained the word *spatula,* you need only type **spatula**.

Figure 6-7:
The Search
Companion.

5. **Type a word or phrase in the file.**

   It can be something from the file's contents — if the file has text content. Otherwise, leave it blank.

   Don't bother filling in the Word or phrase box if you're searching for a graphics file, audio or MP3 file, or video file or a program.

6. **Select the folder to look in.**

   To search all your computer's hard drives, choose Local Hard Drives from the list.

   To search only one hard drive, select it from the list.

   To search a specific folder, such as the Windows or My Documents folder, select it from the list.

   The rest of the settings, hidden in Figure 6-7, are optional. You're now ready to search.

7. **Click the Search button.**

   This action sends Windows off on a merry chase to locate the file you have requested. One of two things happens when it's done:

   No dice. A message tells you that there are no results to display. Oh, well. Try again; click the Back button.

   Eureka! Any files matching your specifications are listed on the right side of the window.

The found files appear on a list. You can double-click a found file to open it. Or, if you want to know which folder the file was hiding in, right-click the file's icon and choose Open Containing Folder from the pop-up menu.

Be sure to close the Search Results window when you're done.

- ✔ The list of files displayed can get quite long. The list's length depends on how specific you are when you tell Windows what to find.

- ✔ If your keyboard has a Windows key, you can press Win+F, where the F means Find. This summons the Search Companion window.

- ✔ In any folder window, you can press Ctrl+E to display the Search Companion.

- ✔ The book *Troubleshooting Your PC For Dummies* (Wiley Publishing, Inc.) contains many more Search Companion options and variations for finding just about any file based on its type, size, or date.

Chapter 7

Make Your Own CDs

· ·

· ·

*T*en years ago, if you had told anyone that a teenager could make more music CDs than the local music store sells, no one would have believed you. The phenomenon is now a national crisis, with the music industry huffing and puffing to Congress about all the money they're losing from people on computers burning their own CDs.

Though you can create your own CD, of either the data or musical variety, it's illegal to copy things you don't own. Becoming your own music store without paying the musicians is theft. But creating your own CDs doesn't always make you a scofflaw. CDs can be freely burned for your own good and personal use. Making data CDs is a good way to archive and protect your data. And burning a few musical CDs of your own albums and using them yourself is perfectly fine. This chapter shows you the details.

Making Your Own Data CD

Yes, you can make a CD, which doesn't involve magnets, a huge, smelly machine in your garage, or the use of special settings on the microwave oven. You need three only things:

- A CD-R disc, one specifically designed for storing computer data
- A CD drive capable of writing to a CD-R disc
- Software to make it all happen

The CD-R discs, you have to buy. The CD drive must come with your computer, though external CD-R drives are plentiful and cheap. The software also comes with Windows, though better software exists on the Internet or up on the shelf at the Software-O-Rama.

Got all that stuff? You're ready to burn!

- CD-R discs are cheap. Buy 'em by the hundreds.
- Some CD-R discs are better than others. I recommend the discs with green-gold surfaces. I don't have much luck with the bluish-green discs.
- CD-R drives are generally also capable of using CD-RW discs. They're called CD-R/RW drives.
- For more information on creating CD-RW discs, see the section "A few words about CD-RW," later in this chapter.

What to put on the CD-R?

The burning question is "What kind of data should you put on a CD-R?" Obviously, you don't want to use a CD-R like a floppy disk or any other external drive. That's because the disc can be used only once. When it's full, it's done! It cannot be erased. Therefore, I recommend using CD-R data discs for *archiving*.

For example, when I'm done writing a book, I archive all the text documents, figures, pictures, —even the contract — on a CD-R disc. Though the files may not equal the disc's

full 600MB capacity, that's fine; it's an archive. With the files safely saved on the CD-R, I can delete them from my hard drive and make that space available for something else. And, if I ever need the files again, they're handy on the archive CD.

Try to archive stuff from your hard drive that you want to keep, but may not need to keep handy, such as e-mail, graphics files, downloads from the Internet, videos, and old work projects.

Mounting the CD-R

Just as floppy disks must be formatted, roads must be paved, and babies properly swaddled in diapers, CD-R discs must be prepared for use. Windows handles this task automatically. It's known as *mounting* the disc.

Floppy disks and Zip disks are mounted by simply inserting them into their appropriate disk drive. For a CD-R, here's what you need to do:

1. **Put a blank CD-R disc into the drive.**

   Windows XP is smart enough to recognize the disc and asks you what to do with it, as shown in Figure 7-1.

Figure 7-1: A blank CD-R is detected.

2. **Select the option Open Writable CD Folder Using Windows Explorer.**

3. **Click OK.**

   Windows mounts the CD-R.

After mounting the CD-R, you can use that disk just as though it were any other disk in your computer system. Files are copied to the disk using any of the file manipulation commands covered in Chapter 6.

  ✔ If you're running other CD-R burning software, it takes over and does I-don't-know-what, but probably something similar to what Windows XP does.

  ✔ If the CD-R drive doesn't recognize the disc, the disc could be defective. Fetch another.

✔ If you're using software other than Windows, ensure that you create a standard CD, one that can be read by any PC.

✔ Some CD-R discs can hold up to 700MB of data or 80 minutes of music. It usually says on the CD-R case, so look when you buy.

Copying files to the CD-R

After Windows has mounted the CD-R, you can work with it just like any disk in your computer system: Copy files to the disc's window. Create folders, even subfolders. Rename and manage files as you normally would.

The trick here is that nothing is written to the CD-R until you direct Windows to burn information to the disc. So, technically (and rather sneakily) you're merely messing with an *image* of what the CD-R will eventually look like; nothing is burnt to the disc yet.

✔ Avoid saving files directly to the CD-R. Instead, save the file first to the hard drive, preferably in the proper folder. After that, you can save a copy of the file to the CD-R. Only after the CD-R has been successfully written should you consider deleting the original file(s) on the hard drive, if at all.

✔ The fewer times you write to the CD-R disc, the more data the disc can hold. Writing to the disc a little bit at a time consumes extra space due to the overhead required to keep track of the information.

✔ See Chapter 6 for the bazillion ways to copy files.

✔ Note that Windows updates its File⇨Send To submenu to include the CD-R drive, which allows for the quick right-click copying of files and folders.

Burning the CD-R disc

As files are prepared for the CD-R disc, Windows pops up a message on the system tray, as shown in Figure 7-2. This is your reminder that files are waiting to be burned to the CD-R.

Figure 7-2:
Files are
awaiting the
flames.

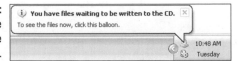

Making sure that the CD-R drive is up to writing a CD-R disc

If you're having trouble mounting a CD-R, check to ensure that Windows is set up to properly use the CD-R drive. Heed these steps:

1. Open the My Computer icon on the desktop.

2. Right-click the CD-R drive icon in the My Computer window.

3. Choose Properties from the pop-up menu.

4. In the CD Drive's Properties dialog box, click the Recording tab.

If you see no Recording tab, you either don't have a CD-R drive or it is defective. Return it to your dealer.

5. Put a check mark by the option Enable CD recording on this drive.

6. Click the OK button.

7. Close the My Computer window.

 By clicking in the bubble (refer to Figure 7-2), you can see the CD-R's window. There, you find the icons prepped for burning, each flagged with an arrow, as shown in the margin.

To burn the files to the CD-R disc, choose File⇨Write these files to CD. This starts the CD Writing Wizard.

Work through the wizard, answering the questions as best you can; fear not — nothing is that difficult. In fact, most of your time is spent waiting for the files to burn, so get a cup of coffee or catch up on your e-mail.

When the files have all been burnt, the disc is automatically ejected from the drive. It's now ready to use, readable on any PC just like any other CD disc.

 ✔ The speed at which the information is written to the CD-R is based on the drive's (hardware) speed rating. The first value in the rating is the speed at which data is written to disc.

 ✔ If you have disk-labeling software, use it to create a unique label for your CD-R. Or, you can write right on the disc using a felt pen, such as a Sharpie.

Messing with files on a burnt CD-R disc

Some CD-burning software may finish the task after the disc is ejected. But with Windows you can continue to mess with the CD-R until it's absolutely full. (In other words, no "final burn" occurs, as it does with some CD-writing software.)

For example, if you want to add more files to the CD-R, you can do so — if the disc has room. The files appear in the CD-R's window; existing files on the CD-R appear as normal, with the files waiting to be burned appearing with the little arrow on them, as shown in Figure 7-3.

Note the Details listing in the lower-left corner of the CD-R disc's window. It tells you how much space is still available (Free Space) on the disc. In Figure 7-3, it shows 237MB — plenty of room!

You can also manipulate the files already on the CD. You can rename and even delete files. Note, however, that messing with those files consumes disc space.

Unlike with a regular disk drive, information is never really erased from a CD-R. So, when you rename a file, Windows simply covers up the old name and creates a new one — which uses disc space. Similarly, when you delete a file from a CD-R, the space used by the file isn't recovered. Keep this in mind if you change anything already burned to the disc.

A few words about CD-RW

CD-RW discs work just like CD-R data discs. All the information in the previous sections applies to CD-RW discs just as it applies to CD-Rs. The main difference is the addition of a command used to reformat the CD-RW disc and start over.

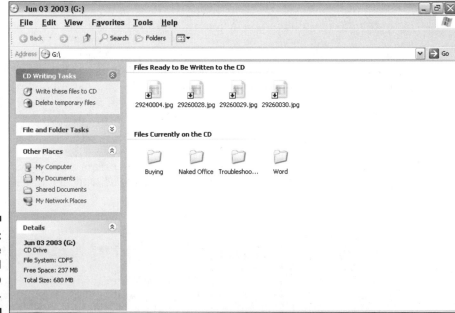

Figure 7-3: Files on the CD and waiting to be burned.

To reformat the CD-RW, open its window (from the My Computer window), and then choose the File⇨Erase this CD-RW. This starts the CD Writing Wizard, which you work through, and eventually it wipes the disc clean.

After reformatting the CD-RW disc, you can use it over again — which is the advantage of the CD-RW over the CD-R (which cannot be reformatted).

- ✔ Most CD-R drives double as CD-RW drives.

- ✔ CD-RW discs are different from CD-R discs. It says "CD-RW" on the label, and the disc is more expensive, which is most obvious when you try to taste this disc.

- ✔ CD-RW discs may not be readable in all CD drives. If you want to create a CD with the widest possible use, burn a CD-R rather than a CD-RW disc.

- ✔ Erasing, renaming, or moving a file after it has been burned to a CD-RW disc wastes disc space, just as doing so on a CD-R disc wastes space. If possible, try to do your file manipulations *before* you burn the files to the disc.

- ✔ The speed at which the drive rewrites the CD-RW disc is the middle number in the drive speed rating-thing.

Using CD-R/RW discs for backing up

CD-R discs, and especially CD-RW discs, are ideal for backing up the data stored on your computer. This operation can be relatively easy:

1. **Open the My Documents folder on the desktop.**

2. **Choose Edit⇨Select All to select all the files and folders in the My Documents folder.**

   In other words, this step selects all the files you have created on your computer.

3. **Choose File⇨Send To⇨CD Drive (G:)**

   Be sure to choose the CD-R/RW drive from the Send To submenu; in these steps, I have picked Drive G, which is the CD-RW drive on my PC.

4. **Burn the CD.**

   Follow the steps in the section "Burning the CD-R disc," earlier in this chapter.

What about DVD-R/RW and the zillion other DVD formats?

Though Windows XP does support some DVD-RAM formats, full support for the garden of DVD-writable formats just isn't there yet. You can buy third-party software to create and burn your own data as well as video DVDs.

Future editions of this book will document how to create your own DVDs as this technology matures and is fully supported by Windows.

When the disc is ejected, you have a complete backup of your files — or at least all those files you have created and stored in the My Documents part of the hard drive.

✔ This trick works if all your stuff fits on a single CD-R or CD-RW disc.

✔ Alas, this trick does not back up your e-mail folders and other personal settings.

✔ To back up all your personal stuff, open the My Computer window, open drive C, and then open the Documents and Settings folder. Copy your account's folder in the window to the CD-R/RW drive. That action backs up not only all your files, but also e-mail and other personal settings.

✔ To do a good backup job, you need backup software that copies files over several CD-R/RW discs. The silly Windows Backup program cannot do this. Instead, you need a third-party backup program. I recommend Retrospect Backup, from Dantz — as long as its software recognizes your CD-R/RW drive.

✔ Try to back up your stuff at least once a week. During the week, consider backing up only your current projects to a Zip disc. Or, if you're using third-party backup software, arrange daily and weekly backup schedules.

✔ Every few months or so, you should consider backing up all your disk drives — the entire computer system. Use software that takes advantage of CD-R/RW disks, such as Dantz Retrospect Backup or Norton Ghost.

✔ CD-RWs make better backup discs than CD-R discs. As with other backup media (floppy disks and tape systems), you can use and reuse the same set of CD-RW discs over and over for your backup procedures.

Burning a Musical CD

Creating the music CD involves three steps:

- ✔ Collect the music or sound files from their sources.
- ✔ Manage the files inside the media software.
- ✔ Write selected files to a music CD.

The first step is to use your media software to collect the music you want to burn to a CD. The music can be downloaded from the Internet, copied from an existing CD, or entered using the PC's sound input from any audio device. The music files are saved on disc and managed by your media software.

Next, you create *playlists,* or collections of the songs you have stored on disk. For example, you can collect a smattering of road tunes and create a playlist of those songs — like building your own album on your computer.

Finally, you simply copy one of your playlists to the CD-R disc. The media software then converts the music files and burns the CD-R.

The following sections detail these steps in Windows Media Player. Note that your version of Media Player may have subtly different options than those I have outlined.

- ✔ I'm particularly fond of the MUSICMATCH Jukebox program as a great alternative to Windows Media Player. Look it up on the Web at www. musicmatch.com.
- ✔ You use specific CD-R discs for recording music, which are often cheaper than the computer CD-Rs. If you plan on creating music only, consider buying some of these cheaper discs.
- ✔ It is assumed that you own whatever music it is that you're copying and that you're using the copies for only your personal use. Making a copy of a commercial CD or copyrighted music and distributing it without paying for it is theft.

Collecting tunes

This is cinchy to do in Windows Media Player. Follow these steps:

1. **Insert a music CD into your CD-ROM drive.**

   This step automatically runs Windows Media Player. If not, from the Start panel, choose Programs⇨Windows Media Player.

In a few moments, information about the CD appears in the Media Player window. (The Internet may even be called up; this isn't necessary, so cancel the operation. Be warned, though, that it's a persistent calling, so consider giving in and connecting anyway.)

2. **Click the Copy from CD button.**

It's on the left edge of the Media Player window, as shown in Figure 7-4.

3. **Click to select the tracks you want to copy from the CD.**

4. **Click the Copy Music button.**

It's in the upper part of the Media Player window, just above the Composer column. (It appears as Stop Copy in Figure 7-4.)

After the songs are copied, they appear in the Media Library. Click the Media Library button. Then, in the Media Library tree structure, you find the album and its copied tracks listed under Audio\Album. Click to select the album title and you find the copied tracks on the right side of the window.

- You can also copy sounds from the Internet in the form of *downloading* MP3 files. See Chapter 26.

- Note that it takes little time to copy over the tracks to the hard drive. That's because the CD-ROM can read from disc many more times faster than it plays the music — that's the last X (multiple) in a CD-ROM drive's speed rating.

Creating a playlist

Before you can burn the music CD you must create a playlist in Windows Media Player. The playlist is a collection of tunes, which doesn't necessarily have to be copied to a CD. For example, if you want, you can create a playlist of all your favorite afternoon songs or driving tunes or cleaning-the-house music. A *playlist* is merely a collection of songs that Media Player can play.

For creating a music CD, however, you probably want to assemble several dozen songs specific to the kind of CD you want to burn. For example, I can create my list of show tune highlights so that I can sing in the car and pretend I'm on Broadway.

To create a playlist in Windows Media Player, follow these simple sample steps:

1. **Click the Media Library button on the left edge of the Media Player window.**

2. **Click the New Playlist button.**

3. **Type a descriptive name for the playlist.**

4. **Click OK.**

    The new playlist is placed in the My Playlists part of the Media Library tree, on the left side of the Media Player window.

    The next step is to add music tracks to the playlist. The music tracks can be found under the Audio branch of the Media Library tree. They're in the All Audio, Album, Artist and Genre branches.

5. **Click an audio source in the Media Library tree.**

    For example, I clicked one of my show tunes albums. The list of songs I copied from that CD appears on the right side of the Media Player window.

6. **Click to select a song, or Ctrl+click to select several songs.**

7. **Click the Add to playlist button.**

8. **Choose your playlist from the drop-down menu.**

    If it doesn't appear, choose the Additional Playlist command; choose your playlist in the dialog box and click the OK button.

9. **Repeat Steps 6 through 8 to collect the songs you want in your playlist.**

10. **Click to highlight your playlist in the Media Library tree.**

    On the right side of the Media Player window, you find all the songs you copied into that playlist.

Figure 7-4: A file is copied from CD to the hard drive.

After the playlist is created, listen to the songs. See whether they're what you want.

To remove a song from the playlist, click to highlight the song and then click the Delete Media button; choose Delete from Playlist from the Delete Media button's menu.

The songs play and are recorded to CD in the order they appear on the playlist. To rearrange the songs, use the up- or down-arrow buttons just above the list.

A playlist can contain many more songs than you eventually end up copying to CD; the CD need not contain all the songs on the playlist.

Burning a music CD

Burning a music CD is a snap after you have created a playlist in Media Player. Here are the steps to take to burn your music CD:

1. **Insert the CD-R into the drive.**

   If Windows attempts to open it or displays the "What the heck do I do now?" dialog box, just cancel out of the operation.

2. **Click the Copy to CD or Device button on the left edge of the Media Player window.**

3. **Ensure that you have your playlist selected on the left side of the window.**

   In Figure 7-5, it's the PCs for Dummies Sample Playlist, though my editor tells me that the *For* should be capitalized. Like, *whatever.*

4. **Ensure that each title you want to copy has a check mark by its name.**

   If you don't want to copy a specific track, remove the check mark. Remember that you don't have to copy them all.

   Keep an eye on the amount of time used by the songs you have selected to copy. Media Player lets you know if you have too many files to copy over. When that happens, you must unselect some songs to make room for others.

5. **Ensure that the CD-R drive is chosen on the right side of the window.**

   It says CD Drive (G:) in Figure 7-5.

6. **Click the Copy Music button.**

   It's in the upper-right corner of the Media Player window.

After clicking the Copy Music button, Windows dutifully copies the tracks you have selected to the CD-R disc. First, the tracks are converted into the proper CD format one at a time. Then the files are copied over to the CD-R.

When the operation is complete, the disc is ejected and is ready to be played in any CD player. The disc's name is the same as the playlist you copied over.

✔ Some older CD players may not be able to read the CD-R music disc.

✔ The speed at which you can write to the CD-R drive is the writing speed. That would be the first number in the drive's speed rating. So, if you have a 40X–16X–48X drive, it creates a 40-minute music CD in only 1 minute.

✔ Unlike data CD-Rs, you cannot add more music to a CD-R after it's been burned once.

✔ Not all sound files can be copied to an audio CD. MIDI files, for example, must be converted into WAV files to be recorded to a CD-ROM. Special software is required in order to make this conversion. Also, some WAV files may be recorded in a low-quality format that makes them incompatible with CD audio. Again, the files must be converted using special software.

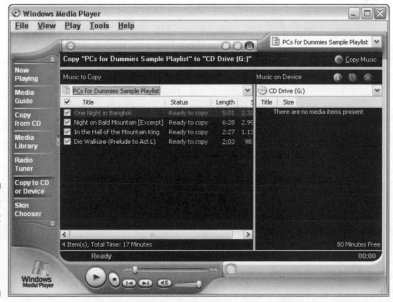

Figure 7-5:
A playlist is being prepared to be burned to CD.

Part III
Your Guide to Computer Hardware and Software

The 5th Wave   By Rich Tennant

Okay, here's your problem. You've got warts on your motherboard.

In this part . . .

1t's part of the eternal conflict. Like the gods versus
men, good versus evil, tastes-great versus less-filling,
and peanut butter versus chocolate, there will be the ever-
lasting battle between computer hardware and software.

Well, actually, no. You see, the software controls the hardware. There is no battle! Understanding the role of hardware
and software is the key to understanding your computer.
Yet, despite the importance of software, the bulk of your PC
and what you need to know about dwells on hardware stuff.
Dumb. Heavy. Mysteriously electronic. Yet, its physical
nature draws us to it, like the moth to the flame or the bee
to the flower or the fly to the piece of — candy bar. With
that in mind, I hereby present the hardware before the software in the hardware-software part of this book.

Chapter 8

Basic Computer Guts

• •

• •

*L*ooks can be deceiving. Spend a night watching the Discovery Channel's "Undersea Predator" special and you'll be convinced of it. Just because it looks innocent and weak doesn't necessarily mean that it's okay to touch. That pretty flower just may be some beast's salivating tongue. The lazy jellyfish could paralyze a bull. And if that's just a scummy rock, why does it have an *eyeball*, Mommy?

Like the mysterious menagerie of undersea creatures, your computer exhibits signs of importance and innocence. For example, you may think that your PC's console is pretty swell and, therefore, it's important. After all, it's got a sleek, aerodynamic case and translucent plastic panels in various colors, or it may be boldly black or thick and intimidating. Even so, the PCs case is merely for show. When it comes to what's really important, you need to peer inside the case. Just like the Sea of Terror, that's where you have to pay attention.

This chapter is about the important stuff inside your PC. There, you can find a veritable sushi bar of electronic things you should know about. Remember: Just because it's important doesn't mean that you should ignore it.

The Mother of All Boards

The computer's case exists primarily to house the largest circuitry board inside your computer. It's the mother of all circuitry boards; hence, it's called the *motherboard*.

Central to the motherboard is the PC's main chip — the *microprocessor,* or *CPU*. Because it's the main chip, all the circuitry on the motherboard is designed to interact with or support the microprocessor. If you think of the motherboard as the downtown of a big city, the microprocessor is the political kingpin.

Just as big cities have train stations and airports, the motherboard also sports various ways to get information in and out. For example, the computer's disk drives connect directly to the motherboard. Expansion slots are on the motherboard, which allow new circuitry to be added. And all those ports on the back of the console? They're directly wired onto the motherboard.

As far as big-city utilities go, the motherboard really needs only the electric company; it has a connection for the PC's power supply, which provides the juice to keep the microprocessor and all the motherboard's diodes, resistors, and mystery chips happily supplied with electricity.

- The *motherboard* is the main piece of circuitry inside your PC.

- CPU stands for *central* *p*rocessing *u*nit.

- The most common items to add to the motherboard are expansion cards, which plug into expansion slots on the motherboard. And to answer that wise guy question: Yes, expansion cards are sometimes called *daughterboards*.

- Computer memory also exists on the motherboard, where it's directly handy to the microprocessor. See Chapter 11.

The Microprocessor

At the heart of every computer beats the *microprocessor*. That's the computer's main chip. It's not the computer's *brain*. (Software is the brain.) Instead, the microprocessor acts like a tiny calculator: It just adds and subtracts (though it does so quickly, like an accountant on espresso).

In addition to doing math, the microprocessor interacts with other elements in the computer. These elements provide either *input* or *output,* which compu-jockeys call *I/O*. Pretty much the whole computer obsesses over this input and output stuff.

✔ *Input* is information flowing into the microprocessor.

✔ *Output* is information the microprocessor generates and spits out.

✔ When your jaw is tired, you can refer to the microprocessor as the *processor.*

✔ Microprocessors no longer look like computer chips. They once did, but now they come in scary-looking black boxes — about the size of an instant camera (but thinner).

Naming a microprocessor

Once upon a time, microprocessors were named after famous numbers. You may have even heard of the 386 or even the 8088. But now, in a move toward rationality, microprocessors are given proper and more powerful names, such as Pentium, Celeron, Athlon, and Duron.

No, those aren't ancient Greeks. They didn't sail on the *Argo.* And they certainly aren't members of the Klingon High Council. They are the names of microprocessors:

Pentium: The premium microprocessor, developed by industry leader Intel.

Celeron: A less-expensive version of the Pentium often used in low-end, or *home,* PCs.

Athlon: An imitation Pentium from Intel rival AMD. The Athlon is just as good as the Pentium, though less expensive.

Duron: AMD's Celeron imitation.

Some names even have suffixes — for example, the Pentium 4, which is the high-end microprocessor now found in most PCs. The Pentium 4 succeeded the Pentium III, so my guess is that someday there will be Pentium 5 (or Pentium V or Pentium Five or whatever).

✔ The Pentium also has some higher-end siblings: the Itanium and Xeon microprocessors, used exclusively in high-end server computers.

✔ Intel is the world's leading manufacturer of computer microprocessors. The company developed the original 8088, which dwelt in the bosom of the first IBM PC.

✔ Little difference exists between a true Intel and a non-Intel microprocessor. As far as your PC's software is concerned, the microprocessor is the same no matter who made it. If you feel better about using a Pentium as opposed to using something from AMD, by all means buy a computer with a Pentium. Really, your software won't know the difference.

The measure of a microprocessor

Microprocessors are gauged by how fast they go. The speed could be miles per hour (mph), but, unfortunately, microprocessors have no wheels and cannot travel distances in any measurable amount of time. Therefore, the speed that's measured is how fast the microprocessor thinks.

Thinking speed is measured in megahertz (MHz) and gigahertz (GHz). The higher the hertz number, the faster the microprocessor. Therefore, a Pentium 4 running at 2.4GHz is slower than a Pentium 4 running at 3.0GHz.

A microprocessor's power is also measured in how many bits it can chew up at once. All Pentium microprocessors can work with 32 bits of information at a time, which makes them very fast. (Older PC microprocessors worked with 16 or 8 bits at once.)

A good analogy with bits in a microprocessor is cylinders in a car engine: The more cylinders the car has, the more powerful the engine is. A future microprocessor may be able to handle 128 bits. That would be very, very powerful.

"Okay, wise guy, so which microprocessor lives in my PC?"

Who knows which microprocessor lurks in the heart of your PC? Better get a big wrench. Better still, right-click the My Computer icon on the desktop. Choose Properties from the pop-up menu. The System Properties dialog box is displayed, similar to the one shown in Figure 8-1.

In Figure 8-1, you can see that the PC sports a Pentium 4 microprocessor running at 1.60GHz. Is that true? Unfortunately, you have no way to tell for certain without opening the console and looking with your own eyeballs. But it has been my experience that what you see in the System Properties dialog box is accurate.

✔ Not every System Properties dialog box displays information as complete as that shown in Figure 8-1. Sometimes, the microprocessor description can be vague, as in x86 Family 6 Model 8 Stepping 3.

✔ The System Properties dialog box also tells you how much memory (RAM) lives inside your computer. In Figure 8-1, the computer has 384MB of memory.

✔ You can change the logo that appears in the System Properties window, such as the IBM that appears in Figure 8-1. Use the Paint program in Windows to open and edit the file OEMLOGO.BMP, which is in the C:\WINDOWS\SYSTEM32 folder. To substitute your own logo, save your image file (which can be anything) under the filename OEMLOGO.BMP in the folder I just mentioned. Make sure that the image isn't larger than about 190 pixels wide and 100 pixels tall.

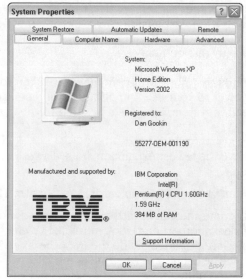

Figure 8-1:
The System
Properties
dialog box.

Expansion Slots

To add more goodies and expand your PC's capabilities, the motherboard sports special long, thin slots. These are *expansion slots,* into which you can plug special *expansion cards.* The idea is that you can expand your system by adding options not included with the basic PC.

Your PC can have anywhere from zero to a dozen expansion slots. Some home systems and most laptops have no expansion slots. That keeps the price down on the home systems and, well, laptops are too petite to worry about hulking expansion cards. Aside from those models, most PCs can have up to eight expansion slots, depending on the size of the console.

Expansion slots come in three delicious flavors: Orangy ISA, Pineapple-y PCI, and Tutti-Fruity AGP.

ISA. The most ancient type of expansion slot is the ISA, which stands for (get this) Industry Standard Architecture. That's because it never really had a name until another, better type of expansion slot came along. ISA slots hang around to be compatible with older expansion cards. Most PCs have one or two ISA expansion slots for compatibility reasons.

PCI. The PCI slot is the most common form of internal expansion for a PC (for a Macintosh too, but that's not the subject here). Chances are good that if you buy an expansion card, it's a PCI card. If given the option, choose a PCI expansion card over an ISA model.

AGP. The final expansion slot is the AGP, or Accelerated Graphics Port. This special type of slot takes only video expansion cards, usually the nice spendy ones that do all sorts of amazing graphics. Not every PC has this type of slot, and if your PC does, it has only one of them.

Expansion slots and the cards that plug into them make it Tinker Toy simple to add new features and power to your PC. And although anyone can plug in a card and expand a computer system, this job is best left to those experts who enjoy such things.

- Small-footprint PCs have the fewest expansion slots. Tower computer models have the most.

- For more information on video expansion cards, see Chapter 12.

- Most expansion cards come squirming with cables. This mess of cables makes the seemingly sleek motherboard look more like an electronic pasta dish. Some cables are threaded inside the PC; others are left hanging limply out the back. The cables are what make the internal upgrading and installation process so difficult.

Tick-Tock Goes the Clock

All computers come with an internal clock. Tick-tock. The clock is battery operated, which enables it to keep track of the time, day or night, whether the PC is plugged in or not.

To check the current time, gander at the far right side of the taskbar. Living on the system tray is the current time. Point the mouse at the time — hold it very still — and the current day and date pop up.

Okay. You can wildly move the mouse about again.

- The format for the date and time varies depending on how your computer is set up. Windows displays a date-and-time format based on your country or region. This book assumes the typical (and I agree, backward) U.S. method of listing the date. The specific format used is chosen in the Control Panel by opening the Regional and Language Options icon.

- If you don't see the time displayed on the system tray, right-click the Start button and choose Properties from the pop-up menu. Click the Taskbar tab in the Taskbar and Start Menu Properties dialog box. Look for the Show the Clock check box near the bottom. Click in that check box. Click the OK button and Windows shows you the time on the taskbar.

Yes, the time is important!

Who cares if the computer knows what time of day it is? Well, because your files are time- and date-stamped, you can figure things out, such as which is a later version of two similar files or two files with the same name on different disks. That's why computers have clocks.

"My clock is all screwy!"

Computers don't always show the proper time. A typical PC loses about a minute or two of time every day. Why? Who knows!

Generally speaking, the clock runs slow or fast because of all the various things going on inside the computer. The more that goes on, the more the clock is wrong. Especially if you put your computer to sleep or "hibernate" it, the clock can get really nuts. (Refer to Chapter 2 for more hibernation information.)

On the positive side, the computer's clock is well aware of Daylight Savings Time; Windows automatically jumps the clock forward or backward, and does so without having to know the little ditty "Spring forward, fall back." Or is it the other way around? Whatever — the computer knows and obeys.

What do you do if the clock is wrong? Why, set it, of course. Keep reading!

Boring details about your PC's battery

All computers have an internal battery, which is part of the motherboard. The battery serves two purposes.

First, the battery is there to keep track of the time. If you notice that the computer's clock is totally off — and I mean by years and years — your computer's internal battery may need replacing.

Second, the battery provides power to a special thing called the *CMOS*. It's a memory location that stores basic information about the computer (disk drives, setup options, and the printer port, for example), information that the computer needs in order to remember even when it's unplugged. So the battery powers the CMOS memory, which keeps track of those things.

Computer batteries are robust little suckers. They typically last upward of five years. When they die, you know because the computer's date is wrong, or the computer may complain that it can't see your PC's hard drives (which seems scary, but is nothing to worry about). When that happens, simply have the battery replaced. Or beg for a new computer. Yeah, that's what I would do!

Setting the clock

To set the date and time on your PC, double-click the time on the taskbar: Click-click. The Date and Time Properties dialog box magically appears, as shown in Figure 8-2.

Manipulate the controls in the Date and Time Properties dialog box to change or set the date or time.

For example, type **10:00** if it's 9:58 or so. Then, when the time lady (or whoever) says that it's 10 o'clock, click the Apply button in the Date and Time Properties dialog box. That action sets the time instantly. Click OK when you're done.

Internet time to the rescue!

If you want to be ultraprecise about setting your PC's clock, you can synchronize your computer with one of the many nuclear clocks on the Internet. To do so, open the Date and Time Properties dialog box, as described in the preceding section. Then click the Internet Time tab (refer to Figure 8-2).

Put a check mark by the option Automatically synchronize with an Internet time server. Optionally, choose a time server from the drop-down list.

Windows automatically adjusts the PC's clock whenever you're connected to the Internet. There's nothing else you need to do — ever!

Figure 8-2:
The Date and Time Properties dialog box.

The PC's Setup program

The Setup program is an important part of all computers, but something you rarely (if ever) need to run. What it does is configure some of the basic pieces of your computer, such as what types of hard drives the system has; in which order to boot the floppy drive, CD-ROM, or hard drive; plus other technical trivia.

The key to using the Setup program is knowing how to start it. When the computer first starts, you see some text messages. One of them says something like `Press <F1> to enter Setup`, though it may be the F2 key, Delete key, or some other key on the keyboard. If you press that key, you run the PC's Setup program.

The BIOS

One more thing found on the motherboard is the computer's BIOS (pronounced "BYE-oss"). The *BIOS* is a special chip that contains the simple instructions for the computer to communicate with its various pieces and parts.

For example, the BIOS contains software to talk to the keyboard, monitor, and expansion slots; display the manufacturer's logo; and do other simple activities. The BIOS isn't as complex as the operating system, but it's necessary in order to get the PC going in the morning.

✔ BIOS stands for Basic Input/Output System.

✔ BIOS is also known as ROM. See Chapter 11 for information on ROM.

✔ In addition to the main BIOS, your computer may have other BIOSes. For example, the video BIOS controls your system's graphics display, and the hard drive BIOS controls the hard disk. Your network adapter may have its own BIOS. Normally, when you see the term *BIOS* by itself, it refers to the PC's main BIOS.

The Source of PC Power

The final goody in your PC gut's need-to-know collection is the *power supply*. It does several things for Mr. Computer:

✔ Brings in electricity from the wall socket, converting it from wild AC current into mild DC current

✔ Provides electricity to the motherboard and everything living on the motherboard

✔ Provides juice to the internal disk drives

✔ Contains fans that help keep the inside of the console cool

✔ Contains or is directly connected to the PC's power button.

The power supply is also designed to take the brunt of the damage if your computer ever suffers from electrical peril, such as a lightning strike or power surge. In those instances, the power supply is designed to die, sacrificing itself for the good of your PC. *Don't panic!* You can easily replace the power supply and discover that the rest of your PC is still working fine.

✔ Thanks to the fans, the power supply is the noisiest part of any PC.

✔ Only if the power supply blows up do you need to replace it. (I really should say "fail" rather than "blow up.")

✔ Power supplies are designed for sacrifice. As such, they're easy to replace.

✔ Power supplies are rated in watts. The more internal hardware stuff your PC has — the more disk drives, memory, and expansion cards, for example — the greater the number of watts the power supply should provide. The typical PC has a power supply rated at 150 or 200 watts. More powerful systems may require a power supply upward of 300 watts.

✔ One way to keep your power supply — and your computer — from potentially going Poof (even in a lightning strike) is to invest in a surge protector, or UPS. Refer to Chapter 2 for details.

Chapter 9

Ports, Jacks, and Holes

· ·

· ·

Come on 'round back, behind your PC. On its rump. There you find a host of holes, a cluster of connectors, and a plethora of plug-in places. They're ugly, like a bag woven with shells that reads "San Diego." Yet, despite the ugliness, despite that it's the side of your PC that faces the wall, those holes are handy. They help you to expand your PC system and to connect various important items to the main console unit.

This chapter is about the holes on your PC's backside. Officially, they're known as *jacks,* probably because some chap named Jack discovered the first hole on the back of an early British, piston-powered computer during "the big one." Another term, equally official, is *port.* It means the same thing as jack, which is just another term for hole. As with most things in a computer, keeping the air clear with a single well-defined and descriptive term is not a top priority.

Holes for Everything

Yup, they look like holes. Fancy holes. Plug-in type holes, as shown in Figure 9-1, which illustrates a typical panel found on the back of most PCs. Here's the list of what the holes are called, which also helps you to understand what connects to them:

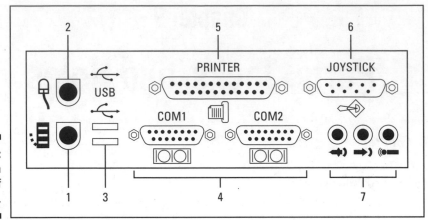

Figure 9-1:
Jacks on
the back of
the console.

1. Keyboard connector

2. Mouse connector

3. USB connector (usually two of them)

4. Serial port connector (usually two of them)

5. Printer (parallel) port connector

6. Joystick port connector

7. Audio connectors (three of them)

The sections that follow elaborate on the different cables and devices that plug into these various holes.

- A hole is really a jack or connector on the back of your PC. Into the jack you can plug any one of a variety of external devices with which your computer can communicate.

- Some jacks are dedicated to certain devices. Other jacks, known as ports, can connect to a variety of different and weird things.

- More ports can be added to any PC through an expansion card. For example, you can add a Firewire port to your computer with a $90 expansion card.

- Your PC may also sport a video port for the monitor. You may find that port with the other ports or on an expansion card. Chapter 12 covers all things video.

- Another common hole, not shown in Figure 9-1, is the networking port, or RJ45 jack. That's where the network cable plugs into the computer. See Chapter 18 for more information.

In Plugs the Keyboard and the Mouse

The keyboard and mouse connectors look the same on most PCs. That's because they are! Even so, one is for the keyboard, and another is for the mouse. The keyboard doesn't work unless it's plugged into the proper hole, and ditto for the mouse.

✔ Tiny pictures by the ports tell you which is which.

✔ If you use a USB mouse, you can plug it into the USB port and leave the mouse port open. Or, you can buy one of those special USB-to-mouse port adapters, which often comes with USB mice.

✔ Some computer mice plug into the serial port rather than into the special mouse port. If so, plug the mouse into serial port 1. Plugging the mouse into serial port 2 conflicts with the PC's dial-up modem.

All Sing Praises to the Glorious USB

The most versatile jack on the back of your PC isn't a jack at all. It's a port — the USB port. Right away, you need to know that it's pronounced "yoo-es-bee," not "uss-ub." USB stands for Universal Serial Bus, from which I could extract several puns, but have elected not to.

The USB port is the most versatile connector on your computer. Unlike most other ports, USB was designed to host a number of different and interesting devices, making it replace just about every other connector on the PC's rump.

If the computer sports a USB port, the whole world of USB devices is open to you. The devices (peripherals) that plug into the USB port are legion: monitors, speakers, joysticks, scanners, digital cameras, floppy drives and other storage devices, modems, anti-gravity facelift straps, and the list goes on. More and more USB devices are appearing every day.

✔ Eventually, USB ports will replace the keyboard, mouse, joystick, COM (serial), and printer ports on all PCs.

✔ USB 2.0 is a second superduper USB standard. It's faster than regular USB and supports high-speed external devices, such as CD-ROM, DVD, and hard drives. If you get a USB 2.0 device, ensure that your PC supports USB 2.0.

Does your PC have a USB port?

 Before you go nuts over USB, first ensure that your PC has USB ports. They're about the size of a breath mint and labeled with the USB symbol, as shown in the margin.

USB ports are found behind the PC, usually along with other ports, as shown earlier, in Figure 9-1. Some PCs have one or more USB ports on the front of the console, sometimes hidden behind a pop-up or sliding door.

✔ Those USB ports on the front of the console are very handy for plugging in game pads.

✔ Don't worry if your PC lacks a USB port. You can always add a few via a USB expansion card. Expect it to cost about $20.

✔ If your computer has USB ports, be sure to buy USB peripherals. This strategy is much better than using the PC's other ports to connect external devices.

USB cables

USB devices connect to the PC's USB ports via cables. It's important to note that though many USB devices come with cables, some (such as printers) do not. Be sure to check the box to see whether a USB cable is included.

 You see two different USB connectors, labeled A and B, as shown in the margin. Most USB cables have an A end and a B end; the A end plugs into the PC, and the B end plugs into the device.

Note that you also see USB cables with two B ends or two A ends. They're used as extensions so that you can link two USB cables to connect a remote device to a PC.

 ✔ You can buy USB cables cheaply on the Internet or not-as-cheaply at any office supply store.

✔ Be mindful that you don't buy an A-A or B-B USB cable when what you really need is an A-B cable.

Connecting a USB device

One reason the USB port is poised to take over the world is that it's smart. Dumb things never take over the world. Witness the Salad Shooter. But I digress.

Unlike other connectors on a PC, when you plug a USB device into a USB port, Windows instantly recognizes it and configures the device for you. You don't even need to turn off or reset your computer. Amazing.

Of course, there's more to adding a USB device. You still need to install software to control the device. Note that sometimes you need to do this before you plug in the USB device, and sometimes you need to do it after.

For example, the Iomega USB-powered Zip drive needs to have its software installed *before* the drive is connected. On the other hand, the Umax USB scanner must be plugged in *before* the software is installed. Be sure to check the manual for the proper sequence.

✔ After USB devices are initially installed, you can plug them in or unplug them as you need them. So, if you have a scanner and joystick hooked up, unplug one and plug in your PC's camera instead. No penalty or glitch occurs by making this change.

✔ Some USB devices don't even need a power cord; the USB device gets its power from the console. These devices are often labeled "USB-powered." Other USB devices, such as monitors, do require a separate power cable.

Expanding the USB universe

Most PCs have two USB connectors. You can plug two USB devices into them. If you have more USB devices, you can unplug and replug devices as necessary. But rather than subject yourself to that kind of a pain, you can get a USB *hub*.

USB hubs allow you to greatly expand your PC's USB universe. The hub, as shown in Figure 9-2, connects to your PC's USB port. But then it turns around and instantly provides even more USB ports for those devices that need them.

✔ If one hub isn't enough, buy another! You can connect hubs to hubs, if you like. As long as the cables fan out from the PC and nothing loops back on itself, it all works.

✔ Note that some USB devices prefer to be plugged directly into the console. These types of devices say so on their box and in the manual.

✔ Using hubs, you can expand your PC's USB universe to the maximum 127 USB devices. You'll probably run out of desk space before that.

✔ Some USB hubs are built into USB devices. A few USB monitors, for example, have USB hubs that add two or four more USB ports. Some USB keyboards have an extra port on them for connecting a USB mouse.

✔ The first hub (your PC) is the *root* hub. Beyond that, you can connect only a certain number of hubs to the computer, depending on your PC's hardware. This maximum number most likely will never be known because the cost of the USB devices required to reach that limit would bankrupt most small countries.

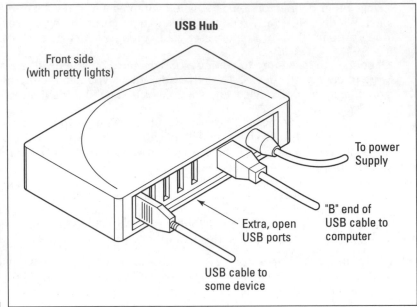

USB Hub

Front side
(with pretty lights)

To power
Supply

"B" end of
USB cable to
computer

Extra, open
USB ports

USB cable to
some device

Figure 9-2:
Add more
USB ports
with a
USB hub.

Even Better than USB Is Firewire

Bigger, faster, wiser, and definitely better named than the USB port is the
Firewire port. *Firewire* is an Apple Computer trademark for what's also known
as the IEEE 1394 High Performance Serial Bus standard. Some folks just say
"IEEE 1394." Others have shortened it to "I-E-E-E" or "Eye triple E" or even the
"Ieeeee!" yelp of pain. But you still can't beat Firewire as a great name.

Firewire is basically a superior and faster version of the USB port. That makes
it ideal for such high-speed operations as digital video, high-resolution scanning, external storage devices, and getting Mom to vacuum the entire house
in fewer than 15 seconds.

Though Firewire is widely used on the Macintosh, it's not considered an inte-
gral part of the PC . . . yet. But if you're into high-speed operations, consider
Firewire as a spiffy alternative to USB (and USB 2.0).

✔ Firewire ports are marked by the Firewire symbol, as shown in the margin.

✔ As with USB devices, you can plug in or unplug a Firewire device without
having to turn your computer off and on.

✔ Firewire uses its own, unique cables, which are not the same as USB
cables. In fact, unlike a USB cable, both ends of the Firewire cable are
the same.

✔ You can also buy Firewire hubs to add even more devices.

✔ The limit on FireWire devices is much less than USB. You can have only 64 devices tangled up on a Firewire port. Still, that's a heck of a lot.

✔ The primitive alternative to Firewire is the *SCSI* port. SCSI ports were once popular for adding both internal and external storage devices to PCs. This port may still be found in some high-end computers, but mostly it's being phased out by other standards. The only vital thing you need to know about SCSI is how it's pronounced: "skuzzy." (I kid you not.)

Serial, or COM, Ports

Cereal ports are named after Ceres, the Roman goddess of agriculture. Wait. Wrong type of cereal.

Before USB, serial ports were the most versatile type of connector on your PC. Into the serial port you could pour, or plug, a mixture of interesting devices, which is why it's called a serial port rather than a this-or-that port.

The serial port on a PC is rarely used now. It's lonely! External dial-up modems, a serial mouse, or a direct PC-to-PC cable is about all you find connected to a serial port today.

✔ Most computers come with two serial ports, dubbed COM1 and COM2.

✔ A serial port can also be called a modem port, or even an RS-232 port.

✔ Unlike with USB ports, you can plug only one item at a time into a serial port. That's okay because most of the serial port's devices are those consistently connected to the PC: modem, mouse, and so on.

The Ever-Versatile Printer Port

Oddly enough, the printer port is where you plug in the computer's printer. The printer cable has one connector that plugs into the printer and a second that plugs into the computer. Both connectors are different, so plugging a printer cable in backward is impossible. (Give Alma a hammer and vice grips, though, and she can do it!)

In addition to yakking it up with a printer, your PC can also use the printer port to communicate with any of a variety of high-speed devices. To do this, daisy-chain the device between the console and printer, as shown in Figure 9-3. Believe it or not, such chicanery works, and — for that one device, anyway — the printer port can prove to be quite versatile.

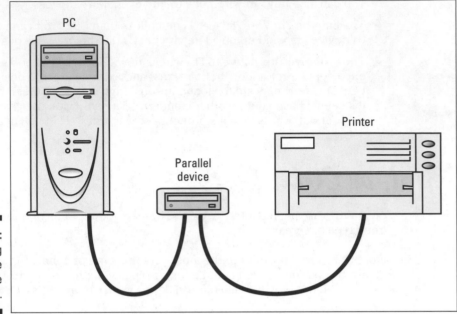

PC

Parallel
device

Printer

Figure 9-3:
Sticking
a device
on the
printer port.

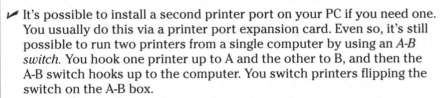

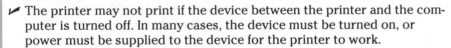

✔ Though only one device can be daisy-chained between the printer and the printer port, the variety of devices is pretty wide; you can connect CD-ROM, CD-R, DVD, Zip, and even hard drives to the PC this way.

✔ Plugging an external device into the printer port doesn't interfere with printing. It seems like it should, but it doesn't.

✔ The printer may not print if the device between the printer and the computer is turned off. In many cases, the device must be turned on, or power must be supplied to the device for the printer to work.

✔ It's possible to install a second printer port on your PC if you need one. You usually do this via a printer port expansion card. Even so, it's still possible to run two printers from a single computer by using an *A-B switch.* You hook one printer up to A and the other to B, and then the A-B switch hooks up to the computer. You switch printers flipping the switch on the A-B box.

✔ For the printer port to work with an external device, you must configure your PC so that the printer port operates in *bidirectional* mode. Have your guru or dealer configure the PC's setup program so that the port is configured as bidirectional (either EPP or ECP, depending on the device's requirements).

✔ For more information on printers, see Chapter 15.

✔ Printer ports are also called *parallel ports,* or to old-time nerds they're known as *Centronics* ports. IBM refers to the printer port as the LPT1 port. People who refer to ports in this manner are *not* getting any flav-o-pops for dessert.

The Super-Scientific A-to-D (Joystick) Port

They aren't called joysticks any more; they're *game controllers*. Some are even *game pads*. That must make it seem more professional in some dimension. Anyway, most PCs have a joystick port into which you can plug a single joystick or an adapter that lets you use two joysticks (game pads, whatever) at one time.

✔ Plugging in the game controller or joystick is only half the job. The other half is using the Control Panel's Game Controllers icon to let Windows and your software know about the joystick.

✔ The joystick port is also where you can plug in the MIDI box for connecting musical instruments to your PC.

✔ Originally IBM dubbed the Joystick port the Analog-to-Digital ("A-to-D") port. It was designed for "scientific" operations, and somehow *joystick* falls under that definition. Even so, a variety of devices can be controlled using the joystick port. I have a friend who controls his model railroad through the joystick port, and the anemometer (one of those twirly wind things) on my office roof connects to my PC via the joystick port.

Audio Connectors

The PC shall not remain silent! To let you hear what it has to say or to tell the computer what exactly to do with itself, the PC has thee audio jacks. Two are for input, one is for output. All are marked with one of the specific, helpful, cryptic icons shown in the margin.

 Line Out/Speaker: This is where you connect the PC's speakers or your headphones, which is why this jack has a headphone icon on it rather than the weird thing shown in the margin.

 Microphone: This is where you plug in an optional microphone, which allows you to record your own voice or the lovely ambient noises of your computer room.

Line In: Unlike the microphone jack, this jack is for connecting sound-producing devices to your PC. For example, using the proper audio cables available at Radio Shack ("You've got questions, we've got answers"), you can hook up your VCR, phonograph, or tricorder to the PC and record audio from that device.

Don't panic if your PC seems to have two sets of these audio jacks. You may find one set on the back panel (refer to Figure 9-1) and another set on an expansion card. That's the DVD-ROM expansion card, and you can bet dollars for donuts that the audio connectors on that expansion card are the ones you want to use, not the silly jacks on the back panel.

See Chapter 17 for more information about sounds in your PC.

Chapter 10

All about Disks and Drives

- -

- -

*B*ehold the disk drive. It toils and it spins. And why do they spin? Like the moon spins about the earth, disk drives spin because they're happy. Or it could be the disk drive motor. Scientists have yet to clear up the issue.

Another important hardware goody dwelling in your PC console's bosom is the disk drive. This is your PC's storage device; the software side, you're probably already familiar with if you have read the chapters in Part II. This chapter covers the more technical and grimy side of the drives from a pure hardware perspective.

Different Types of Disk Drives for Different Needs

In the beginning was the floppy disk. And it was good.

When the microcomputer first dawned in the late 1970s, the main storage medium was a cassette recorder with a special cassette tape. Then came the floppy drive, which was faster and more reliable than cassette tape.

Eventually, the hard drive (always on the scene) came down in price until it was a standard fixture on all PCs. Then came the CD-ROM drive, first a novelty for "multimedia" computers, but now standard fare on all PCs.

The most recent standard addition to the PC's disk drive hive is the DVD-ROM drive, which is essentially a higher-capacity CD-ROM. Oh, and you see other interesting and odd flavors of disk drives. The following list summarizes the most common types and how they're used:

- **Floppy drives:** A floppy drive eats floppy disks, which, sadly, store only a puny 1.44MB of information. That was enough space 10 years ago. Today, it's useless, which is why floppy drives soon will be phased out of the PC's design.

- **Hard drives:** The PC's primary long-term storage device is the hard drive. These drives store many gigabytes of information, more than enough for Windows, your software, and all the data you can create and take from the Internet. Unlike other types of drives, the hard drive cannot be removed from the computer.

- **CD-ROM drives:** A CD-ROM drive eats discs, which look just like music CDs. Computer CDs can store hundreds of megabytes of information, and all new computer software comes on CDs. Unlike with hard drives and floppy disks, you cannot write information to a CD-ROM disc. The *RO* in CD-ROM means read-only.

- **DVD drives:** Now standard on many computer systems, the DVD, or DVD-ROM, drive eats DVD-ROM discs, which look just like regular CD-ROM discs but store much more information. DVD-ROM discs can store as much information as 20 CDs, or about enough space to store a full-length movie or a copy of every promise ever made by all American politicians. (Well, maybe not.)

- **Zip drives:** Zip drives eat Zip discs, which work much like floppy disks, although they can store 100MB, 250MB, or 750MB of information per disk. That makes them a better — and cheaper — removable storage option than the floppy disk.

Beyond these basic types of disk drives, you may find other drives, common or not, spinning and humming inside your PC. The variety is too bizarre to mention here.

Here are some general disk drive thoughts for you to ruminate:

- The drive is the device that reads the disk.

- Zip-a-dee doo-dah!

- The disk is the thing that contains the data — the media inside the drive.

- The information is stored on the disk, similar to the way a movie is stored on a videocassette.

- Zip drives are not related to the ZIP file format (known as a *compressed folder* in Windows). The ZIP file format is used to compress files downloaded from the Internet or from other users. A *Zip drive* is a device that reads and writes to removable Zip discs.

Land of the Floppies

Despite the near obsolescence of floppy disks, you may one day have to deal with one. I still occasionally use them myself. I have a drawer full of them. When someone needs me to mail a disk, I see whether it fits on a floppy and use it rather than burn a CD-R. Despite the cost, there's something about putting a 1MB file on a 600MB CD-R that irks me. Anyway. . . .

The following sections cover various fun floppy facts.

Floppy drives eat floppy disks

The floppy disk, or diskette, measures 3½ inches square and is about ⅛ inch thick. The disk may also be referred to as *IBM formatted* or *DS, HD*. It's all the same type of disk, the only one you can buy in most places and the only one your PC's floppy drive eats.

Here are some floppy disk points to ponder:

- ✔ It's tempting to use these disks as beverage coasters. Don't. Moisture can seep underneath the sliding metal thing and freak out the disk inside.

- ✔ A floppy disk must be *formatted* before you can use it. Fortunately, most floppy disks are already formatted when you buy them. If not, refer to Chapter 4 for formatting information.

- ✔ No, the *IBM* on the label of a preformatted box of disks doesn't mean that they're only for IBM-brand computers. If you have a PC, you can use an IBM disk.

- ✔ Keep floppy disks away from magnets, including telephone handsets, radio and TV speakers, executive-style paper-clip holders, desk fans, photocopiers, MRI machines, and the planet Jupiter.

- ✔ Avoid extreme temperatures. Don't leave a disk sitting on the dash of your car or even on a windowsill. And, even if the novel thought occurs to you, don't store your disks in the freezer.

- ✔ Don't touch the disk surface; touch only its protective cover.

- ✔ When you're mailing a disk, don't use a floppy disk mailer from the drugstore. Don't fold the disk in half and mail it in a standard-size envelope. Instead, buy a photo mailer, which is the same as a floppy disk mailer but doesn't cost as much.

- ✔ Floppy disks are great for transporting files from one computer to another. However, the small capacity of the floppy disk (only 1.4MB) limits the size and number of files you can move.

✔ Floppy disks are extremely unreliable. In fact, the more you use a floppy disk, the higher the chance that you will lose information on the disk.

✔ Never save any file to a floppy disk. Place only *copies* of files on floppy disks.

In and out goes the floppy disk

To use the floppy disk, you must insert it into your PC's floppy drive. To do so, stick the floppy disk into the drive with the label facing up and the shiny metal piece going in first. The disk should make a satisfying *thunk* noise when it's in place.

To remove the floppy disk, push the button near the floppy drive slot. This causes the drive to spit out the disk like a vile sinner — though the disk doesn't come all the way out. Grab the disk and pull it out the rest of the way. Put the disk away.

✔ Never remove a disk from a floppy drive when the floppy drive light is on. Wait.

✔ Before you eject a floppy disk, make sure that you're not using any files on that disk. If you eject a disk that still has open files on it, Windows asks you to reinsert the floppy disk so that it can finish writing information. That can be annoying.

✔ Be careful not to insert the floppy disk into the Zip drive slot. The Zip drive slot is larger than the floppy drive slot. If you have both, be sure to put floppies in the floppy drive.

Write-protecting a floppy disk

You can protect floppy disks in such a way as to prevent yourself or anyone else from modifying or deleting anything on the disk. To *write-protect* a 3½-inch disk, locate the little sliding tile on the disk's back corner. When the tile covers the hole, the disk can be written to. If you slide the tile off the hole (so that you can see through it), the disk is write-protected and cannot be written to. You can read from the disk and copy files from it, but forget about changing the disk's contents.

Driving a Hard Disk

Because of their expense at the time, hard drives weren't part of the original IBM PC specification. In fact, it was the IBM model PC/XT that contained the first hard drive, a 10MB monster. Back in 1983, that was really something.

Since that original 10MB unit, hard drives have become standard equipment on all PCs, though their size is now measured in gigabytes (GB) and not in megabytes (MB). Like that original hard drive unit, however, today's hard drives can still be found inside the PC's console case. All you can see of the hard drive is its tiny activity light, which blinks as information is written to or read from the drive.

See Chapter 11 for the definitions of gigabyte and megabyte.

Hard drive technical blather

Hard drives contain hard disks. However, unlike a floppy or CD-ROM disk, the disks inside a hard drive are *not* removable. That's because the hard drive is a hermetically sealed unit. No air can get in or out. The mechanism that reads and writes information is therefore precise, with lots of information written to and read from the disk reliably.

Inside the hard drive are the hard disks themselves. Most hard drives have two or more disks, or *platters,* each of which is stacked on a spindle. A device called a *read-write head* is mounted on an actuator arm that allows it to access both sides of all the disks in the hard drive at once. Figure 10-1 attempts to illustrate this concept.

Multiple units, multiple letters

Your PC has room for more than one physical hard drive. The second hard drive, if it's added, becomes drive D in your computer system. (Chapter 4 discusses this subject.) However, it's possible to divide a single physical hard drive into smaller units or *partitions*.

For example, a physical drive C has a 60GB capacity. That drive can be divided into three partitions of 20GB each. So the single physical drive becomes three *logical* drives: C, D and then E. Windows handles this all well and it sees the drives partitions separately — despite the fact that the three logical drives exist on a single physical drive.

Though you may hear the term *partition* bandied about and notice your disk partitions while using various disk utilities, don't get hung up on them. If partitioning was done to your hard drive, it was most likely done by your dealer. I don't recommend that you repartition or otherwise mess your hard drive, which is considered an advanced thing to do with a computer.

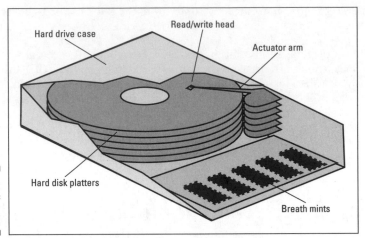

Figure 10-1:
The guts of
a hard drive.

Working the Shiny Media CD-ROM and DVD Drives

CD-ROM drives eat special discs, which I call CDs, or computer CDs. The computer CDs look exactly like music CDs, although they store many megabytes of computer information. The CD-ROM drive can access that information, making it available to you just like it was on a hard disk or floppy. Oh, and it can play music CDs.

A DVD drive (also called a DVD-ROM drive by those who have more time to type than I do) looks and acts just like a CD-ROM drive. In addition to reading computer CDs and music CDs, the DVD drive can access computer DVD and video DVD discs.

- ✔ The *RO* in CD-ROM means Read-Only. You can only read information from a CD-ROM disc. You cannot add new information to the disc or erase or change information already on the disc.

- ✔ Ditto for DVDs: You can only read from them. You cannot record new information on a DVD.

- ✔ DVD is an acronym for Digital Versatile Disc. Or, it may be Digital Video Disc.

- ✔ A typical CD holds up to 640MB of information. A typical music CD can store up to 80 minutes of music.

- ✔ DVD technology is now capable of storing 4GB of information on a disc. Some future versions of DVD discs are rumored to be able to hold more than 17GB of information (barely enough for Excel 2010, most likely).

✔ The speed of a CD-ROM drive is measured in X. The number before the X indicates how much faster that drive is than the original PC CD-ROM drive (which plays as fast as a musical CD player). So, a 32X value means that it's 32 times faster than the original PC CD-ROM drive.

✔ Three Xs are in a CD-R/RW drive's rating:

  • The first is the drive's write speed, or how fast a CD-R can be written to.

  • The second X is how fast the drive can rewrite to a CD-RW.

  • The final X is how fast the drive can be read from.

✔ The special CD-R/RW and DVD-RW drives allow you to create your own CDs or DVDs. Chapter 7 covers this fun activity.

✔ Yes, there is such a thing as a DVD-R/RW or DVD-RAM disc. The formats for these discs aren't really settled yet: Some types are read/write, and others are more like CD-Rs. Also, the capacity of these discs is all over the map. Hopefully, someday they will be standardized, like CD-R/RW drives. Until then, if you want to create a DVD, refer to whatever software you're using for the format it recommends. Then buy that type of DVD drive.

Inserting a CD or DVD

You can stick a CD or DVD into the drive in two ways, depending on which type of disk drive the computer has.

Tray type: The most popular type of CD-ROM or DVD drive uses a slide-out tray to hold the disc. Start by pressing the drive's eject button, which pops out the tray (often called a *drink holder* in many computer jokes). Drop the disc into the tray, label side up. Gently nudge the tray back into the computer. The tray slides back in the rest of the way on its own.

Slide-in type: Another type of disk drive works like the CD player in most automobiles; the drive is merely a slot into which you slide the disc: Pushing the CD into the slot causes some gremlin inside the drive to eventually grab the CD and suck it in all the way. Amazing.

When the disc is in the drive, you use it just like any other disk in your computer.

✔ Generally speaking, the disc is always inserted label side up.

✔ An exception to the label-side-up rule is a DVD with data recorded on both sides. For example, some DVD movies have the TV version on one side and the wide-screen or letterbox version on another. If so, make sure to put the proper side up into the drive.

✔ Some CDs are clipped. That is, they aren't round discs, but rather are business card size or some other special shape. These discs work fine in the tray type of CD-ROM/DVD drive, but don't insert them into the slide-in type of drive.

Ejecting a CD or DVD

Follow these steps to eject a disc from the CD-ROM or DVD drive:

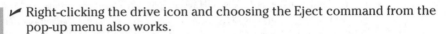

 1. **Open the My Computer window.**
 2. **Click to select the CD-ROM or DVD drive icon.**
 3. **Choose File⇨Eject from the menu.**

    The disc spits from the CD-ROM drive.

 ✔ Right-clicking the drive icon and choosing the Eject command from the pop-up menu also works.

 ✔ You can also eject a disc by pushing the manual eject button on the CD-ROM or DVD drive. However, this method doesn't ensure that Windows is done with the drive. To avoid any particularly nasty error messages, use only the steps outlined in this section for ejecting a CD or DVD.

 ✔ In times of urgency, such as when the computer is locked up (or turned off), you can eject a CD or DVD by pushing a bent paper clip into the tiny hole — the "beauty mark" — on the front of the CD or DVD drive. That manually ejects the disc when the computer is too stupid to do it by itself.

Starting your PC from a CD-ROM

The original PC came with only floppy disks. To start the computer, you had to insert a DOS *boot floppy* to get the system up and running. When the hard drive came along, the computer was designed to start from it as well; if no floppy disk was in the drive, the computer would look for startup instructions on the hard drive. And that's the way it has been for years.

In addition to being able to start, or *boot,* from a floppy disk or the hard drive, modern PCs can also start themselves from a *boot CD,* if one is left in the CD-ROM drive.

To start your PC from a CD-ROM drive, you need a bootable CD, such as the *System Restore* disc, which may have come with your PC. That's a CD you can use to start your computer in times of dire emergency. Put the bootable CD into the drive and then restart Windows. When the computer starts up again, it looks on drive A for a startup disk and then goes to the CD-ROM drive. When the disk is found, the computer starts itself using that disk.

- To *boot* a computer is to start it. A *boot* disk is a startup disk, or a disk used to start the computer.

- You need to start from a CD only if directed to do so by some procedure, book, or manual.

- Some PCs may ask whether you want to boot from the CD-ROM drive, Yes or No. Press Y to do so or N to continue starting up with the hard drive.

- The PC's Setup program sets the order in which the computer looks for a startup disk. Refer to Chapter 8.

The Zip Disk Solution

For the past several years or so, Zip disks have been all the rage. Zip drives are offered as an option on many new PCs, and you can add a Zip drive internally or externally to just about any PC.

Zip disks store 100MB or 250MB or 750MB per disk, depending on which Zip drive you have. The disks are about 4 inches square, only slightly bigger than a floppy disk.

These high-capacity, removable disks are great for backing up files, storing files long-term, or transporting large files between two computers.

- Zip drives come with many new PCs.

- You can add a Zip drive to your PC at any time, either internally or externally.

- The 100MB Zip drives can read only 100MB disks. You must have a 250MB Zip drive to read 250MB disks; these drives can also read the 100MB disks. The 750MB Zip drives can read all three disk formats.

- Zip disks are a great way to move lots of information or massive files between two computers.

- Zip disks are expensive. Yowie! Buy them in bulk to get any type of deal on them. And make sure that you buy the PC-formatted Zip disks, not the Macintosh Zip disks.

Inserting a Zip disk

Zip disks go into the drive with the label side up and with the shiny metal part stuck in first.

Don't force the Zip disk in! If it doesn't fit, you have the disk in the wrong orientation. Inserting the disk is especially frustrating if the disk drive is mounted sideways.

You must push the Zip disk all the way into the drive. After a certain point, the disk becomes locked into place. Stop pushing at that point.

Only when the Zip disk is in the drive can you read or write information to it.

Ejecting a Zip disk

To eject a Zip disk, locate the drive in the My Computer window. Click to select the drive and then choose File⇨Eject from the shortcut menu. This command works just like ejecting a CD or DVD disc.

In times of woe, you can remove a Zip disk from a dead Zip drive. Poke the end of a bent paperclip into the tiny hole near the Zip disk drive's opening. Press hard enough and the Zip disk pops up. But do this only in times of dire need.

Chapter 11

Memory (RAM-a-Lama Ding-Dong)

• •

• •

A s human beings, we're lucky. We have a seemingly endless memory capacity. No one has ever checked into a hospital because their brain was full and they could no longer remember things. Although memory loss can happen, and brain damage isn't something to laugh at, our brains can simply never be "full." To bad it isn't the same for your PC.

Memory is a valuable resource, up for grabs inside your PC. Some programs you run gobble up memory faster than 4-year-olds scramble after the goodies dispersed by a ruptured piñata. Obviously, the more memory in your PC, the better. This chapter tells you how much is enough and how to add more, if you deem it necessary.

What Is Memory?

All computers need memory. That's where the work gets done. The microprocessor can store information inside itself, but only so much. It needs extra memory to jot things down, just like humans need sticky notes and yellow legal pads.

🗸 The more memory in your PC, the better. With more computer memory, you can work on larger documents and spreadsheets, enjoy applications that use graphics and sound, and boast about all that memory to your friends.

✔ The term RAM is used interchangeably with the word *memory*. They're the same thing. (In fact, RAM stands for *Random Access Memory,* in case you have been working any crossword puzzles lately.)

Using memory

Memory in your computer is used for storage — fast and changeable storage because all memory is accessible by the microprocessor. The software you run tells the microprocessor how to interact with memory, what to store in memory, and what to do with the stuff stored in memory.

It works like this: Whenever you create a document with your word processor, each character you type is placed in a specific location in memory. After it's there, the microprocessor doesn't need to access it again unless you're editing, searching or replacing, or doing something active to the text.

After you create something in the PC's memory, you save it to disk. When you need to access the information again, it's opened up and loaded back into memory from disk. After the information is there, the microprocessor can again work over it.

✔ Turning off the power makes the *contents* of memory go bye-bye. The memory chips themselves aren't destroyed.

✔ Your disk drives provide long-term storage for information. It's necessary because computer memory is lost when the power is turned off or when you restart Windows. See Chapter 4 for more information.

✔ When you open a file on disk, the computer copies that information from disk into the computer's memory. Only in memory can that information be examined or changed. When you save information back to disk, the computer copies it from memory to the disk.

✔ Always save your stuff to disk. Make it your mantra: "Save! Save! Save!"

Measuring memory

Memory is measured by the byte. A *byte* can store a single character. For example, the word *goat* is 4 bytes long and requires 4 bytes of computer memory storage. The word *bruise* is 6 characters long and requires 6 bytes of memory to store.

Bytes, however useful, are puny. Although the experimental hobby computers of the 1970s may have had 256 or 1,000 bytes, PCs now have many times that amount. So, rather than waste time talking about millions or billions of bytes, handy abbreviations and swanky computer jargon are used to refer to a specific quantity of memory, as shown in Table 11-1.

Table 11-1		Memory Quantities	
Term	*Abbreviation*	*About*	*Actual*
Byte		1 byte	1 byte
Kilobyte	K or KB	1,000 bytes	1,024 bytes
Megabyte	M or MB	1,000,000 bytes	1,048,576 bytes
Gigabyte	G or GB	1,000,000,000 bytes	1,073,741,824 bytes
Terabyte	T or TB	1,000,000,000,000 bytes	1,099,511,627,776 bytes

The terms in Table 11-1 can still be obscure. To help you visualize them, think of a *kilobyte* (KB) as being about a page of typewritten text. One *megabyte* (MB) of information is required in order to store one minute of music on a CD or as much text information as in an encyclopedia.

The *gigabyte* (GB) is a huge amount of storage — one billion bytes. And the *terabyte* (TB) is 1 trillion bytes, or enough RAM to dim the lights when you start the PC.

Other trivia:

- ✔ The term *giga* is Greek, and it means *giant*.
- ✔ The term *tera* is also Greek. It means *monster!*
- ✔ A specific location in memory is an *address*.
- ✔ Hard disk storage is also measured in bytes.
- ✔ A PC running Windows XP requires at least 256MB of memory to work properly.
- ✔ A typical hard drive now sold stores between 40 and 80 *gigabytes* of data.
- ✔ Bytes are composed of eight bits. The word *bit* is a contraction of *bi*nary digi*t*. Binary is base 2, or a counting system that uses only ones and zeroes. Computers count in binary, and their bits are grouped into clusters of eight for convenient consumption as bytes.

Chips off the old block

Memory dwells on the PC's motherboard, sitting very close to the microprocessor for fast access and ready dispatch. Memory comes in the form of tiny chips called *DRAM* chips. They're permanently attached to teensy-tiny memory expansion cards called *DIMMs*.

Boring details on RAM, ROM, and flash memory

RAM stands for *Random Access Memory*. It refers to memory that the microprocessor can read from and write to. When you create something in memory, it's done in RAM. RAM is memory and vice versa.

ROM stands for Read-Only Memory. The microprocessor can read from ROM, but it cannot write to it or modify it. ROM is permanent. Often, ROM chips contain special instructions for the computer — important stuff that never changes. For example, the BIOS is in ROM (see Chapter 8). Because that information is stored on a ROM chip, the microprocessor can access it. The instructions are always there because they're not erasable.

Flash memory is a special type of memory that works like both RAM and ROM. Information can be written to flash memory, like RAM, but it isn't erased when the power is off, like RAM. The memory cards and sticks used by digital cameras are flash memory. That way, the images stay in the camera even when the camera's batteries run out (which is often).

A real DIMM is slightly smaller than the image shown in Figure 11-1. It also has chips on both sides, which is why it's a DIMM, or *Dual*-Inline-Modular-Memory, thing, and not a SIMM, or Single-Inline-Modular-Memory thing.

Figure 11-1:
DIMM's
about
this big.

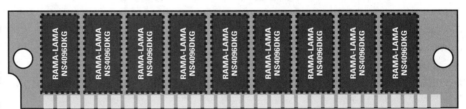

Each DIMM card contains a given chunk of RAM, measured in one of the magical computer memory values of 4, 8, 16, 32, 64, 128, or 256 megabytes.

DIMM cards are plugged into memory slots on the motherboard, and each slot is a *bank* of memory. So, a PC with 256MB of RAM may have four banks of 64MB SIMMs installed.

✔ DRAM stands for Dynamic Random Access Memory. It's pronounced "dee-ram," and it's the most common type of memory chip installed in a PC.

✔ Other types of memory chips exist, each with a name similar to DRAM, such as EDORAM or NIFTYRAM or DODGERAM. Most of these are merely marketing terms designed to make one type of memory sound better or faster than another.

Some Memory Q&A

Here are some common questions people ask me about computer memory. All these are real questions asked by this book's readers over the years. Those that aren't real questions, I just made up.

"How much memory is in my PC right now?"

This information may be a mystery to you, but it isn't a secret to your computer. The System Properties dialog box shows you how much memory lives inside the beast: Right-click the My Computer icon on the desktop and choose Properties from the shortcut menu that appears. The System Properties dialog box appears (refer to Figure 8-1).

The amount of memory (shown as RAM) appears right beneath the type of microprocessor that lives in your PC. In Figure 8-1(you have to look in Chapter 8), it says that the computer has 348MB of RAM — plenty. Click the OK button to close the dialog box.

"Does my PC have enough memory?"

Knowing how much memory is in your PC is one thing, but knowing whether that amount is enough is entirely different!

The amount of memory your PC needs depends on two things. The first, and most important, is the memory requirement of your software. Some programs, such as photo-editing programs, require lots of memory. It says right on the box how much memory is needed. For example, the Photoshop photo-editing program demands 192MB of RAM.

To test to see whether your PC has enough memory, do this:

1. **Start a bunch of programs — maybe three or four large programs.**

   For example, start Microsoft Word, Microsoft Excel, a graphics program (such as Photoshop), and perhaps some other program, like Internet Explorer or Outlook Express.

2. **Press Alt+Esc.**

   This keyboard command switches from one program to the other. As it does, listen to your computer to hear any hard drive access, or "rumbling."

3. Repeat Step 2 until you have switched between all open programs.

The rumbling you hear is the sound of virtual memory at work, which means that Windows is supplementing RAM with disk storage (discussed in the next section). That means your PC could use some more RAM.

Close any programs you have opened.

✔ Generally speaking, all PCs should have at least 256MB of RAM, which is what you need at minimum to run Windows XP.

✔ One sure sign that your PC needs more memory: It slows to a crawl, especially during memory-intensive operations, such as working with graphics.

✔ Not enough memory? You can upgrade! See the section "Adding More Memory to Your PC," later in this chapter.

"What is virtual memory?"

Running out of memory is quite impossible, despite whatever limited amount is in your computer. That's because Windows uses a clever technique to prevent memory from ever becoming full: It creates virtual memory.

Virtual memory works to augment the physical RAM in your computer by swapping out vast chunks of memory to the hard drive. Because Windows manages both memory and hard drive storage, it can keep track of things quite well, swapping chunks of data back and forth.

The only problem with virtual memory is that the swapping action slows things down. Although it can happen quickly and often without your noticing, when memory gets tight, virtual memory takes over and things start moving more slowly.

✔ The solution to avoid using virtual memory is to pack your PC with as much RAM as it can hold.

✔ Windows never says that it's "out of memory." No, you just notice that the hard drive is churning frequently as the memory is swapped into and out of the disk drive.

✔ Virtual memory is controlled from the System Properties dialog box: Open the Control Panel's System Properties icon. In the System Properties dialog box, click the Advanced tab. Click the Settings button in the Performance area. In the Performance Options dialog box, click the Advanced tab and then click the Change button at the bottom of the dialog box. Finally(!), you see the Virtual Memory dialog box, where you can change the settings, if you want. Unless you're having problems, the settings shown there are fine as listed.

"What is video memory?"

Memory used by your PC's video system is known as *video memory*. Specifically, it's memory chips that live on the video adapter card. These chips are used specifically for the computer's video output and help you see higher resolutions, more colors, 3-D graphics, bigger and uglier aliens, and girlie pictures your husband downloads from the Internet late at night.

Like regular computer memory, you can upgrade video memory if your PC's video card has room. See Chapter 12 for more information on video adapters.

Adding More Memory to Your PC

No electronic equivalent of Geritol for your computer exists. If you think that your PC has tired RAM or didn't have enough memory in the first place, you can always add more.

Adding memory to your computer is Lego-block simple. The only difference is that the typical Lego block set, such as the Medieval Castle or Rescue Helicopter set, costs less than $100. Your computer, on the other hand, may cost 5 to 20 times that much. Adding memory isn't something to be taken lightly.

Upgrading memory involves five complex and boring steps:

1. **Figure out how much total memory you need.**

   Your PC should have at least 256MB, which is enough to run Windows XP. After that, you can upgrade the RAM to 512MB, 640MB, 768MB, 1,024MB, or 1GB of RAM and beyond.

2. **Figure out how much memory you can install.**

   This step is technical. It involves knowing how memory is added to your computer and in what increments. If you have an empty bank of memory, this step is quite simple. But if your PC doesn't have any empty memory banks, it can be complex — and expensive. Better leave this task to your dealer or computer guru.

3. **Buy the memory.**

4. **Pay someone else to plug in the chips and do the upgrade.**

   Oh, you can do it yourself, but I would pay someone else to do it.

5. **Gloat.**

After you have the memory, brag to your friends about it. Heck, it used to be impressive to say that you had 640K of RAM. Then came the "I have 4 megabytes of memory in my 386 or 8 megabytes of memory in my 486." Now? Anything less than 256MB and your kids will roll their eyes at you.

- ✔ A shocker: You may think that upgrading from 256MB to 512MB RAM requires the addition of only 256MB of more memory. Wrong! Suppose that your PC has four memory slots and each has only a 64MB DIMM in it. Therefore, to upgrade, you have to ditch all those DIMMs and buy either four 128MB DIMMS (the cheapest option) or two 256MB DIMMS (the next cheapest) or one single 512MB DIMM (the most expensive option, but the most logical for future expansion).

- ✔ My favorite place to get memory chips online is `www.crucial.com`. The Web site asks a series of questions and then provides memory solutions to solve your problems exactly.

- ✔ If you want to try upgrading memory yourself, go ahead. Plenty of easy books on the subject of upgrading memory are available, as well as how-to articles in some of the popular magazines. Some places that sell memory, such as Crucial.com, even have well-written how-to booklets that come with the memory. I still recommend having someone else do it, however.

Chapter 12

Amazing Monitors and Glorious Graphics

. . . .

In This Chapter

▶ Understanding monitors and graphics adapters

▶ Adjusting your monitor

▶ Setting the graphics resolution and colors

▶ Changing the desktop background (wallpaper)

▶ Adding a screen saver to Windows

▶ Using a theme

▶ "Sleeping" a monitor

▶ Copying graphics from the screen

. . . .

*L*ike a big, ugly zit on the end of your nose, the monitor is the first thing you notice on a PC. It's what you stare at when you use the computer. And the monitor is what makes the best target if you ever decide to shoot your computer. (Keep in mind that the monitor is only the messenger; what you really want to destroy is the console.)

If your computer were a person, the monitor would be its face. This chapter is about your PC's face, both the hardware part and how Windows can manipulate that face to make it more pleasing for you. Bye-bye, zit!

What's in a Name?

Is it a monitor? Is it a screen? Is it a display? Each term refers to that TV-like thing you use to view information from your computer. But which term is correct?

The *monitor* is the box. There are two types: CRT, which is bulky like a TV set, and LCD, which is thin and flat like a Rodeo Drive model (but with more personality). Either way, it's a monitor. So, if the whole thing falls on the floor, you can say "The monitor fell on the floor. It was an accident."

The *screen* is the part of the monitor that displays an image. It's the glassy part of a CRT or the plastic-film part of an LCD monitor. The screen is there whether the computer is turned on or off. The screen is what you need to clean after you sneeze.

The *display* is the information that appears on the screen. This term is confusing because you could say "My screen says the computer doesn't like me," and it means the same thing as "My monitor says the computer doesn't like me" or even "The display is showing how much the computer loathes my presence." However it's put, the computer doesn't like you.

- ✔ CRT stands for cathode ray tube. Note that it's *cathode* ray tube, not *catheter* ray tube.

- ✔ LCD stands for liquid crystal display. It isn't a hallucinogenic.

- ✔ For games, CRT monitors are better because they're faster than LCD monitors. If it means that you can dodge more Cacodemons on a CRT, good for you!

Monitors versus Adapters

The monitor is only half the video system in your PC. The other half is known as the *graphics adapter*. It's the circuitry that runs the monitor, controlling the image the monitor displays.

Figure 12-1 illustrates the monitor/adapter relationship. The graphics adapter exists either as part of the motherboard or on an expansion card plugged into the motherboard. A cable then connects the monitor to the console. The monitor, of course, plugs into the wall.

The monitor itself is rather dumb. The graphics adapter really makes things happen on the monitor. Between the two, the graphics adapter is what determines your PC's graphics potential.

- ✔ Your PC needs both a monitor and a graphics adapter.

- ✔ In some PCs, particularly laptops, the graphics adapter is built into the motherboard.

- ✔ Most laptops let you add an external monitor using an external graphics port.

- ✔ USB monitors connect to the PC through the USB port.

- ✔ If your PC has more than one monitor (and it can, you know), it must have one graphics adapter for each monitor or a special graphics adapter that supports multiple monitors.

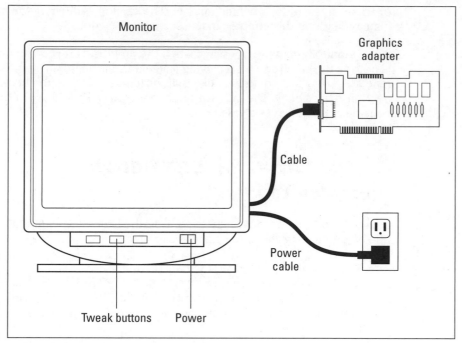

Monitor

Graphics
adapter

Cable

Power
cable

Figure 12-1:
The monitor
and graphics
adapter.

Tweak buttons   Power

Getting to Know and Love Your Monitor

A PC's monitor is really a *peripheral*. It's a separate device that need not be sold with the computer (the console). Some dealers offer a range of different monitors for sale with a computer. When you buy a new computer, you can bring along your old PC's monitor — as long as it's still in good shape.

Despite all the features and technical mumbo-jumbo, all monitors serve the same function: They display information the computer coughs up.

The physical description

Each monitor has two tails. One is a power cord that plugs into the wall. The second tail is a video cable that connects to the graphics adapter port on the back of the console.

You usually find the monitor's on–off button on the front of the monitor, most likely near the lower-right corner. (It's a total bias against left-handed people, part of the larger adroit conspiracy.)

Additional buttons adorn the front of the monitor, which you use to control the monitor's display. These buttons may be visible, like a row of ugly teeth, or they may be hidden behind a panel. The section "Adjusting the monitor's display," later in this chapter, discusses what they do.

Some monitors display a message when the monitor is turned on and the PC is not (or the monitor isn't receiving a signal from the PC). The message may read No Signal or something like that, or it may urge you to check the connection. That's okay. The monitor pops to life properly when you turn on the console and it receives a video signal.

All the technical information you need to know

Lots of technical nonsense is used to describe a monitor's abilities. Of that pile of jargon, only the following terms are really necessary:

✔ **Size:** Monitors are judged by their picture size, measured on a diagonal, just like TVs. Common sizes for PC monitors are 15, 17, 19, and 21 inches. The most common size is 17 inches, though I love the 19-inch monitors and absolutely swoon over the 21-inch monsters! Oooooooo! (That's me swooning.)

✔ **Dot pitch:** This term refers to the distance between each dot, or *pixel,* on the screen (as measured from the center of each pixel). The closer the dots, and the tinier the dot pitch value, the better the image.

✔ **Interlace/non-interlacing:** You want a monitor that is *non-interlacing,* which means that the image appears on the monitor in one swipe rather than two. An interlacing monitor flickers, which makes your eyeballs go nuts.

✔ **Flat screen:** All LCD monitors are flat, but some CRTs have a flat picture tube. That's what a flat-screen monitor is: glass, but flat. It produces a better image than curved CRT monitors, but it is *not* the same thing as an LCD.

Other aspects of the display — such as resolution, colors, and video memory — are all part of the graphics adapter hardware, not the monitor. These terms are covered elsewhere in this chapter.

Oh, and other terms, ugly and verbose, are used to describe a monitor. Most of them are shopping terms, which doesn't do you any good after you own the monitor.

Adjusting the monitor's display

In the early days, you were lucky if your PC's monitor had contrast and brightness knobs. The adjustments you can make to your monitor now are endless. Sometimes, you make adjustments using a row of buttons that adorn the front of your monitor, looking almost like a second keyboard. Other times, you use a combination of generic buttons, similar to the annoying way digital clocks are set.

Generally, the buttons on your monitor are of two types.

The first type has a menu button and then two or four control buttons adorned with arrows or plus and minus symbols. Pressing the menu button pops up an onscreen display, such as the one shown in Figure 12-2. You use the buttons to manipulate the display and adjust the monitor.

Figure 12-2: A typical onscreen display.

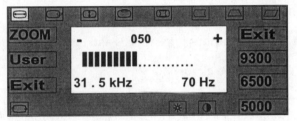

The second type, often hidden behind a flap or door, has specific buttons with icons that adjust specific things, as shown in Figure 12-3. The idea is to use these buttons to adjust what the icons represent. Sometimes, you have to press more than one button to make a specific adjustment.

Figure 12-3: Icons on the typical PC monitor.

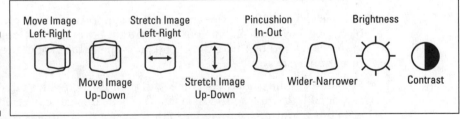

- ✔ This is one area of the PC that I really wish they would standardize.
- ✔ The onscreen information appears over any other image displayed on the monitor. Don't let it freak you out.
- ✔ Use the buttons to adjust the image size to make full use of the monitor's display area.

✔ Monitors may also display frequency information (31KHz/60Hz, for example) when they change screen modes, such as when you play a game and the screen changes to another resolution.

✔ Most monitors also have a Save or Store button, which remembers the settings you have entered, making them permanent. Use it.

All about Graphics Adapters

The secretive, internal part of a PC's video system is its graphics adapter. It's an expansion card that plugs into your PC's motherboard and gives your computer the ability to display lovely text and graphics.

Graphics adapters come in various price ranges and have features for artists, game players, computer designers, and regular Joes like you and me and guys named Joe. Here's the quick roundup:

✔ The main measure of a graphics adapter is how much memory (video RAM) it has. Adapters can come with 0MB (which you don't want) all the way up to 64MB or more video memory.

✔ The 0MB graphics adapters "share" video memory with main memory. Obviously, for anyone interested in playing games or creating computer graphics, this is a bad deal.

✔ The more memory the graphics adapter has, the higher the resolutions it can support and the more colors it can display at those higher resolutions.

✔ Many graphics adapters are advertised as supporting 3-D graphics. That's okay, but they work only if your software supports the particular 3-D graphics offered by that graphics adapter. (If so, the side of the software box should say so.)

✔ High-end graphics adapters come with their own graphics microprocessor, or GPU (graphics processing unit). These devices can really boost graphics performance — and also the price of the graphics adapter.

✔ If your PC has a DVD drive, you need a graphics adapter capable of producing the DVD image on the monitor. A graphics adapter typically has an S-Video Out port on it, which lets you connect a TV to the computer for watching things on a larger screen.

Adjusting the Display in Windows

The monitor gets all the credit, but the graphics adapter does all the work. The graphics adapter controls what you see on the screen. You, the human (in case you forgot), can control the graphics adapter by using Windows. Specifically, the Display icon in the Control Panel is your door to the graphical world displayed on the monitor.

The following sections discuss various strange and wondrous things you can do with the display in Windows. Some would call this "messing around" or "dinking." I refer to it as "necessary and frequent tuning." It also helps to wear a white lab coat and safety goggles to appear professional while you make adjustments.

Summoning the Display Properties dialog box

You tweak the display in Windows through the Display Properties dialog box. Here's how you muster it:

1. **Right-click the desktop.**

2. **Choose Properties from the pop-up menu.**

   The Display Properties dialog box appears, ready for action, as shown in Figure 12-4.

 You can also summon the Display Properties dialog box by opening the Display icon in the Control Panel, but in half a dozen years of using Windows, I have rarely done that.

Figure 12-4: The Display Properties dialog box.

Some Display Properties dialog boxes may have custom tabs for your display adapter. For example, some versions of the ATI adapter may add tabs for doing special things with that graphics adapter. I don't cover those things here, mostly because ATI doesn't send me any free stuff.

To preview any changes made in the Display Properties dialog box, click the Apply button. Your monitor may blink or flicker, and Windows asks whether everything is okay. Click the OK button if it is.

Adjusting the display size (resolution) and colors

The monitor's dimensions cannot change, but you can adjust the amount of stuff you see on the screen by increasing its resolution. Likewise, if you find the display too tiny to read, you can decrease the resolution. These activities are handled on the Settings tab in the Display Properties dialog box, as shown in Figure 12-5.

The Screen Resolution slider sets the display resolution, measured in pixels horizontally and vertically. (A *pixel* is a dot, or *picture element,* on the display.) The larger the numbers, the more information is displayed. Smaller values yield less information, but make everything appear bigger.

Use the preview window at the upper center of the dialog box to get an idea of how the new resolution affects the display.

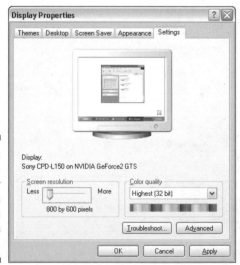

Figure 12-5:
Change
your
monitor's
resolution
and colors
here.

Making things easier to see

If you have trouble seeing small things, adjust the display so that they appear as big as possible: Choose a low resolution, such as 800 x 600 or even 640 x 480. Take advantage of the various View➪Zoom commands available in applications, which greatly enlarge the text or subject matter.

You can also direct Windows to use larger icons on the display. In the Display Properties dialog box, click the Appearance tab and then click the Effects button. In the Effects dialog box, put a check mark next to the Use Large Icons option. Click OK.

The Color Quality area sets how many colors are available at a specific resolution. The colors range from 16 (which is pretty dern ugly) to the Highest rating, also known as 32 bits.

- ✔ The resolution and color settings are related. Higher resolutions have fewer colors, so you may want to set the color setting first and then see which resolutions are available for that setting.

- ✔ You need only the highest color settings if you plan to use graphics applications, such as photo editing.

- ✔ Higher resolutions work best on larger monitors.

- ✔ Some LCD monitors allow only selected resolutions, such as 800 x 600 or 1024 x 768.

- ✔ The maximum resolution and color settings depend on the graphics adapter and not on the monitor size. The more video RAM the graphics adapter has, the more options are available.

- ✔ Some computer games automatically change the monitor's resolution to allow the games to be played. This is okay because the resolution should return to normal after playing the game.

Changing the background (wallpaper)

The background, or *wallpaper,* is what you see when you look at the desktop. It can be a solid color, or it can display any graphics image stored on your hard drive or found on the Internet. This process is all handled on the Desktop tab in the Display Properties dialog box, as shown in Figure 12-6.

To use a solid color, choose (None) from the top of the scrolling Background list and then select a color using the Color button. Yes, you can choose from only 20 colors; I hope you can find something to match the drapes.

Figure 12-6:
Select
desktop
wallpaper
here.

Images are more fun than solid colors, and Windows gives you a host of image files to choose from on the Background scrolling list. You can click to select an image and then see how it looks in the preview at the top of the dialog box. If you can't find the image you're looking for, use the Browse button to go fetch one from a specific location on the disk.

If the image doesn't quite fill the screen, you can use the Position button to adjust it. Choose Tile to have the image pattern replicate to fill the screen; the Stretch option forces an image to resize itself and cover the whole desktop.

✔ The Browse dialog box works just like the Open dialog box. Refer to Chapter 5.

✔ To set an image from the Web as your wallpaper, right-click the image and choose the Set As Background command from the pop-up menu.

✔ Creating your own wallpaper is easy. You can do so in the Windows Paint program, or you can use a scanned image or a shot from a digital camera. See Chapter 19 for specific instructions.

Adding a screen saver

The *screen saver* is an image or animation that appears on the monitor after a given period of inactivity. So, after your computer sits there lonely and feeling ignored for 30 minutes, for example, an image of a fish tank appears on the monitor to amuse any ghosts in the room.

To set a screen saver, you use the Screen Saver tab in the Display Properties dialog box, as shown in Figure 12-7. Choose a screen saver from the drop-down Screen Saver list. Use the Settings button (if it's available) to adjust the screen saver's action. The preview window shows you what the screen saver looks like teensy; use the Preview button to see what the screen saver looks like full-screen.

Figure 12-7:
Select a
screen
saver here.

One key setting is the Wait box, which tells Windows how many idle minutes pass before the screen saver kicks in.

Make your settings and then click the OK button. If you don't touch the mouse or keyboard after the given amount of Wait time, the screen saver appears on your monitor.

- ✔ A safe key to press for switching off the screen saver is Ctrl. Unlike other keys on your keyboard, this key doesn't mess with any application that appears after the screen saver vanishes.

- ✔ A cool way to switch off the screen saver is to pound your desk with your fist. That jostles the mouse and deactivates the screen saver.

- ✔ Windows XP lacks a screen saver password option. The equivalent is to check the box next to the On resume, display Welcome screen option. That effectively prevents anyone without an account on the system from getting access (as long as all the accounts are password-protected).

- ✔ Beware of downloading screen saver files from the Internet. Although some of them are legitimate screen savers, most of them are invasive ads or programs that are impossible to uninstall or remove. If you download this type of screen saver, you're pretty much stuck with it. Be careful!

✔ The problem the original screen savers tried to prevent was known as *phosphor burn-in*. It can still happen on monitors now, but only if the same image is displayed for months. LCD monitors are not susceptible to phosphor burn-in.

Doing it all at once with a theme

If you would rather not adjust the display piecemeal, you can use the Themes icon in the Control Panel to set all your PC's graphics (as well as sound and mouse options) to a specific theme. Or, you can create and save your own theme. The secret is in opening and gawking at the Theme tab in the Display Properties dialog box (refer to Figure 12-4).

To set a theme, choose one from the Theme drop-down list. You see how it affects the display in the lower, Sample, part of the dialog box. The theme applies a window style, text, colors, a background, and screen saver all at once.

TIP

If you prefer to have your own theme, be smart about it and save it to disk. After choosing all the settings you like, click the Save As button on the Themes tab of the Display Properties dialog box. Create a special folder named Themes in the My Documents folder, give your theme a name, and then save it in that Themes folder.

✔ The benefit of saving your own theme is that you can instantly recall its settings from the Themes tab in the Display Properties dialog box. That way, if someone else messes with things, you can recover quickly.

✔ Themes are also available for your PC's sound settings (see Chapter 17) and the mouse pointer selection (see Chapter 13). Note that they're called *schemes,* not themes, in those dialog boxes.

Putting the monitor to sleep

As an alternative to using a screen saver, you can take advantage of your PC's power-management abilities and simply turn the monitor off after a given amount of time. To make it happen, click the Power button at the bottom of the Display Properties dialog box, on the Screen Saver tab (refer to Figure 12-7). Doing so displays the Power Options Properties dialog box.

Look for the Turn Off Monitor option in the Power Options Properties dialog box. Set a time interval after which the PC automatically shuts off the monitor. If you don't want the monitor shutting itself off, choose Never.

Click OK to close the Power Options Properties dialog box.

✔ If you're using a screen saver, set the value *greater than* the time after which the screen saver kicks in.

✔ I forgo the screen saver and merely choose to turn off my monitor after an hour of inactivity.

Power Options

✔ You can also get to the Power Options Properties dialog box by opening the Power Options icon in the Control Panel.

Taking a Screen Dump

A screen dump isn't a pile of old monitors somewhere in the desert. *Dump* is an ancient Ming dynasty computer term. It refers to copying raw information from one place to another, a pouring out of the old bit bucket, as it were.

A *screen dump* is the process of sending the information on your computer screen off to the printer or to a file. Under DOS, the magic Print Screen key on the keyboard initiated this procedure. In Windows, the Print Screen key does kind of the same thing, though the image isn't immediately printed.

In Windows, when you press the Print Screen key, you take a snapshot of the desktop. Click! All that graphical information is saved as a graphics image on the Clipboard. You can then paste the image into any program that can swallow graphical images, such as Windows Paint or Microsoft Word. Even though nothing prints, you still get a dump of what was on the screen.

To see how this process works, follow these steps:

1. **Press the Print Screen key.**

2. **Start the Windows Paint program.**

   Find it on the Start panel by choosing Programs⇨Accessories⇨Paint.

3. **Choose Edit⇨Paste in the Paint program.**

   The desktop image is pasted into the Paint program, ready for editing, saving to disk, or printing.

TIP

If you press the Alt+Print Screen key combination, only the frontmost, or "top," window is copied to the Clipboard.

Chapter 13

The Mouse in Your PC House

*A*fter modem jokes, more computer mouse jokes are told than anything else. And, like the modem jokes, none of the mouse jokes is worth repeating. In fact, having a mouse with your computer is so common that the silly thing doesn't really need much explaining any more; hence, no more funny jokes about Maude thinking that it's a foot pedal or Dave using the mouse upside down. Keep in mind that this mouse chapter could have been packed with lots more humor along with your regularly expected good information.

Why a Mouse?

Your computer's mouse is an *input* device. Although the keyboard (another input device) can do almost anything, you need a mouse to control graphics and graphical whatnots on the screen — especially in an operating system like Windows.

✔ Your PC may have come with a specific mouse, but you can always buy a better replacement.

✔ The plural of computer mouse is *mice*. One computer has a mouse. Two computers have mice.

✔ Doug Englebart invented the computer mouse at the Stanford Research Institute in the 1960s. (Apple computer didn't "invent" it for the Macintosh.) Doug received only $10,000 for his invention, but in 1997 he won the $500,000 Lemelson–MIT Prize for American Innovation.

Just your basic, generic mouse

Many species of computer mice exist. Beyond the common bar-of-soap model are upside-down mice, mice with too many buttons, radio mice, pen mice, and on and on. They all sport common features yet fill the basic service of helping you work the various graphics gizmos in Windows and in various applications.

Standard buttons: The standard PC mouse has a minimum of two buttons, left and right. The left button, which falls under your right hand's index finger, is the *main* button. That's the button you press when the instructions say to *click* the mouse. Pressing the other button, the right button, is specifically called out as a *right-click*.

The wheel button: Other buttons crop up on PC mice depending on the brand and type of mouse. The most common button is the *wheel* button, positioned between the left and right buttons. The wheel can be rolled up or down or even pressed to manipulate various goodies on the screen.

Other buttons: The Microsoft IntelliMouse Explorer, as shown in Figure 13-1, has two additional buttons, used for browsing the Web. These thumb buttons on the mouse's left flank let you browse backward and forward between Web pages and perform other functions in other applications.

✔ The PC's mouse plugs into the mouse port on the back of the console (refer to Chapters 1 and 9). The USB mouse plugs into the USB connector, or into the mouse port if an adapter is used.

✔ Designate a special mouse area on your desk and keep it clear of desk debris so that you have room to move the mouse around. An area about the size of this book is typically all you need in order to roll the mouse around.

✔ I once saw a mouse with 52 buttons on it, allowing you to use it as a keyboard. (I wonder why the thing never caught on?)

✔ The wheel button is turned to scroll a document. When the button is pressed, it can be used to scan-and-pan to drag a document up, down, left, or right. When used with the Ctrl key, the wheel button often zooms in or out of a document, making it appear larger or smaller on the screen.

✔ A variation on the standard mouse is the *trackball,* which is like an upside-down mouse. Rather than roll the mouse around, you use your thumb or index finger to roll a ball on top the mouse. The whole contraption stays stationary, so it doesn't need nearly as much room and the cord never gets tangled. This type of mouse is preferred by graphic artists because it's often more precise than the traditional soap-on-a-rope mouse.

✔ Another popular mouse variation for the artistic type is the stylus mouse, which looks like a pen and draws on a special pad. This mouse is also pressure sensitive, which is wonderful for use in painting and graphics applications.

Optical versus mechanical

The mouse works by detecting its movement on your desktop. The detection method is either mechanical or optical.

The traditional mouse is mechanical, using a ball that rolls as you move the mouse. Sensors inside the mouse body detect the movement and translate it into information the computer interprets.

Optical mice have no moving parts. They use an LED sensor to detect table-top movement and then send off that information to the computer for merry munching.

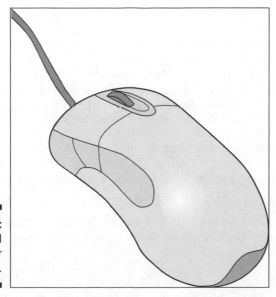

Figure 13-1:
A typical computer mouse.

Because they lack moving parts, optical mice last longer than mechanical mice and they're easier to clean. Plus, the optical mouse doesn't require a special surface to move on; any nonreflective surface works, such as your pant leg (or even a friend's pant leg).

- A mechanical mouse works best when moved across a *mouse pad,* which is a small piece of plastic or foam rubber that sits on your desk. Also, it reminds you to keep that area of your desk clean.

- The best mouse pads have rough surfaces, which the mechanical mouse's ball can grip well.

- Though the optical mouse doesn't need a mouse pad, you must slide it over a surface that isn't too shiny or uniform in color. If you notice that the mouse isn't responding properly, you need to use a mouse pad of sorts (anything flat that isn't reflective or a solid color).

- Though many gamers prefer joysticks or game pads, a few enjoy using a mouse instead. In that case, the mechanical mouse is considered a better choice than the optical one. Mechanical mice are more responsive, whereas optical mice have a tendency to jump when moved quickly.

Cordless mice

Though the latest rage in computing is all wireless, wireless mice have been around for quite some time. You can find two types of wireless mice, which really depends on how messy your computer desktop grows.

The infrared (IR) wireless mouse: This type of mouse requires a line of sight to work; the mouse sends bursts of IR light to the base station, which picks up the signals the same way your TV remote transmits information to the TV set. Like the TV remote, however, if the mouse's batteries are low or something is blocking the line of sight, the remote mouse doesn't work. In that case, say "Stupid mouse!" and throw it out the window.

The radio frequency (RF) wireless mouse: Unlike IR wireless mice, the RF variation works without the mouse being able to see the base station. In fact, you can hide the base station behind the PC (or a pile of manuals and sticky notes).

- Cordless mice require power, which comes in the form of batteries. They must be replaced or recharged occasionally, or else the mouse doesn't work.

- Stupid mouse!

- Try to buy a cordless mouse that features a cradle, or "nest," for the mouse to rest in when you're not using it. That way, the mouse doesn't

get lost, wander off, or serve a new purpose as the Power Ranger's latest vehicle.

✔ The best mouse cradles also double as battery chargers.

✔ Some new model cordless mice are also 3D mice, which can be pointed at the computer screen like a TV remote; desktop optional.

Basic Mouse Operation

The computer's mouse controls a graphical mouse pointer or mouse cursor on the screen. When you move the mouse around by rolling it on your desk, the pointer on the screen moves in a similar manner. Roll the mouse left and the pointer moves left; roll it in circles and the pointer mimics that action; drop the mouse off the table and your computer bruises. (Just kidding.)

✔ You don't need to squeeze the mouse; a gentle grip is all that's necessary.

✔ The first time you use a mouse, you want to move it in wild circles on your desk so that you can watch the pointer spiral on the screen. This urge takes a long time to wear off (if it ever does).

✔ When the mouse cord becomes tangled, raise the mouse in your hand and whip it about violently.

✔ The best way to learn how to use a computer mouse is to play a computer card game, such as Solitaire or FreeCell (both of which come with Windows). You should have the mouse mastered in only a few frustrating hours.

Point the mouse

When you're told to "point the mouse," you move the mouse on the desktop, which moves the mouse pointer on the screen to point at something interesting (or not).

Click the mouse

A *click* is a press of the mouse button. The point-the-mouse operation is implied when you click the mouse.

For example, you may read "Click the mouse on the OK button." Here is what you do:

1. **Look for the graphical button on the screen with the word OK on it.**

2. **Move the mouse so that the mouse pointer on the screen is pointing at or hovering over the word** OK.

3. **With your index finger, click the mouse button.**

   You hear an audible click as you press and release the mouse button. The OK graphic on the screen also reacts, confirming the entire operation.

The button you click is the *left* mouse button, the one under your index finger. That's the main mouse button.

✔ When clicking the button, push it down once and release it. Don't hold it down continuously. (It makes two clicks — one when it's pushed and another when it's released. Is your hearing that good?)

✔ You also click the mouse to *select* something. The instructions say "Click to select," or even only "Select the Drive C icon." That's clicking.

✔ Sometimes, you may be asked to press a key combination along with clicking the mouse. A popular combo is Ctrl+click, which means to press and hold down the Ctrl (control) key on your keyboard before you click the mouse button.

Double-click the mouse

A *double-click* is two rapid clicks in a row. This works just like the single click described in the preceding section, though in Step 3 you click twice.

✔ Double-clicking is done in Windows to open something. For example, you double-click the My Documents icon to open its window.

✔ Try not to move the mouse around between the clicks; both clicks have to be on the same spot.

✔ Oh, and you can triple-, quadruple-, and quintuple-click. It's all the same idea: Click the mouse more than once in the same spot. (I have never needed a sextuple-click.)

✔ If you double-click your mouse and nothing happens, you may not be clicking fast enough. See the section "Double-clicking doesn't work!" later in this chapter.

Drag the mouse

You drag with the mouse to select a group of items on the screen or to pick up and move something.

To drag with the mouse, follow these steps:

1. **Point the mouse cursor at the thing you want to drag.**

2. **Press and hold the mouse's button.**

   Press and hold the button down — don't click it! This action has the effect of picking up whatever the mouse is pointing at on the screen.

   If a drag isn't picking up something, it also selects objects by drawing a rubber-band-like rectangle around them.

3. **Move the mouse to a new location.**

   The drag operation is really a *move;* you start at one point on the screen and move or drag the icon or object to another location.

4. **Release the mouse button.**

   Lift your finger off the left mouse button. You're done dragging.

When you release the mouse button, you let go of whatever it was you were dragging.

✔ You can also drag to select a group of items. In this case, dragging draws a rectangle around the items you want to select. Refer to Chapter 6.

✔ Dragging is used in many drawing and painting programs to create an image on the screen. In this sense, dragging is like pressing a pen tip or paintbrush to paper.

✔ You can also drag using the right mouse button instead of the left. This action is usually called a right-drag.

✔ Releasing the mouse button to let go of the item/object (Step 4 above) is also known as a *drop*. This is where the term "drag and drop" comes from.

✔ Sometimes you may be asked to press and hold a key while dragging, referred to as a Ctrl+drag (Control+drag) or Shift+drag or some other key combination. If so, press that key — Ctrl, Shift, Alt, or whatever — *before* you first click the mouse to drag something.

Dinking with the Mouse in Windows

 In Windows, the mouse is controlled, manipulated, and teased by using the Mouse icon in the Control Panel. Opening that icon displays the Mouse Properties dialog box, as shown in Figure 13-2, where you can make mousy adjustments.

Figure 13-2:
The Mouse
Properties
dialog box.

Note that the Mouse Properties dialog box may differ, depending on which mouse your PC uses. Although some tabs are generically the same, some are specific to the mouse hardware.

The following sections cover some of the more interesting things you can do in the Mouse Properties dialog box in Windows.

Messing with the mouse pointer

You don't have to put up with the same silly mouse pointer as everyone else. No, the mouse pointer can be changed as often as teenage fashions and with about as much contemplation and reason. This process is handled on the Pointers tab of the Mouse Properties dialog box, as shown in Figure 13-3.

The scrolling list shows the different pointers that appear when Windows is busy selecting text, resizing something, or losing a file, for example. All those pointers can be changed.

To change an individual pointer, follow these steps:

1. **Click the pointer you want to change, such as the Normal Select pointer.**

2. **Click the Browse button.**

    The Browse dialog box displays a list of alternative pointers for you to choose from.

3. **Click to select an alternative pointer as shown in the Browse dialog box.**

Figure 13-3:
Choose
another
mouse
pointer.

4. **Preview the pointer in the Browse dialog box's Preview window.**

   Note that some pointers are animated. Also, some pointers are larger than others, making them easier to see.

5. **To select a pointer, click the Open button.**

   You return to the Mouse Properties dialog box, where your pointer is set in place.

6. **Repeat these steps to select other pointers for other mouse situations in Windows.**

7. **Click the OK button when you're done.**

   Try out your new pointers.

One way to change all the pointers at once is to choose a pointer scheme from the drop-down list. It works like choosing a graphics theme in the Display Properties dialog box (refer to Chapter 12), though the settings here affect only the mouse pointer.

✔ If you like your new mouse pointer settings, click the Save As button to save your pointer collection as a scheme on disk.

✔ If you're not satisfied with the selection of mouse pointers Windows offers, you can download cursor files from the Internet. Use your favorite search engine to look for "cursor files" on the Web. See Chapter 24 for more information on searching the Web.

✔ You can also create your own cursor types, if you're game. Various free utilities you can find on the Internet create plain as well as animated cursors. Search the Web for "cursor creation software" to find a bunch of different utilities to choose from.

"I can't find the mouse pointer!"

The Pointer Options tab in the Mouse Properties dialog box, as shown in Figure 13-4, contains a number of options to help you locate a lonely or lost mouse pointer. These options can come in handy, especially on larger displays or when the mouse pointer is floating over a particularly busy desktop.

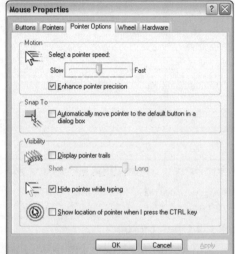

Figure 13-4: Ways to find a wayward mouse.

> ✔ The pointer trails option displays a comet trail of mouse pointers as you move the mouse about. Jiggling or circling the mouse makes lots of visual racket, allowing you to quickly locate the mouse pointer.

> ✔ The Ctrl key location option allows you to find the mouse pointer by tapping either Ctrl key on the keyboard. This action makes a radar-like circle appear, zeroing in on the cursor's location.

> ✔ You can also employ the Snap To option, which specifically jumps the mouse pointer to the main button in any dialog box that appears (though I find this option annoying).

> ✔ Consider changing the mouse pointer to something *larger* (refer to the preceding section). In fact, the Magnified scheme is designed to display the mouse in a particularly easy-to-find way.

"Double-clicking doesn't work!"

If you can't seem to double-click, one of two things is happening: Either you're moving the mouse pointer a little bit between clicks or the double-click *rate* is set too fast for human fingers to manage.

The *double-click rate* is set in the Mouse Properties dialog box, on the Buttons tab, as shown earlier, in Figure 13-2. Practice your double-clicking on the tiny folder icon off to the right. Use the Slow-Fast slider to adjust the double-click speed to better match your click-click timing.

To test your timing, first click the Apply button, which resets Windows to your new mouse specifications. Then double-click the folder graphic in the test area. If the graphic changes, you have a proper double-click speed set.

"I'm left-handed, and the buttons are backward!"

Where is that left-handed class action suit, anyway?

In Windows, you can adjust the mouse for southpaw use on the Buttons tab, as shown earlier, in Figure 13-2. Put a check mark by the box labeled Switch primary and secondary buttons. That way, the "main" mouse button is under your left index finger.

✔ This book and all manuals and computer books assume that the left mouse button is the main button. *Right-clicks* are clicks of the right mouse button. If you tell Windows to use the left-handed mouse, these buttons are reversed. Keep in mind that your documentation doesn't reflect that.

✔ Left-handed mice are available that are sculpted to fit your left hand better than all those right-hand-oriented biased mice on the market.

✔ No setting is available for ambidextrous people, wise guy!

Chapter 14

The Keyboard Chapter

*R*egardless of what you see in science fiction, computers of the future will still have keyboards attached to them. Dictation eventually may eliminate a lot of typing, but you need a keyboard for tasks that dictation could never muster, like entering passwords. So it's safe to say that the PC keyboard will be around for a while and that it's a good thing to bone up on.

Fear not your keyboard! Despite its surplus of more than 100 keys, it's not that difficult to master. The keys have letters, numbers, or punctuation symbols on them. Other keys have complete words to describe their functions. When you consider that a piano has only 88 keys and takes years to master, your 100+ key keyboard is a cakewalk. Why, it can be mastered in, well, the time it takes to read this chapter!

Yes, Your PC Needs Its Keyboard

Your keyboard is the direct line of communication between you and your computer. The computer has no ears. You can try yelling. The computer has no eyes. You can wave your arms. But the computer hears or sees nothing unless you type something on the keyboard. It's the computer's primary input device.

Your typical PC keyboard

The typical PC keyboard is shown in Figure 14-1. It's known as the *Enhanced 104-key keyboard.* Yes, it has 104 keys on it. You can count them yourself, if you have the time.

Variations on this keyboard are available. Some keyboards are ergonomic and have a more natural shape. Some come with extra buttons on them, such as Internet buttons. See the section "Special keys on special keyboards," later in this chapter, for more information.

Basic keyboard layout

Four main areas are mapped out on your PC's keyboard, as shown in the preceding section, in Figure 14-1:

Function keys: These keys are positioned on the top row of the keyboard. They're labeled F1, F2, F3, and on up to F11 and F12.

Typewriter keys: These keys are the same type of keys you would find on an old typewriter: letters, numbers, and punctuation symbols.

Cursor-control keys: Often called *arrow keys,* these four keys move the text cursor in the direction of their arrows. Above them are more cursor-control keys — the six-pack of Insert, Delete, Home, End, Page Up, and Page Down.

Numeric keypad: Popular with accountants, bank tellers, and airline ticket agents, the numeric keypad contains calculator-like keys. This keypad also doubles as a cursor keypad; the Num Lock key determines its behavior.

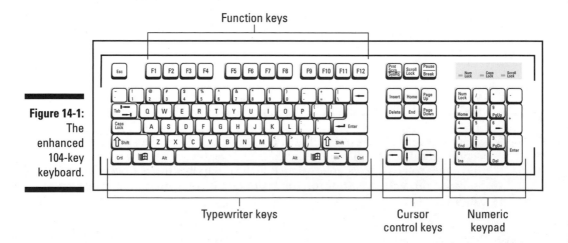

Figure 14-1: The enhanced 104-key keyboard.

When you press the Num Lock key and the Num Lock light is on, the Numeric keypad is used to enter numbers. When the Num Lock light is off, the numeric keyboard serves to double the function of the cursor-control keys: PgUp and PgDn stand for Page Up and Page Down; Ins for Insert and Del for Delete.

✔ See the section "The Lock sisters," later in this chapter, for more information on the numeric keypad's duplicity.

✔ The cursor-control keys are used to move the text cursor around, which typically looks like a blinking toothpick when you type or edit text in Windows. The mouse pointer is often called a cursor, though the cursor keys don't move it around.

✔ Note that the words *Break* and *SysRq* share the same keys as *Print Screen* and *Pause*. Sometimes, they're written on the key cap, and sometimes on the side of the key. Either way, these are dual-function keys; press the Alt key to activate the second function: Alt+Print Screen equals SysRq, and Alt+Pause equals Break.

✔ The Print Screen key may also be labeled PrtScr or Print Scrn.

"Must I learn to type to use a computer?"

No one needs to learn to type to use a computer. Plenty of computer users hunt and peck. In fact, most programmers don't know how to type; they sit all hunched over the keyboard and punch in enigmatic computer languages using greasy, garlic-and-herb potato-chip-smeared fingers. But that's not being productive.

As a bonus to owning a computer, you can have it teach you how to type. The Mavis Beacon Teaches Typing software package does just that. Other packages are available, but I personally love the name Mavis Beacon.

Trivia: A computer software developer once halted all development and had his programmers sit down and learn how to touch-type. It took two whole weeks, but afterward they all got their work done much faster and had more time available to break away and play games.

Specific Keys from Any to the Bizarre

Your computer keyboard is a virtual playground of buttons — some famous, some mysterious and some non-existent. The following sections mull over the lot, highlighting what's important and ignoring what's not.

Know your ones and zeroes

On a typewriter, the lowercase letter *L* and the number 1 are often the same. In fact, I remember that my old Royal upright lacked a 1 key altogether. Unfortunately, on a computer, a big difference exists between a one and a little *L*.

If you're typing 1,001, for example, don't type l,00l by mistake — especially when working with a spreadsheet. The computer gags.

The same holds true for the uppercase letter *O* and the number 0. They're different. Use a zero for numbers and a big *O* for big *O* things.

Sometimes, zero is displayed with a slash through it, like this: Ø. That's one way to tell the difference between O and 0, but it's not used that often.

"So where is the Any key?"

Though the message isn't as common as it was in the olden days, you may someday see "Press any key to continue" displayed on the screen. So where is the elusive *Any* key?

Any key refers to, literally, *any* key on your keyboard. Why beat around the bush? When a message says to press the Any key, press the Spacebar.

- ✔ If you can't find the spacebar or you think that it's the place where you order drinks on the starship *Enterprise,* press the Enter key.

- ✔ So why does the message say, "Press any key" rather than "Press the Spacebar to continue"? I guess it's because the idiot programmers want to make things *easy* for you by giving you the whole keyboard to choose from. If that's really the case, why not just break down and say "Slap your keyboard a few times with your open palms to continue"?

The all-powerful Enter key

All PC keyboards have two keys labeled Enter. Both keys work identically, with the second Enter key placed by the numeric keypad to facilitate the rapid entry of incorrect numerical values.

- ✔ Pressing the Enter key is the same as clicking OK in a dialog box.

- ✔ In your word processor, press Enter only at the end of a paragraph.

- ✔ In a Web browser, you press the Enter key after typing a Web page address to view that page (well, eventually).

✔ Don't press Enter after filling in a text box inside a dialog box. Use the Tab key to move from text box to text box. This rule also applies when using some database programs; use the Tab key to skip merrily between the fields. La, la, la.

✔ No Return key is on the PC's keyboard. It never was. The reason I bring this subject up is that occasionally some reference tells you to "Press Return." When that happens, press the Enter key instead.

✔ The difference between Enter and Return is only semantic. *Enter* has its roots in the electronic calculator industry. You pressed Enter to enter numbers or a formula. *Return*, on the other hand, comes from the electronic typewriter. Pressing Return on a typewriter caused the carriage to return to the left margin. It also advanced the paper one line.

The Tab key

The Tab key is used in two different ways on your computer, neither of which generates a diet cola beverage.

In a word processor, you use the Tab key to indent paragraphs — just like the old typewriter's Tab key.

In a dialog box, you use the Tab key to move between the various graphical gizmos. Use Tab rather than Enter, for example, to hop between the First Name and Last Name fields. This advice also holds true for filling in a form on the Internet: Use the Tab key, not Enter, to fill in the blanks.

✔ The Tab key often has two arrows on it — one pointing left and the other, to the right. These arrows may be in addition to the word *Tab*, or they may be on there by themselves to confuse you.

✔ The arrows move both ways because Shift+Tab is a valid key combination. For example, pressing Shift+Tab in a dialog box moves you "backward" through the options.

✔ The computer treats a tab as a single, separate character. When you backspace over a tab in a word processing program, the tab disappears completely in one chunk — not space by space.

Where's the Help key?

Whenever you need help in Windows, whack the F1 key. F1 equals help — there's no way to commit that to memory.

For those forced to do math on the computer

Clustered around the numeric keypad, like campers roasting marshmallows around a fire, are various keys to help you work with numbers. Especially if you're dabbling with a spreadsheet or other number-crunching software, you find that these keys come in handy. Take a look at your keyboard's numeric keypad right now, just to reassure yourself.

What? You were expecting a ×_or ÷ key? Forget it! This is a computer. It uses special oddball symbols for mathematical operations:

✔ + is for addition.

✔ –is for subtraction.

✔ * is for multiplication.

✔ / is for division.

The only strange symbol here is the asterisk, for multiplication. Don't use the little *x!* It's not the same thing. The / (slash) is okay for division, but don't waste your time hunting for the ÷ symbol. It's not there.

The Lock sisters

The three Lock sisters are special keys designed to change the way other keys on the keyboard behave:

Caps Lock: This key works like holding down the Shift key, but it produces only capital letters; it doesn't shift the other keys like a typewriter's Shift Lock key would do. Press Caps Lock again and the letters return to their normal, lowercase state.

Num Lock: Pressing this key makes the numeric keypad on the right side of the keyboard produce numbers. Press this key again and you can use the numeric keypad for moving the text cursor around on the screen.

Scroll Lock: This key has no purpose in life. Some spreadsheets use it to reverse the function of the cursor keys (which move the spreadsheet rather than the cell highlight). Scroll Lock does little else that's significant or famous.

✔ The Caps Lock, Num Lock, and Scroll Lock keys have lights. When the light is on, the key's feature is turned on.

✔ Caps Lock affects only the keys A through Z; it doesn't affect any other keys.

✔ On most computers, the Num Lock key is already on when the computer starts. Annoying, huh?

✔ If you type **This Text Looks Like A Ransom Note** and it looks like tHIS tEXT lOOKS lIKE a rANSOM nOTE, the Caps Lock key is inadvertently turned on. Press it once to return everything to normal.

✔ If you press the Shift key while Caps Lock is on, the letter keys return to normal. (Shift kind of cancels out Caps Lock.)

Some shifty keys

Three keys on your keyboard are *modifier* keys. These keys work in combination with other keys to do various interesting and unbelievable things:

Shift: Hold down the Shift key to make capital letters. By pressing the Shift key, you also can create the %@#^ characters that come in handy for cursing in comic strips. When you release the Shift key, everything returns to normal, just like on a typewriter.

Ctrl: The Control key, abbreviated as Ctrl, is also used like the Shift key; you press it in combination with another key. In most Windows programs, the Ctrl key is used with various letter keys to carry out specific commands. For example, if you hold down the Ctrl key and press S (Ctrl+S), you activate the Save command. Likewise, in most programs, you press Ctrl+P to print, and so on for each clever letter of the alphabet.

Alt: Like the Shift and Ctrl keys, the Alt key is used in combination with other keys to carry out commands. For example, holding down the Alt key and pressing the F4 key (Alt+F4) closes a window on the desktop. You press and hold the Alt key, tap the F4 key, and then release both keys.

These keys may even be used solo for special purposes, together, or in all sorts of strange and forbidden combinations.

Here are more thoughts on these moody keys on your keyboard:

✔ Even though you may see Ctrl+S or Alt+S with a capital *S,* it doesn't mean that you must press Ctrl+Shift+S or Alt+Shift+S. The *S* is written in uppercase simply because Ctrl+s looks like a typesetting error.

✔ Don't be surprised if these shift keys are used in combination with each other. I have seen Shift+Ctrl+C and Ctrl+Alt. Just remember to press and hold the Shift keys first and then tap the letter key. Release all the keys together.

✔ Some manuals use the notation ^Y rather than Ctrl+Y. This term means the same thing: Hold down the Ctrl key, press Y, and release the Ctrl key.

Weird Windows keys

The 102nd, 103rd, and 104th keys on your 104-key keyboard are specialty keys. Two of them have the Windows logo on them, and the third sports what's called the *Context menu.* These keys sit on the bottom row of your keyboard, between the Alt and Ctrl keys on either side of the Spacebar (refer to Figure 14-1).

The Windows key can be used alone or as a shift key in combination with other keys.

Used by itself, the Windows key pops up the Start menu thing. See the section "Using the Win key," later in this chapter, for information on using the Windows key in combination with other keys.

Pressing the Context key displays the shortcut menu for whatever item is selected on the screen. It's the same as right-clicking the mouse when something is selected. Obviously, this key is next to useless.

Slashing about

Two slash keys are on your keyboard, and you can easily be confused.

The forward slash (/) leans forward (duh!), like it's falling to the right. You use the slash primarily to denote division, such as 52/13 (52 divided by 13).

The backslash (\) leans to the left. You use this character in *pathnames,* which are complex and discussed only near the end of Chapter 5, where no one can find them.

Together, these characters can be used to create the pattern on Charlie Brown's shirt: /\/\/\/\

Escape from Windows!

The one key that says "Hey! Stop it!" to Windows is the Escape key, labeled Esc on your keyboard.

Pressing the Esc key is the same as clicking Cancel or No Way in a dialog box. This key closes most windows, but not all, just to keep you guessing.

- ✔ Esc can be a good pinch hitter to try first when something goes awry.
- ✔ To close any window or quit any program, use the mysterious Alt+F4 key combination.

Don't bother with these keys

Some keys on the keyboard meant something to some old program, now long forgotten, but they still hang around on the keyboard for historical reasons or because the keyboard removal person is on holiday. Here are a few antiques not worth mentioning:

Pause: Honestly, the Pause key doesn't work in Windows. Some games may use it to pause the action, but it's not a consistent thing.

SysRq: The System Request ("Ah! That's what it means!") key was supposed to be used for a "future operating system." But that future never came to be. No, aliens from Galaxy P stole that future operating system, which explains the implosion of Galaxy P several years back. Despite that situation, the SysRq key lingers on the PC's keyboard to remind us of that intergalactic disaster.

Break: The Break key does nothing. And why is the key named Break? Why not call it the Brake key? Wouldn't that make sense? Who wants a computer to break, anyway? Golly.

Special keys on special keyboards

If 104 keys on the keyboard just aren't enough, you can venture out and buy special keyboards that sport *even more* keys. Or, perhaps your computer came with that type of keyboard. Typically, this type has a row of buttons along the top, right above the function keys. These buttons carry out specific tasks, such as connecting to the Internet, scanning images, or adjusting the computer's sound volume.

Specialty keyboard buttons are *nonstandard:* They don't come with the typical PC keyboard and must be supported by using some special program run on the computer. That program controls the keys and their behavior. If the keys don't work, it's a problem with the special program and not anything that Windows or your computer is doing wrong.

Using the Keyboard in Windows

Windows isn't totally limited to using the mouse for getting things done. Plenty of key combinations empower your fingers with electrifying commands designed to jolt Windows into obedience. The following sections highlight some favorites.

Bizarre yet useful Windows key combinations

Yea, Windows shudders at any of the keyboard commands listed in Table 14-1.

Table 14-1	Windows Key Combinations
Key Combo	*Command*
Alt+Tab	Switch to the next window/program
Alt+Shift+Tab	Switch back to the preceding window or program
Alt+Esc	Cycle through running programs
Ctrl+Esc	Display the Start panel
Alt+F4	Close the current window
Alt+↓	Display a drop-down list
F10	Activate the menu bar
Alt+Enter	Display a window's Control menu

Don't memorize this list! Instead, put a bookmark on this page and refer to it whenever you want to make the mouse seethe with jealousy.

The kindergarten keys

Common keyboard commands are shared by just about every Windows program. These commands started with the common kindergarten keys, which are called that because they serve the basic functions of Cut, Copy and Paste. In Windows, you can use more than just those three keyboard combinations in the common set, as shown in Table 14-2.

Table 14-2	Common Keyboard Commands
Key Combo	*Command*
Ctrl+A	Select All
Ctrl+B	Make text bold
Ctrl+C	Copy selected item(s)

Key Combo	Command
Ctrl+F	Summon Search/Find command
Ctrl+I	Make text italics
Ctrl+N	Start a new document
Ctrl+O	Open a document or display Open dialog box
Ctrl+P	Print or display Print dialog box
Ctrl+S	Save document
Ctrl+U	Underline text
Ctrl+V	Paste copied or cut item(s)
Ctrl+W	Close window
Ctrl+X	Cut select item(s)
Ctrl+Y	Repeat command
Ctrl+Z	Undo last action

Using the Win key

The Windows key serves the same purpose as pressing Ctrl+Esc: It pops up the Start menu thing. You can also use the Windows key in combination with other keys for a few quick shortcuts, as shown in Table 14-3.

Table 14-3	Windows Key Shortcuts
Key Combo	**Function**
Win+D	Display the desktop (minimizes all Windows)
Win+E	Start Windows Explorer
Win+F	Display the Find Files/Search Results dialog box
Win+L	Lock windows or displays logon screen
Win+M	Minimize open windows
Win+Shift+M	Unminimize windows
Win+R	Display the Run dialog box
Win+Break	Display the System Properties dialog box

Windows text-editing keys

Any text in a dialog box, window, or input box or in the Notepad program can be edited by using simple keys on the keyboard. Table 14-4 summarizes these handy keys for you.

Table 14-4	Windows Editing-Key Shortcuts
Key Combo	*Function*
Cursor keys	Move the toothpick cursor in the key's direction: up, down, left, right
End	Move the toothpick cursor to the end of the line
Home	Move the toothpick cursor to the start of the line
Ctrl+←, Ctrl+→	Move the toothpick cursor left or right one word
Delete	Delete the character to the right of the toothpick cursor
Backspace	Delete the character to the left of the toothpick cursor
Insert	Switch between insert and overtype modes
Shift+[cursor key]	Select text in the direction of the cursor key

Proper Typing Attitude

Repetitive anything can be bad: smoking, eating, drinking, running for Congress, and typing on your computer keyboard. This problem can be serious, especially if you rely on your computer for your job.

Many typists suffer from *carpal tunnel syndrome,* also called repetitive stress injury (RSI).

RSI is a soreness caused when muscles chafe against each other in a small wrist passage called the carpal tunnel (the names Lincoln Tunnel and Holland Tunnel are already copyrighted by the state of New York). The carpal tunnel collapses and changes from a horseshoe shape into something narrower that causes the muscles (tendons, actually) to touch each other, and therein lies the rub.

Various solutions are available for this problem. Some sufferers wear expensive reinforced gloves that, if they don't help alleviate the pain, at least draw sympathetic stares from onlookers. Crunching your wrist by squeezing your palm below the thumb and little finger can help. But the best thing to do is to avoid the problem in the first place.

Here are several things you can do to avoid RSI:

Get an ergonomic keyboard: Even if your wrists are as limber as rubber tree plants, you may want to consider an *ergonomic* keyboard. That type of keyboard is specially designed at an angle to relieve the stress of typing for long — or short — periods of time.

Use a wrist pad: Wrist pads elevate your wrists so that you type in a proper position, with your palms *above* the keyboard, not resting below the Spacebar. Remember Sister Mary Lazarus and how she whacked your slouching wrists? She was right!

Adjust your chair: Sit at the computer with your elbows level with your wrists.

Adjust your monitor: Your head should not tilt down or up when you view the computer screen. It should be straight ahead, which doesn't help your wrists as much as it helps your neck.

- ✔ Ergonomic keyboards cost a little more than standard keyboards, but they're well worth the investment if you type for long hours, or at least want to look like you type for long hours.

- ✔ Some mouse pads have built-in wrist elevators. They're great for folks who use mouse-intensive applications.

- ✔ Many keyboards come with adjustable legs underneath for positioning the keys to a comfortable angle. Use them.

Chapter 15

P Is for Printer

. . . .

. . . .

*T*his chapter is brought to you by the letter *P*. P is for *printer;* the PC's printer, to be precise. People are particularly picky about printers. Primarily, printers provide printouts. Past that, printers proudly employ private memory, plus personal processors. Perchance other printers sport peer-to-peer networking prowess. Put another way, the PC's printer is the perfect peripheral for persons pining for picture-perfect productivity.

Presenting the printer chapter, which provides particular specifics and points to ponder on your PC's printer.

Hello! I'm Mindy, and I'll Be Your Printer

Printers print. They produce an image on paper, which can be text, graphics, color ink, black ink, or a combination of these. The printer's job is an important one because it's often the last step in the creative process; the result of your PC labors is to print something on paper — to get that all-important *hard copy,* something you can show the world.

Yea, verily I say, the printer isn't something to be ignored.

Two basic models: Inkjet and laser

You can splatter ink on paper in many ways. For your PC, the two most popular methods are classified into the two most common types of computer printers: inkjet and laser.

Inkjet printers are the most popular type of computer printer now sold. They produce high-quality text or graphics on just about any type of paper. Their low price makes them quite affordable; you can pay from less than $100 to several hundred dollars, depending on which extra features you need.

Figure 15-1 illustrates a typical inkjet printer, which looks a lot like my inkjet printer. I have flagged important things in the illustration.

Inkjet printers work by literally lobbing tiny balls of ink on paper. The teensy-tiny ink balls stick to the paper, so this type of printer needs no ribbon or toner cartridge; the ink is jetted out directly, which is how the printer gets its name.

On the higher end of the market, *laser* printers are found primarily in the office environment. More expensive than inkjet printers, laser printers are also more robust and better able to meet the demands of a business environment, home or office.

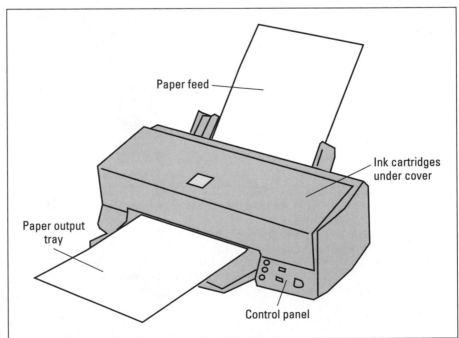

Paper feed

Ink cartridges under cover

Paper output tray

Figure 15-1:
A typical inkjet printer.

Control panel

Figure 15-2 illustrates a typical laser printer, which usually resembles a squat photocopy machine. As with a copy machine, paper is fed into the laser printer via a tray. The paper scrolls through the printer, and the final result snakes out the back or top.

Laser printers work like photocopiers. The difference is that the computer creates the image and etches it using a laser beam rather than use a mirror and the magic moving bar of light you see whenever you try to photocopy your face.

✔ Some specialized inkjets are photo printers, capable of photographic-quality output. These printers add more ink colors to the standard four colors most inkjets use.

✔ Inkjet printers are by no means messy. The ink is dry on the paper by the time the paper comes flopping out of the printer.

✔ Low-end inkjet printers cost less because they're dumb; they contain no internal electronics to help create the image. Instead, the computer is required to do the thinking, which slows things down a tad. When you pay more for an inkjet printer, the smarts are usually included with the printer.

✔ High-priced printers offer a higher-quality output, faster speed, more printing options, the ability to print on larger sheets of paper, and other amazing options.

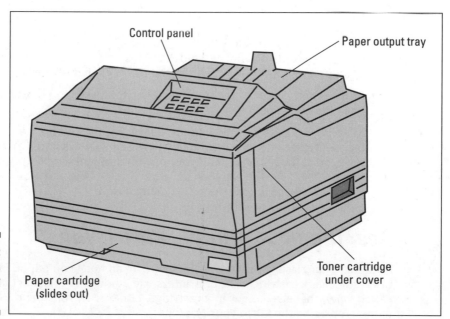

Figure 15-2:
Your typical, squat laser printer.

Control panel

Paper output tray

Paper cartridge (slides out)

Toner cartridge under cover

Examining your printer's control panel

Every printer has a control panel somewhere on its body. The fancy models have LCD screens that display lots of text: `Printer jammed`, `I'm out of paper`, or `You're plagiarizing`, for example. Other printers, less fancy, may just have an on–off button and a page eject button. Whatever. Find your printer's panel now.

You should locate two buttons on the panel:

- ✔ On-Line or Select
- ✔ Form Feed

The purpose of the On-Line or Select button is to tell your printer whether to ignore the computer. When the printer is offline or deselected, the computer can't print. This seems odd because the printer is still on, but because it's offline or deselected, it doesn't print.

The Form Feed button is used to eject a page of paper from the printer. For example, if you stop printing and only half a page is printed, you can use the Form Feed button to eject that page.

- ✔ The computer can print only when the printer is online or selected.

- ✔ You take the printer offline if, for example, you have to unjam it or want to eject a page of paper. Sometimes, you have to turn the printer off when it jams.

- ✔ If your printer seems to lack a control panel, it's probably controlled via a software control panel in Windows. This is the printer's feature and not a part of Windows, so refer to the printer's manual for instructions.

- ✔ Printers with larger LCD control panels often use menu buttons to help you choose the online or form-feed options.

- ✔ Keep your printer's manual handy. For example, I put my printer's manual right beneath the printer, where I can always find it. You may never read the manual, but if your printer suddenly pops up and displays `Error 34`, you can look up what `Error 34` is and read how to fix it. (The voice of experience is talking here.)

Feeding your printer, Part 1: Ink

Both inkjet and laser printers use ink to create an image on paper. Inkjet printers use ink cartridges; laser printers use a powdery ink substance, called *toner,* that also comes in a cartridge. Either way, you spend lots of money replacing the ink in your printer.

One reason that they say inkjet printers are so cheap is that the printer company makes its money back when you have to buy the ink cartridges. When the cartridges run dry, you must buy new ones. Even if only 1 color in a 3-color cartridge is gone, you must replace the whole thing. Replacement cost: $25. And that's cheap! I have paid $50 for some ink cartridges.

To replace a cartridge in an inkjet printer, first remove the old cartridge. Carefully unwrap the foil around the new cartridge. Remove any tape or covering, per the package's instructions. Then insert the ink cartridge into the printer, again following the instructions for your specific ink printer. Put the old cartridge into the new cartridge's box and properly dispose of it.

Laser printers require drop-in toner cartridges. They're easy to install and come with their own, handy instructions. Just don't breathe in the toner or else you'll die. Some manufacturers sell their cartridges with return envelopes so that you can send the old cartridge back to the factory for recycling or proper disposal.

- ✓ Several online and mail-order dealers offer cheap prices on ink and toner cartridges, better than you find locally or in an office supply superstore.

- ✓ Make a note of what type of inkjet cartridges your printer uses. Keep the catalog number somewhere handy, such as taped to your inkjet printer's case, so that you can always reorder the proper cartridge.

- ✓ If the ink cartridge has nozzles, you can refill it on your own. Refill kits are sold everywhere, and they're cheaper than continually buying new cartridges. However, the kits work best if the cartridge has nozzles. If the cartridge is just a storage bin, you're better off buying a new one.

- ✓ Always follow carefully the instructions for changing cartridges. Old cartridges can leak and get messy ink all over. I suggest having a paper towel handy and putting the used cartridge in a plastic baggie while you walk to the trashcan.

- ✓ You don't always have to print in color with an inkjet printer! You can also just print in black ink, which saves the (often spendy) color cartridge from running low. The Print dialog box (covered later in this chapter) often has an option that lets you choose whether you want to print with color or black ink.

- ✓ When the laser printer first warns you that `Toner [is] low`, you can get few more pages out of it by gently rocking the toner cartridge. Rock it back and forth the short way (not end to end), which helps redistribute the toner dust.

- ✓ Buy rubber gloves (or those cheap plastic gloves that make you look like Batman) and use them when changing an ink or toner cartridge.

- ✓ Another option for an empty laser printer toner cartridge is recharging. You can take it to a special place that cleans the old cartridge and refills it with fresh new toner. This process works and is often cheaper than buying a whole new cartridge.

✔ Never let your printer toner get low or ink cartridges go dry. You may think that squeezing every last drop of ink saves you money, but it's not good for the printer.

Feeding your printer, Part II: Paper

Next to consuming ink, printers eat paper. Fortunately, paper isn't as expensive as ink, so it doesn't bankrupt you to churn through a ream or two. The only issue is where to feed in the paper. Like feeding a baby, there is a right end and wrong end.

For inkjet printers, load the paper in the tray, either near the printer's bottom or sticking out the top.

Laser printers require you to fill a cartridge with paper, similar to the way a copy machine works. Slide the cartridge all the way into the printer after it's loaded up.

Confirm that you're putting the paper in the proper way, either face down or face up. And note which side is the top. Most printers have little pictures on them that tell you how the paper goes into the printer. Here is how those symbols translate into English:

✔ The paper goes in face down, top side up.

✔ The paper goes in face down, top side down.

✔ The paper goes in face up, top side up.

✔ The paper goes in face up, top side down.

This info helps you when loading things such as checks for use with personal finance software. If the printer doesn't tell you which way is up, write *Top* on a sheet of paper and run it through the printer. Then draw your own icon, similar to those shown above, that help you orient the pages you manually insert into the printer.

✔ Always make sure that you have enough printer paper. Buying too much isn't a sin.

✔ When in doubt, buy standard photocopier paper for your printer.

✔ Avoid thick papers because they get jammed inside the printer. (They can't turn corners well.)

✔ Some printers are capable of handling larger-size paper, such as legal or tabloid sizes. If so, make sure that you load the paper properly and tell your application that you're using a different-size sheet of paper. The File⇨Page Setup command is responsible for selecting paper size.

✔ Avoid using erasable bond and other fancy dusted papers in your printer. These papers have talcum powder coatings that gum up the works.

✔ Don't let the expensive paper ads fool you: Your inkjet printer can print on just about any type of paper. Even so, the pricey paper *does* produce a better image.

✔ My favorite type of inkjet paper is *laser paper*. It has a polished look to it and a subtle waxy feel.

✔ The best (and most outrageously expensive) paper to buy is special photographic paper. Using this paper with your printer's high-quality mode prints color images that look just like photographs. But at $1 per sheet, this kind of paper is best used for special occasions.

✔ Another fun paper: iron-on transfer paper. With this paper, you can print an image (reversed) and then use an iron to *weld* that image to a T-shirt. This technique is popular for those "These are my grandkids" types of T-shirts you see fat guys wear at the county fair.

Setting Up Your Beloved Printer

Printers are one of the easiest devices to set up and configure:

1. **Turn everything off: computer, printer — everything.**

2. **If necessary, remove all packing materials from the printer.**

   Refer to the printer's setup guide for what to yank out and toss. Obey that manual first if its instructions differ with those in this book.

3. **Plug the printer into the PC's console.**

   Start with the printer cable. Oops! The printer didn't come with a cable? Ugh. You need to buy a cable.

   Plug one end of the cable into the printer; the other goes into the computer's *printer port*. If you have a USB printer, plug the USB cable into your console's USB port.

4. **Plug the printer into the proper power socket.**

   Do not plug the printer into a UPS. And you should plug laser printers directly into the wall, not into a power strip or UPS. Refer to Chapter 2 for more information.

There. You're done with hardware installation. You can now turn the printer on. (The printer has to be on for Windows to recognize it.) If this printer is new, continue the setup operation by reading the section "Installing a New Printer (the software part)," a little later in this chapter.

Most of printers, like computers, can now be left on all the time. The printer automatically slips into a low-power sleep mode when it's no longer needed. However, if you don't print often (at least every day), it's perfectly fine to turn off your printer.

✔ If your PC has more than one printer port, plug your printer into LPT1, the first printer port.

✔ Some USB printers demand to be directly connected to the computer, not plugged into a USB hub.

✔ You can connect a number of printers to a single computer. As long as the computer has a second printer port or uses another USB port or even the network, multiple printers work fine.

✔ If you have some type of device (CD-R/RW, DVD, scanner, or whatever) connected to your PC's printer port, you need to plug the printer into that device and not into the console directly. The device has two connectors on its rump. One is labeled for the cable that goes to the console; the other is labeled for the printer. (Refer to Chapter 9 for more information on using the printer port this way.)

✔ The printer cable can be no more than 20 feet long. That length is ridiculous, of course, because the best place for your printer is within arm's reach.

Windows and Your Printer

The printing action in Windows happens inside the Printers and Faxes folder. To get there, open the Printers and Faxes icon inside the Control Panel. This action opens the Printers and Faxes folder, as shown in Figure 15-3.

Your Printers and Faxes folder undoubtedly looks different from what you see in Figure 15-3. It may be empty, for example. Otherwise, you notice a few interesting things:

The default printer: Though I hate the term *default*, Windows puts a check mark by your PC's primary printer. Though the window may be full of printers, the one with the check mark is the one you use first. The others are manually chosen in the Print dialog box.

The Fax machine: This icon represents your PC's fax modem — if you have one. Sending a fax works just like printing.

A shared printer: Printers with the sharing hand icon are connected to your PC, but are available for use by others on the network.

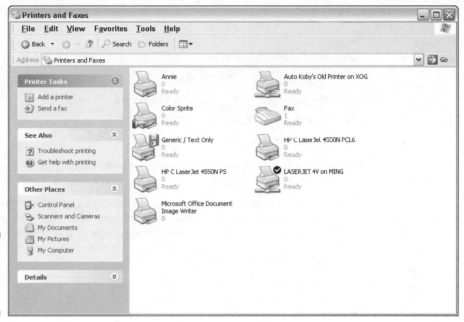

Figure 15-3:
The Printers
and Faxes
folder.

 A network printer: Printers with plumbing beneath them exist elsewhere on the network. You can use them just like any other printer, but it's a walk to get your document after it prints.

The printer icon is generic. All printers appear in the Printers and Faxes window using the same icon, so you cannot tell really what type of printer it is by looking at its icon in the window.

Installing a new printer (the software part)

Most likely, you set up Windows to work with your printer when you first brought your PC home or installed Windows XP. If not, or if you just purchased a new printer, you need to tell Windows about it.

First, start by connecting the printer, as described earlier in this chapter. Or, refer to your printer's manual if it has more specific instructions with fancy illustrations and silly cartoons or political humor.

Second, if you're using a USB printer, you're done. You have nothing else to do. Ditto for a Firewire or IR (infrared) computer. Just plug the printer in and turn it on. Windows recognizes it instantly, or it may ask for a CD. Either way, keep an eyeball on the screen for what to do next, if anything.

Third, if you're using a standard printer, you have to slug it through these steps:

1. **Open the Printers folder.**

   Refer to the preceding section.

2. **Choose File—>Add Printer from the menu.**

   The Add Printer Wizard starts.

3. **Click the Next button.**

   The steps that follow vary, depending on your printer. Here are my words of wisdom to help you through the rest of the wizard:

   • Select only the network printer option if you're on a network. In that case, your network manager sets things up for you, so you're basically done now. If not, or if you have a home network, note that Windows XP automatically finds and installs network printers as part of the network setup.

   • You need to know how the printer connects to the computer. As stated earlier in this chapter, that's most often through the printer port, LPT1.

   • Windows may ask for its distribution CD to load the printer driver files. If you don't have the CD, try using the location `C:\Windows\Options\CABS`. Windows may be able to find the files there.

   • If your printer came with its own CD, you may need to install programs from that CD to begin or finish the printer installation. Refer to the documentation that came with the CD.

4. **The final installation step is to print a test page on your printer.**

   Personally, I'm shocked that the test page isn't a catalog and order form for Microsoft products. But it ensures that your printer is connected properly and everything is up to snuff. It's gratifying to see that page print.

Opening your printer's window

After installation, your printer shows up as an icon in the Printers and Faxes window. Double-click to open that icon and you see your printer's window, similar to what's shown in Figure 15-4.

Any documents waiting to be printed appear in the window, in the order they were "sent" to the printer, from the top down. To remove a document, you select it and then choose Document⇨Cancel from the menu. That's about the most important thing you do here.

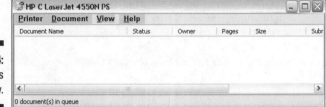

Figure 15-4:
A printer's
window.

When the printer's window contains documents waiting to be printed, a small printer icon appears on the system tray. You can double-click this icon to quickly display your printer's window.

Basic Printer Operation

Under Windows, printing is a snap. All applications support the same print command: Choose File⇨Print from the menu, click OK in the Print dialog box, and — zit-zit-zit — you soon have hard copy.

The Print dialog box is similar for most programs. Figure 15-5 shows a typical Print dialog box. You start by choosing a printer; the default printer is already chosen in the top of the dialog box. Otherwise, you can choose any printer listed, which echoes the selections available in the Printers and Faxes window (refer to Figure 15-1).

You can also set the number of pages to print (the Page Range Option) and the number of copies to print in the Print dialog box.

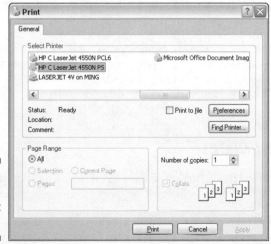

Figure 15-5:
A typical
Print
dialog box.

A Properties, Settings, or Options button in the Print dialog box lets you set specific aspects of printing, such as whether to use color, how to render graphics, and other printer features.

Many other printing options are in the Page Setup dialog box, covered in the next section.

- ✔ The common keyboard shortcut for the Print command is Ctrl+P.

- ✔ Many applications sport a Print toolbar icon. If so, you can click that button to quickly print your document.

- ✔ The Print toolbar icon doesn't summon the Print dialog box. It just prints the entire document. To summon the Print dialog box, you must use Ctrl+P or choose File➪Print from the menu.

Setting printing options

The printing options not found in the Print dialog box (refer to Figure 15-5) are in the Page Setup dialog box instead. To see this dialog box, choose the File➪Page Setup command. Figure 15-6 shows a sample, though many Page Setup dialog boxes are different.

For example, to print "longways," choose the Landscape option in the Page Setup dialog box. A preview window shows you how the document will be laid out.

Setting the paper size is also chosen in the Page Setup dialog box. There, you can choose between Letter, Legal, and a number of other sizes. Note that making this change requires you to manually load that size paper into the printer; just choosing legal-size paper doesn't automatically transform the letter-size paper already in the printer.

Finally, the Page Setup dialog box is where you enter information about the page's margins. Note that laser printers cannot print on the outside half-inch of the page. Depending on how your page fits into an ink printer, either the top or bottom margin must be sacrificed (and not printed on) so that the feed mechanism grabs the paper. This margin varies from half an inch to one full inch.

Printing the screen

Even though the keyboard has a button named Print Screen, it doesn't send a copy of the screen to the printer — at least not directly.

If you really need a printed copy of the Windows desktop or some window on the screen, refer to the section in Chapter 12 about taking a screen dump. After pasting the image into the Paint program, print the image.

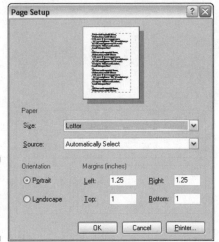

Figure 15-6:
The Page
Setup
dialog box.

Feeding an envelope

To stick an envelope into your printer, just shove it into the special slot. Oftentimes, you must open a hatch on the front of the printer to reveal the slot. A special illustration on the hatch tells you which way to place the envelope: face up or down and top right or top left. Then you tell your software to print the envelope and — *thwoop!* — there it goes and comes back again, complete with a nifty address.

✔ Obviously, feeding an envelope to a printer is different for each type of printer.

✔ Pay attention to how the envelope feeds in. Does it go in longways or wide-ways, up or down, top or bottom?

✔ Each program has, also obviously, a different command for printing envelopes. Typically, you have to tell the program how the envelope goes into your printer so that it knows in which direction to print the address.

✔ Some printers require you to press the On-line or Select button to print the envelope. For example, on my printer I set up everything and stick the envelope in the hatch, and then I print with my software. After a few seconds, the printer's display says "Manual feed!" which I properly interpret to mean "Press my On-line button, doofus!" which I do, and then the thing prints.

Chapter 16

Modem Mania

• •

• •

Modems have become such standard equipment in a computer that trying to buy a PC without one is like trying to buy a lawn mower without the blades. Although once used for computer-to-computer communications, modems are now required equipment in order to get on the all-powerful, alluring, and seductive Internet — a must for the twenty-first century.

Although the Internet is covered in Part IV of this book, this chapter dwells on the hardware that is the model of modern modem mania.

What Does a Modem Do?

A *modem* is a translator. What it does is transform the crude language of ones and zeroes inside the computer into something that can be sent out over the phone lines, over your cable TV wire, or even straight up into outer space. Then, at the other end of the line, another modem retranslates those signals into information the computer can understand, and — long story short — you have two computers talking with each other.

The function of a computer's modem has narrowed pretty much now to Internet communications. Although you can still use the modem to talk directly with any other computer and a modem, most folks simply use their modems to connect with the Internet and that's that.

✔ See Part IV of this book for more information about the Internet.

✔ Modems are controlled by software, just as the printer or an external disk drive hardware is dominated by software. You have no buttons to push on a modem or other options worth setting.

✔ The modem gets its name from what it does: translate digital information from your computer into analog signals (sounds) that can be sent over common phone lines. Converting the digital information into analog is called *modulation*. Converting back the other way is *demodulation*. So, the device is a modulator–demodulator, or modem, for short.

✔ High-speed modems don't modulate or demodulate now because they communicate entirely with digital signals. Yet they're still called modems.

Modem Features

Modems come in all sizes and styles from manufacturers far and wide. Generally speaking, however, only two types are available: the traditional dial-up modem and the high-speed broadband modems. These are explained, cussed, and discussed in the sections that follow.

The traditional dial-up modem

Nearly all PCs come with a dial-up modem preinstalled. It's the traditional computer modem, designed to use the phone lines to transmit and receive information. The modem is inexpensive, but it's also the slowest type available.

Although external modem models are available, most modems sold with PCs live within the console. The modem resides on an expansion card plugged directly into the motherboard. There, it assumes one of the serial (COM) ports and cooperates with the PC's other electronics.

Unless a faster alternative is available in your area, the dial-up modem is your PC's only type of modem. That's not bad: Today's models are fast and reliable, and having a dial-up modem beats not having any Internet access.

On the plus side, even if you do have high-speed modem access (see the next section), the dial-up modem can still be used as your PC's fax machine or as a backup connection.

✔ Dial-up modems cost nothing extra to use, and you incur no surcharges or fees to operate them. If your local phone calls are included on your phone bill, so are the phone calls the computer makes.

✔ If your modem makes a long distance call, regular long distance charges apply.

✔ Some foreign countries do charge per call for Internet access.

✔ Windows comes with faxing software so that you can use your modem like a fax machine. When printing, choose the Fax "printer" from the list. Then follow the steps in the Fax Wizard to send your document as a fax. To get started receiving a fax, open the Fax icon in the Printers and Faxes window (though it's more complex than that).

✔ The plain old telephone system modem is also known as a *POTS* modem. POTS stands for Plain Old Telephone System.

Faster than a speeding phone bill: Broadband modems

High-speed modems fall under the category of *broadband* modems. These modems use special means to connect to the Internet at top speeds. Their only downside is that you must live in an area that provides broadband service and you pay more for access than you do with a dial-up modem.

Three common broadband services are available: cable, DSL, and satellite. Each comes with its own modem:

Cable: This type of modem is the fastest you can buy, often faster than the computer can keep up with! The only downside is that when more of your neighbors begin using their cable modems, the overall speed decreases. But at 2:00 a.m., your cable modem *smokes!*

DSL: This type of modem gives you fast access by taking advantage of unused frequencies in existing phone lines. The modem hooks up to the phone line, but all other phones on that line require special filters. This type is easy to install and, next to cable, gives you the fastest connection speeds.

Satellite: Combined with an outdoor antenna and a subscription to the satellite service, this is one of the fastest modem options available. Try to get a satellite modem that provides both sending and receiving abilities. Avoid satellite service that is "download only."

You pay three times for broadband modems. First, you may pay initially for the modem itself. This isn't bad because DSL modems cost about $100 and most cable companies rent their modems. Satellite modems, however, are spendy because they also include the satellite dish and its hardware.

Second, you have to pay the company that provides the service: your phone company for DSL, your cable company for cable, and your satellite company for a satellite modem.

Finally, you have to pay your ISP for access as well. This isn't the case with some cable and phone companies that provide both the broadband service and Internet access. If you have a different ISP, you have to pay them separately. (See Chapter 22 for more information on what an ISP is.)

✔ Broadband is synonymous with high-speed Internet access.

✔ DSL stands for Digital Subscriber Line. It has variations, such as ADSL and other *something*-DSL options. Your phone company knows more about this matter than I do. Basically, everyone calls it DSL, no matter what.

Fast, faster, fastest

Modem speed is measured in *kilobits per second*. That's kilo*bits,* not kilo*bytes*. To give you an idea of how fast that is, 100 kilobits is about as much information as you see on a line of text in this book. If this book were appearing on your screen through your modem, one line per second, you would have a connection that flies by at 100 kilobits per second, or 100Kbps.

The slowest modem you can buy now is a dial-up model that whizzes out information at 56Kbps. That modem can transmit approximately 14 pages of printed information every second.

The fastest modem you can buy (or rent) is a cable modem that whizzes along at 5,000Kbps. That's many, many pages of information per second, or enough speed to display a real-time video image with sound.

✔ A modem's speed rating is for comparison purposes only. Rarely do modems crank out information as fast as they're rated. It happens, but rarely. For example, a 56Kbps dial-up modem usually chugs along at about 48Kbps.

✔ Values over 1,000Kbps may be written as 1Mbps, or one megabit per second. Sometimes, the M and K are written in lowercase: kbps and mbps.

✔ For dial-up modems, the connection speed is displayed by Windows whenever the modem connects. You can also point the mouse at the tiny modem icon on the system tray.

✔ You can gauge your modem speed online by visiting a site such as www. dslreports.com.

What's a null-modem?

A *null-modem* isn't a modem at all. In fact, it's either a tiny adapter or a cable that works like a standard serial port (COM) cable, but with its wires reversed. Also called *twisted pair*, a null modem is designed to connect two computers up for direct communications.

For example, if you're moving files from an older PC to a newer system and the older system lacks network access or a CD-R (both of which make transferring files easier), you can purchase a null modem cable at an office supply store along with file transfer software and use them to send files between the two systems.

Connecting a Modem

Setting up a modem is so easy that a 65-year-old retired male doctor could do it. The following sections tell you how.

Hooking up a dial-up modem

A dial-up modem connects to the phone jack on the wall just like a telephone does. The key is to look at the back of your computer, where one or two phone jacks appear.

Figure 16-1 shows what the back of the internal modem may look like. Two phone jacks are there. Plug one end of the phone cable into the Line hole. Plug the other end of the phone cable into the wall jack.

Figure 16-1:
Important
stuff on the
back of an
internal
modem.

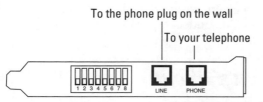

To the phone plug on the wall

To your telephone

1 2 3 4 5 6 7 8   LINE   PHONE

If the internal modem has only one phone jack, well, then, by golly, it plugs into the wall.

It doesn't matter which end of the phone cord goes into the wall or modem; plugging in a modem is just like plugging in a phone. If a phone is already plugged into the wall, unplug it. Then plug it into the Phone hole in the back of your modem.

How do you know you got things right? Try it! If the modem doesn't dial out, just swap the cords.

Connecting a broadband modem

Cable, DSL, and satellite modems are external, so they all must be plugged into a wall socket somewhere. As a suggestion, I recommend plugging them into a UPS, which helps keep their signals going during intermittent power outages.

One end of the broadband modem is plugged into the input source. For DSL, that's the jack on the wall for the phone line that carries the DSL signal. For cable modem, it's the TV cable. For satellite, it's also a TV-cable-like thing, but one that comes in from a satellite dish.

The other connection on the broadband modem plugs into the networking jack or Ethernet port on your PC. Or, if your PC is on a network, you only have to plug the broadband modem into a network switch or hub, in which case all the computers on the network can access it.

✔ Be sure to put the filters, or "dongles," on each phone that shares the line with the DSL modem. If you don't, you have difficulty hearing phone conversations on that line.

✔ Generally speaking, broadband modems are left on all the time. There's no point in turning them on or off. In fact, doing so may cause the broadband service to phone you up to see whether everything is okay.

✔ The Ethernet port exists on the back of an NIC, or network interface card, which can be an adapter plugged into an expansion slot or just another jack on the back of the console. Chapter 18 explains the details, but I have to mention NIC here because it's mentioned in many DSL/cable/satellite modem manuals.

Telling Windows about your dial-up modem

After setting up your modem, you must tell Windows about it. For dial-up modems, open the Control Panel's Phone and Modem Options icon. Click the Modems tab and you see where you can add, remove, or adjust the modems connected to your PC, as shown in Figure 16-2.

Figure 16-2:
Tell Windows
all about
your new
modem in
the Phone
and Modem
Options
dialog box.

To add a new modem, click the Add button. Work through the wizard to have it detect and install your modem. My advice is to *not* have Windows automatically detect your modem; just select it from the list of manufacturers and models or use the CD that came with the modem.

✔ The best way to use a modem is with its own phone line. Just about every house or apartment can have a second line added without your having to pay for extra wiring. If so, have your phone company hook up that line and use it for your modem. Why? Because. . . .

✔ You can't use your phone while your modem is talking. In fact, if somebody picks up another extension on that line, it garbles the signal, possibly losing your connection — not to mention that the human hears a horrid screeching sound. Also see the section, "Dialing Rules from Here to Eternity," later in this chapter.

✔ If Windows ever seems to lose track of your modem, restart your PC. Often, that helps Windows find a lost modem. If you have an external dial-up modem, turn it off and then on again and Windows may suddenly find it.

Telling Windows about your broadband modem

This job is done in the Control Panel's Network Connections window. However, it's closely linked to configuring the Internet for your PC, so the real instructions are in Part IV of this book.

The universal broadband modem fix

Broadband modems are fairly robust and reliable, but they do occasionally go down. An easy and simple fix is to turn your modem off, wait, and then turn it back on again. Often, that supplies the kick necessary to get the modem up and running.

Also necessary for a broadband modem is some type of firewall. No, it's not that the lines get so hot that your computer could burn; a *firewall* is a piece of hardware or software designed to limit access to your computer, which is vital for a high-speed connection. Again, this topic is covered in Part IV of this book.

Dialing Rules from Here to Eternity

Broadband modems don't travel. If you're going on a trip somewhere, don't plan on taking your DSL modem with you. Sadly, it just doesn't work anywhere else. No, on vacation or work, you most likely have to take your laptop with you and use its dial-up modem. When this happens, you need to tell Windows about the new dialing location.

Even if you aren't traveling, you should become familiar with setting a dialing location in Windows. In addition to merely saying "I'm here," the dialing location dialog box is where you tell Windows how to deal with long distance in your part of the woods — which is becoming a nationwide issue as we slowly run out of telephone numbers. Keep reading.

Setting a location for your dial-up modem

Even if you don't ever plan on moving your computer, follow these steps to set a location for your dial-up modem:

1. **Open the Control Panel's Phone and Modem Options icon.**

2a. **If no location is entered, click the New button to create a new location.**

2b. **If locations are entered, select the current one and click the Edit button; you're done.**

3. Type a name for the Location in the Location name box.

For example, if you're calling from home, type **Home**. If the computer is in your office, type Office.

After creating a location, you can use the Edit Location or New Location dialog box, similar to what's shown in Figure 16-3, to set some modem dialing rules. These rules are covered in the sections that follow.

Dealing with call waiting

Call waiting is a handy feature to have, but it can be disruptive too. The call waiting tone disconnects a dial-up modem, which people generally find disruptive.

To disable call waiting, use the Edit Location dialog box, as shown in Figure 16-3. Put a check mark by the item To Disable Call Waiting, Dial. Then choose from the drop-down list the proper numbers to dial, such as *70, or enter whatever numbers your phone company uses.

 Another way to deal with call waiting is to use software that lets you hear who's calling you while you're online. Visit www.callwave.com for more information on that type of product.

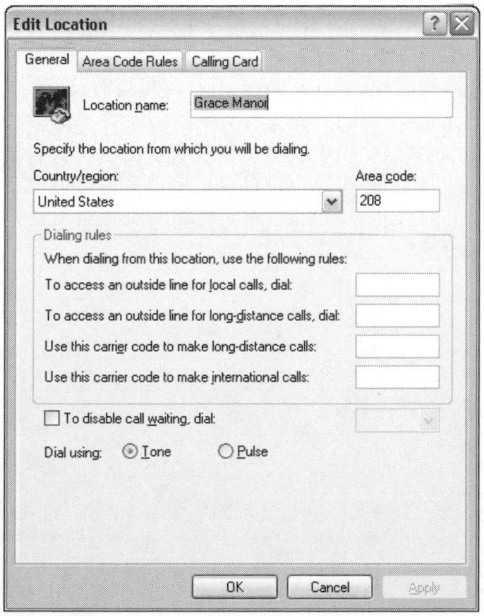

Figure 16-3:
Set dial-up
modem
rules here.

Dealing with "local" long distance

Phone companies seem to delight in forcing us to dial our own area codes for *local long distance*. To deal with this situation, use the Area Code Rules tab in the Edit Location dialog box (refer to Figure 16-3). Click the New button to display the New Area Code Rule dialog box and then fill in the items required for dialing area codes that are required for your part of the country.

Dialing out from a hotel

Whenever I go traveling, I create a new location for my laptop and enter it on the list in the Phone and Modem Options dialog box. That way, I can configure my laptop's dial-up modem for each location individually — plus, when I visit that place again, I have the rules and information already set up so that I can use my modem.

The first step to using a modem in a hotel is to create a new location in the Phone and Modem Options dialog box, on the Dialing Rules tab.

In the New Location dialog box (refer to Figure 16-3), enter the hotel name or city location, country, and then area code.

Next, carefully enter the dialing rules for the hotel. For example, to access an outside line, you dial 9 or 8 in most hotels. Note that in hotels, you sometimes don't need to dial a prefix number to make a local call.

Save the information for your new location and then click to highlight it back in the Phone and Modem Options dialog box. Your laptop's modem is then set to dial out. Now you only have to put up with the outrageous hotel phone bill.

Chapter 17

The Hills Are Alive with the Sounds of PC

. . . .

In This Chapter

▶ Discovering your PC's sound hardware

▶ Understanding sound file types

▶ Using the Windows Media Player

▶ Setting the volume

▶ Recording your own sounds

▶ Making the PC talk and listen

. . . .

Do, re, mi, fa, so, la, ti, DOS!

The first IBM PC had a speaker, but it could only *BEEP*. Games could play silly songs but nothing musically sweet. After all, the PC was a *business* computer, serious and aloof; it had no time for silly stuff, like audio, and sounds to blow off the roof!

Despite that all-business attitude, a few companies began creating *sound cards* for the PC. At first, they were fashioning a "multimedia computer," which needed to play sounds and support the swanky new CD-ROM drive (circa 1992). Then, over time, the sound circuitry became part of the motherboard. Throw in a pair of stereo speakers and a subwoofer, and you have the melodic PC of today, which is the subject of this noisy chapter.

Your PC Can Make Noise

Even if you have an antique PC that lacks sound circuitry, it can still make noise: Just toss it through a window! (Sadly, this noise-making trick works only once for each PC and window.)

All PCs now have either built-in sound smarts or sound expansion cards that let them do more than just BEEP the internal speakers. The following sections cover the necessary sound features of the common PC.

- ✔ Refer to Chapter 1, which shows how to find the audio input and output jacks on your PC's console. If you have those jacks, your PC can make sound.

- ✔ Chapter 9 discusses how to connect audio devices to the PC's audio jacks.

- ✔ Refer to my book *Troubleshooting Your PC For Dummies* (Wiley Publishing, Inc.) if you're having trouble hearing sounds from your PC.

The hardware that brings on da noise

Your PC comes with sound circuitry either included directly on the motherboard or on an expansion card plugged into an expansion slot (also on the motherboard). That sound circuitry can do some amazing things.

The first thing the sound circuitry does is to play *wave sounds,* which are the recorded sounds you hear when you turn on your computer or run a program. They're also the sounds you hear when you play a computer game: a ding-dong for a correct answer, your opponent saying "ouch," or the sound of spent shotgun shells hitting a concrete floor. They're all wave sounds.

The second thing the sound circuitry does is to play music on a built-in synthesizer. Special music files, known as *MIDI* files, direct the synthesizer to play all sorts of songs, from classical music to sitcom themes. Depending on the sophistication of the sound circuitry, the synthesizer can produce quite realistic-sounding music.

Third, the sound circuitry helps amplify and play music from your computer's CD-ROM drive.

Finally, you can use the sound circuitry to record and play back your own sound files.

- ✔ Sounds are recorded, and that information is saved in special sound files stored on disk. See the section "The types of files that contain noise," later in this chapter, for the details.

- ✔ If you're into audio, you can buy special superduper sound cards that provide more features and better recording/playback abilities than the run-of-the-mill PC sound circuitry.

Speakers here and there

Your PC's sound circuitry isn't worth squat if your computer lacks the means for you to hear the sounds. For that, you need speakers.

All PCs come with a single el cheapo speaker inside the console. That speaker is good for beeping only; the sound circuitry doesn't connect to it. To take advantage of your PC's sound circuitry, you have to connect some external speakers.

Here are my external-speaker thoughts:

- ✔ Speaker quality isn't important. Any cheap-o set of stereo speakers works on a PC.

- ✔ Run your speakers electrically rather than through batteries. If your speakers didn't come with an AC power adapter, you can usually buy one.

- ✔ Speakers built into the PC's monitor suck.

- ✔ If sound is important to you, invest in some decent speakers. Sound kits are available that offer good-quality speakers plus perhaps a subwoofer to help boost the bass signal.

- ✔ *Subwoofer?* It's a speaker box, typically sitting on the floor beneath your PC. It amplifies sounds at the low end of the spectrum. Subwoofers give oomph to the bass in music, and for games they truly add emphasis to the horde of football players sacking your quarterback.

- ✔ Surround sound kits are available for PCs. Note that these kits work only with software (mostly games) that supports the numerous speakers. The Dolby 5.1 standard, for example, supports five speakers and one subwoofer; the five speakers are left, center, right, rear-left, and rear-right. The Dolby 6.1 standard adds a sixth speaker, at rear-center.

- ✔ If you put speakers on your desk, remember that they contain magnets. If any stray floppy disk comes too close, especially behind the speakers, it loses data.

Microphone options

Any cheesy microphone works on a PC. If sound quality is important to you and you're using your PC as a digital audio studio, you will spend money on microphones and mixers and all that. But if that's not you, any old microphone will do.

If you plan on using voice over the Internet or dictation, get a microphone-headset combination. That way, you can chatter without having to mess with holding the microphone or setting up a mic stand near your PC.

Having Fun with Sound in Windows

If you have time to waste, you can turn your smart business computer into a goofy business computer by adding sounds to Windows. This is one area where you can waste oodles of time. Of course, keep in mind that this is Important Computer Configuration, not something you're having fun with.

The types of files that contain noise

Sound recorded on a computer is merely raw data — digital information recorded on a hard drive as opposed to analog information you find on a cassette tape. Like other data, sound is kept in a file. Three primary types of audio files are used for the PC: WAV, MP3, and MIDI.

WAV: This is a basic *wave,* or audio, file, which simply contains a digital sound sampling. Most sounds you hear in Windows, or even sounds you record yourself, are WAV files, pronounced "wave" *files.*

MP3: These special compressed WAV files take up less space on disk. A typical MP3 file occupies 1MB of disk space for every minute of sound contained inside. These files contain mostly audio tracks from CDs or other sound sources; any type of sound can find its way into the MP3 format.

MIDI: This synthesized music file format doesn't contain sound. Instead, the MIDI ("MIH-dee") files contain instructions read by the sound circuitry's synthesizer, which then plays back the song as a musician would read sheet music.

You can find other sound file formats as well, such as AU and AIFF and too many more to mention. The three in the preceding list are the most popular with Windows.

- Windows keeps its sound files in the My Music folder, which you find inside the My Documents folder. Music files you download from the Internet are saved there, although I encourage you to create even more folders within the My Music folder for specific categories, or "albums" of music.
- See Chapter 26 for information on obtaining MP3 files from the Internet.
- MIDI stands for Musical Instrument Digital Interface. It's the standard for electronically recording music. By using the proper software, plus maybe some MIDI musical instruments, you can create your own MIDI files.
- Software exists to record sounds as well as convert the sounds from one file format to another. I have nothing specific to recommend, so to find this type of software, search Google (www.google.com/) for "sound conversion software."

✔ By the way, sound files takes up huge amounts of room on a disk. That's why most digitized sounds are limited to short bursts, like golf swings and grunts.

Say hello to the Windows Media Player

To play any sound file in Windows, whether it's a WAV, MIDI, MP3 file, or whatever: Just double-click to open the file. The sound plays in the Windows Media Player program.

Use the controls in Media Player to start, stop, and repeat the audio files you open. Media Player works just a stereo or CD player, and the buttons are labeled the same.

✔ There's no point in explaining the Media Player here; the program invites play, and I encourage you to poke and click the mouse at various parts of Media Player to see what happens.

✔ Refer to Chapter 7 for information on creating playlists of music in Media Player.

✔ A great alternative to Media Player is the MUSICMATCH Jukebox program, available from `www.musicmatch.com`.

The Windows sounds playground

Just to be goofy, Windows lets you assign sounds to various events, actions, or things you do inside the Windows operating system. The playground where that happens is the Sounds and Audio Devices Properties dialog box, found on any Control Panel near you:

1. **Open the Control Panel's Sounds and Audio Devices icon.**

2. **Click the Sounds tab.**

    The dialog box sports a scrolling list of events, which are various things done by Windows or your applications. You can apply a specific sound to any of those events so that when such-and-such an event takes place, a specific sound is played.

    For example, the Critical Stop event — a bad one in Windows — is highlighted in Figure 17-1. The sound associated with that event appears on the Sounds drop-down list as `Windows XP Critical Stop.wav`. That's the WAV file that plays when Windows stops critically.

3. **Select an event to assign a sound to.**

    For example, select the New Mail Notification, which is the sound that plays when Outlook Express picks up new e-mail.

4. Test the current sound, if any.

To test the sound, click the Play button.

5. Assign a new sound.

To assign a new sound to an event, click the Browse button. That lets you "go out on disk" to seek out a specific sound.

You can also choose from one of the preselected sounds on the Sounds drop-down list (where `Windows XP Critical Stop.wav` appears in Figure 17-1).

6. Click the OK button when you're done assigning sounds.

Windows comes with preassigned sound schemes. You can choose them from the Scheme drop-down list to set a whole buncha sounds all at once.

Figure 17-1:
Assigning
sounds to
events.

You can create your own, personalized sound scheme by saving your particular favorite sounds as their own scheme. To do this, after assigning your individual sounds, click the Save As button in the Sounds and Audio Devices Properties dialog box, on the Sounds tab. Give the scheme a name and then click OK. That way, you can instantly recover your favorite sounds by choosing that same scheme again.

✔ To remove a sound from an event, choose (None) from the top of the Sounds drop-down list.

✔ If you can't find an event on the list, you cannot assign a sound to it.

✔ The Sounds and Audio Devices Properties dialog box is used to assign *sounds* to events — specifically, WAV files. Windows isn't equipped to play MIDI or MP3 files for certain events.

✔ The best source for sounds is the Internet, where you can find Web page libraries full of sound samples. Go to Google (`www.google.com/`) and search for "Windows WAV file sounds" to find them.

✔ Don't be embarrassed whenever you call tech support for some reason and each time that they tell you to open this or that window, Mary Poppins says "Spit-spot!"

✔ See the section "Recording Your Own Sounds," later in this chapter, for more information about recording sounds.

Adjusting the volume

Setting how loud your PC plays sounds is done in two places. The first place is a hardware place: the sound volume knob on your PC's speakers or on the subwoofer — though that's not always the case.

The second spot for adjusting the volume is the Volume icon, found on the system tray.

To set the volume, click the Volume icon once. Use the slider in the pop-up window to increase (up) or decrease (down) the volume. Or, just click the slider bar to get an idea of how loud the sound is set now.

To mute the sound, click to put a check mark in the Mute box.

Click anywhere else on the desktop to make the pop-up window go away.

If the Volume thingy doesn't appear on the system tray, open the Control Panel's Sounds and Audio Devices icon. Click the Volume tab and click to put a check mark next to the option labeled Place volume icon in the taskbar.

Using the volume master control

To specifically control the volume or individual sound-producing devices, you need to use the volume master control, as shown in Figure 17-2. It's where you can set the volume for various types of sound sources in Windows, mute specific sources, or adjust stereo settings. It's powerful and mysterious, like that special flavor ingredient that makes you crave KFC.

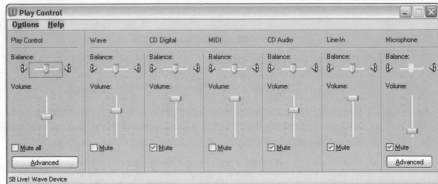

Figure 17-2: The master volume control.

The master volume control displays a whole window full of squeaking and squawking things in Windows, each with its own volume setting slider and Mute button. Set things individually as you see fit.

For example, if you detest having MIDI music play while you're on the Internet (or anywhere), just mute that one item. All other sounds in your system continue to play, but MIDI sounds are muted.

✔ Yes, I know that the window is named Play Control in Figure 17-2, but I prefer calling it the master volume control. Someday, Microsoft will see the light and agree with me on this subject.

✔ Use the Options⇨Properties command to set which sound-producing devices in your PC appear in the volume master control window.

Recording Your Own Sounds

Thanks to the sound input jacks on the PC's console, you can use your computer to record any type of sound. All you need is a *patch cable* to connect a sound-producing device to the audio inputs on your PC.

✔ To record your own voice, plug a microphone into the Mic In or amplified line-input jack.

✔ To record from any other device, plug it into the Line In or unamplified input jack.

You need, on the software side, a program that lets you record from the sound circuitry inputs. Windows has a silly little program that does this, named Sound Recorder.

Run the Sound Recorder program from the Start panel by choosing Programs⇨Accessories⇨Entertainment⇨Sound Recorder. The Sound Recorder's window appears, as shown in Figure 17-3.

Figure 17-3:
The Sound
Recorder.

Get ready at the mic, or cue up the other sound source, and then click the Record button. Watch the timer! You have only 60 seconds.

To stop, click the Stop button.

To hear yourself, click the Play button.

Save your work to disk by choosing the File⇨Save As command, just as you would with any file in any application.

- ✔ I say that Sound Recorder is silly because it lets you record only one minute of sound at a time. To record for longer than a minute, visit this Web page: www.wambooli.com/help/pc/sound_recorder/.

- ✔ Better, more sophisticated sound-recording programs than Sound Recorder often come with your PC's sound card, such as the SoundBlaster Wave Studio. I can also recommend N-track Studio, from Fasoft (www.fasoft.com), which is more of a professional-level program.

- ✔ Sound files are huge! Although playing and collecting sounds is fun, be aware that they occupy lots of disk space.

Getting the PC to Talk and Listen

Sound. Speakers. Microphone. Perhaps the day you can actually yell at the PC and have it be moved by your passion isn't too far away. Until then, consider the following sections on the state of the PC's cybernetic mouth and ears.

Can it talk?

Your PC is more than capable of speaking. The sound card can be programmed to emulate the human voice. But if you're looking for fun software to make that happen, you have to turn to the Internet and search for speech software.

One speech program I can recommend is TextAloud MP3. You can read more about this program at www.wugnet.com/shareware/spow.asp?ID=447.

Windows XP comes with a speech program named Narrator. Rather than a toy, however, Narrator is designed to be a tool to assist the visually impaired with using a computer. To run Narrator, from the Start panel choose the Programs command and then Accessories⇨Accessibility⇨Narrator. The program starts, and begins by immediately reading the window it starts in. To close Narrator, keep closing its windows until it's gone.

Does it listen?

Some programs let you talk to your PC. You talk and the program fairly accurately interprets your speech as text right on the screen. The technology has been available for about ten years now, yet it's still crude, in my opinion.

Eats till Vera crew din myopia non.

The biggest problem with dictation is that you must train the computer to understand your voice. It requires — at minimum — three hours of reading aloud into the computer while it analyzes your speech patterns. (That's a long time; keep a glass of water handy.) On the plus side, the more you train the PC, the better it gets at interpreting your speech. Do you have the time to invest?

✔ Speech recognition software is included with Microsoft Office XP and Office 2003. The programs add two new icons on the Control Panel: Speech and Text Services. Each one controls how the PC communicates, either reading text or accepting audio input.

✔ Another popular dictation package is Dragon Naturally Speaking, at www.scansoft.com.

✔ Dictation works best with a headset microphone.

✔ People who get the most from dictation software spend at least 9 to 12 hours training the computer to understand them.

✔ For a fast typist, such as myself, talking software doesn't really work. I find talking mode and typing mode to be two different things. Also, I change my mind a lot, which means that I'm always editing my own text as I write it, something the dictation software is rather poor at.

Chapter 18

Networking Nonsense

· ·

· ·

*B*ack when the earth was new, when smoldering volcanoes percolated on the horizon, lumbering beasts known as *mainframes* served pale, gaunt men in lab coats. Using an array of wires, these mainframes were connected to remote locations where *dumb terminals* sat and eagerly suckled on the digital brew they were fed. Computing was centralized. Control was absolute. The mainframe was one and all, the only computer. The mortals sat at dumb terminals that were mere nodes. Oh, those were the days!

Today, each computer comes with its own set of smarts, yet there are still many reasons to connect them. Especially in today's environment where you may have two or more computers in your home, connecting them makes a lot of sense, requires very little (and inexpensive) hardware, and is something just about anyone can do. This chapter shows you the ropes.

The Big Networking Picture

Forget the hardware. Forget the software. Computer networking is about one thing: sharing resources.

A computer system has many resources: memory, disk storage, the video system, and so on. Networks allow you to share two common computer resources: hard drive storage and printers.

The biggest bonus to networking is, of course, communications. Primarily, that involves the Internet. As with disk storage and printers, you can share a modem and an Internet connection between several networked computers. So, in a multicomputer family, everyone can enjoy the benefits of a broadband modem as well as the sole color printer.

✔ Like everything in a computer, networking is a combination of hardware and software. The hardware, you may need to purchase, as described later in this chapter. The networking software comes with Windows XP.

✔ Networking PCs as described in this chapter creates what's known as a *peer-to-peer network* — that is, a network with no central humongous computer or evil file server. That type of file server network isn't covered in this book, but rather in other expensive books, some written in English.

✔ You can network Macintosh and Linux computers into your PC network, though, again, this subject was deemed too frightening to be covered in this book.

✔ Yep, networking is a big topic. If you're new to it, read this chapter. Even afterward, I recommend that you have an expert set things up for you or at least have that person available on the phone when things don't work right the first time — because they usually don't.

The Networking Hardware

To make networking happen, you need at least two PCs. People have tried networking with just one computer, but that really doesn't work well (though the speed tests came back "excellent"). Each PC must be equipped with its own networking hardware. In addition to that, other hardware is required in order to connect the computers and get them all talking.

If you enjoy looking at pictures as opposed to reading text, Figure 18-1 provides a grand overview.

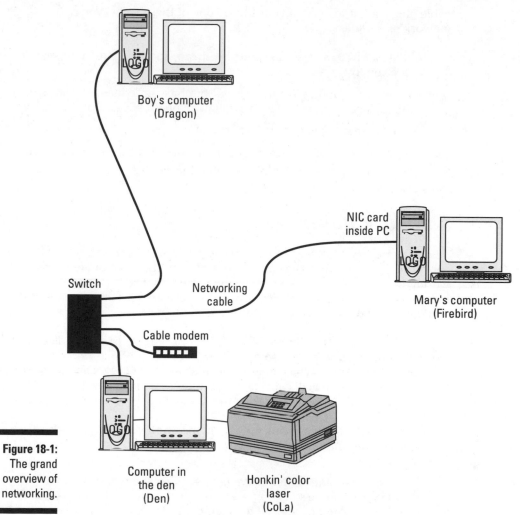

Figure 18-1:
The grand
overview of
networking.

Boy's computer
(Dragon)

NIC card
inside PC

Switch

Networking
cable

Mary's computer
(Firebird)

Cable modem

Computer in
the den
(Den)

Honkin' color
laser
(CoLa)

Saint NIC

As far as the PC goes, the most important piece of networking hardware is
the *Network Information Card,* or *NIC.* Also called an Ethernet card or network
adapter, the NIC comes as either an expansion card plugged into a socket or
as part of the PC's motherboard circuitry.

The way to tell whether your PC has a NIC is to look 'round back for the RJ-45
adapter jack. This hole looks like a large phone cord hole, though network

cable plugs into it instead. If your PC has one of these jacks, you're in networking business.

- Adding a NIC to a PC is easy; they're cheap, and you can find one at any office supply store.
- Wireless NICs don't have RJ-45 jacks, but have antennas instead. The wireless kind is more expensive than wire-based NICs.
- Get a NIC that configures at 10 or 100 Mbps (megabits per second).
- Your NIC needs only an RJ-45, or *twisted pair,* adapter. You don't need to pay extra for a NIC with other networking adapters.

Network hoses

To connect everything, you can use network wires or cable. These cables carry the signal between the computers and a central location. In an ideal world, the cables would simply plug into a wall jack, like the phone does, but your home or office likely isn't wired for networking, which means that you have to find some other way to run the network hoses.

Network hoses are officially known as CAT5, or Category 5, cables. They contain eight wires and can also be used to wire in telephones as well as networking computers. The cables come in a variety of colors and lengths — and I hear that the new fall cable fashions are just *stunning!* Each end of the cable has an RJ-45 connector, making them easy to plug in and unplug.

- You can get creative wiring up your home or office with networking cable. I crawl under my house to wire it all up, and I use the attic and outside walls.
- It's possible — and rather convenient — to run networking cable through your home's heating ducts. If you choose to do it this way, be sure that you buy special high-temperature cable, rugged enough to stand being inside a heating duct.
- Yes, heating ducts are filthy.
- If wiring drives you batty, be smart and go with a wireless type of network, as described in the upcoming section "Wireless networking."

Hubs, switches, and routers

All the wires from the networked PCs and their NICs, or the signals from wireless network connections, gather at a central location known as a hub. The *hub* is nothing more than a box with holes in it, into which all the networking hoses from all the computers are plugged. The hub contains smarts enough to pass along the signals carried on those wires to the other computers on the network.

Smarter and faster than a hub is a switch. And, smarter and faster than a switch is a router.

A *router* is the most sophisticated of the network connection devices, required in situations with lots of computers on the network, to help them resolve important who's who and "Where the heck am I going?" questions. If you have a broadband (high-speed) Internet connection and more than one computer trying to use that connection, getting a router is a good idea.

Wireless networking

Network hoses are optional; it's entirely possible to equip your PCs with wireless gear, which requires no network hose anywhere; just erase all the tiny lines drawn between the computers in Figure 18-1 to get an idea of what's up with that.

If you're starting out, simply get wireless NICs for your PCs. That eliminates the need for any wires (and it keeps your heating ducts chaste).

If your PCs already have NICs, you can buy access points to plug them into, though it's cheaper to refit all the PCs with wireless connections than to mess with too many odd bits and pieces.

You also need a wireless hub or switch to pick up the signals from all the PCs. Ensure that the hub has at least one RJ-45 connector for a high-speed modem or for bridging over to a wire-based hub or switch.

- ✔ Ensure that your wireless connection has at least 128-bit WEP encryption for security.

- ✔ Also get a wireless connection that adheres to at least the 802.11b standard. No matter which manufacturer makes the wireless NIC, as long as it's 802.11b-compatible, it will work.

- ✔ To connect a wireless network to a wired network, you need either a hardware *bridge* to connect the two networks or a computer equipped with a software access point, which then acts as a bridge.

Windows Networking Central

On the software side, Windows offers several locations from which you can install, monitor, control, or manipulate the network. The following sections highlight these fun and exciting locales.

The Network Connections window

Before your computer can access other resources on other computers, it must be connected to a network — either a local network or the Internet. Those connections show up in the Network Connections window. To get there, open the Network Connections icon on the Control Panel.

The Network Connections window is shown in Figure 18-2. In the figure, you see categories for two types of connections. The first are dial-up connections, used to connect to the Internet through a dial-up modem. The second is a Local Area Network (LAN) connection, through which the computer connects to communicate with other computers.

✔ Yes, you can have more than one dial-up connection to the Internet. I have a backup for when my main ISP goes offline.

✔ Note the Network Tasks pane. Two tasks are there: one to create a new connection and another to set up a home network. Both choices run wizards that walk you through the setup process.

✔ Also note the helpful Network Troubleshooter in the See Also pane.

A networking connection's Properties dialog box

Like most icons in Windows, each networking connection in the Network Connections window has its own Properties dialog box. You can use this dialog box to review or change the networking settings — advanced stuff, but it's something you may need to do because networks live to be messed with.

To see a Properties dialog box, right-click an icon in the Network Connections window. Choose Properties from the pop-up menu. The General (or Networking) tab of the Properties dialog box is shown in Figure 18-3. That's where networking options are set and controlled.

In Figure 18-3, you can see that the Local Area Network (LAN) talks to the PC through a 3Com Ethernet NIC. The network connection uses three components, listed in the middle of the dialog box. Look, but don't touch!

In fact, that's about as far down this rabbit hole as you need to go; any additional information here should be supplied specifically by the instructions you received to set up your network.

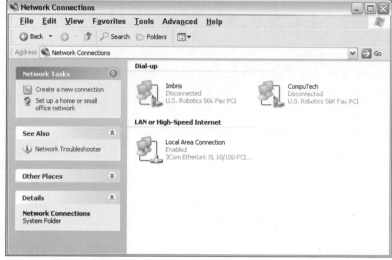

Figure 18-2: The Network Connections window.

My Network Places

The My Network Places icon on the desktop allows you to open a window and view any shared folders that are up for grabs on the network. This folder's contents appear only after the network has been completely set up. Windows XP searches the network and finds any folders marked for sharing. It then lists all those folders in the My Network Places window, as shown in Figure 18-4.

Figure 18-3: A connection's Properties dialog box.

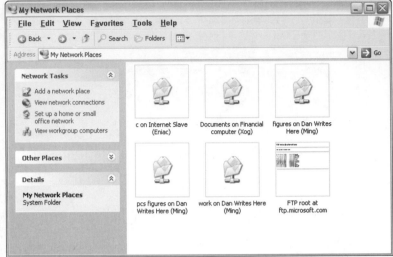

Figure 18-4:
The My
Network
Places
window.

In Figure 18-4, you see five folders available for sharing from other computers. The folders have three names: the folder name, the computer description, and the computer name in parentheses. So c on Internet Slave (Eniac) is the folder named C (actually, drive C) on the computer named Eniac, which is given the nickname Internet Slave.

Also note that an FTP location on the Internet has been saved in the My Network Places folder. In Figure 18-4, the FTP site at Microsoft has been copied into the folder. This is a weird and tangential thing I did, which has no bearing whatsoever on networking.

✔ The shared folders listed in the My Network Places window are *not* mapped to your hard drive. They are merely available on the network. To map a folder to a disk drive letter on your own PC, refer to the section "Mapping in a network drive," later in this chapter.

✔ Don't worry about adding folders to the My Network Places window; it's done automatically every time you turn on the PC. That's one of the advantages of using Windows XP.

✔ You can open the icons in the My Network Places folder. Opening an icon for a folder causes Windows to access the network and then report back the contents of that folder. But on your computer, you see the folder's contents displayed just as though it were a folder on your own computer.

✔ Just as shared folders on the network automatically show up in the My Network Places window, printers shared on the network automatically appear in the Printers folder. (Refer to Chapter 15.)

✔ The View Network Connections item in the Network Tasks panel opens up the Network Connections window; refer to the preceding section.

- ✔ The My Network Places folder is named the Network Neighborhood in other versions of Windows. Both terms refer to the same thing.

- ✔ You can change the view in the Network Neighborhood window just as you can in any Windows Explorer window: Choose a new view from the View menu. Figure 18-4 shows Thumbnails view.

Looking at your workgroup

The My Network Places window shows you only which folders have been shared (or are "up for grabs") on the network. To see all computers available or attached to the network, you need to visit the Workgroup window. Follow these steps:

1. **Open the My Network Places icon on the desktop.**

2. **Choose the View workgroup computers item from the list of network tasks.**

The workgroup appears in the window, such as the Cat workgroup shown in Figure 18-5. You see the three computers that happened to be connected in my office's Local Area Network: Eniac, Ming, and Vishnu. (Xog is hibernating, so that computer — like any other computer not turned on — doesn't show up in the window.)

If you open a computer's icon, you see a list of folders and printers on that particular computer, resources available for sharing.

Opening the computer Ming that's shown earlier, in Figure 18-5, displays the three folders and printer it's sharing, as shown in Figure 18-6.

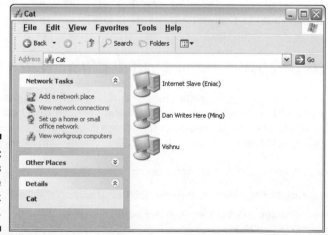

Figure 18-5: Computers in the network workgroup.

Figure 18-6:
Folders and
printers
shared on
a network
computer.

✔ See the following section for more information on giving your network
computer a name.

✔ A *workgroup* is a collection of computers, such as the Cat group shown
earlier, in Figure 18-5. Networks can be divided into workgroups to help
organize situations with many, many computers. For small offices and
the home, this type of workgroup organization isn't necessary, but you
still need to create a single workgroup for your computers.

✔ Note that the pathname to a network computer begins with two backslashes, followed by the computer's name. In Figure 18-6, the pathname
for the network computer named Ming is \\Ming. A file on that computer has the network pathname \\Ming\Work\proposal.pdf, where
Work is the name of a folder shared on that computer and proposal.pdf
is a filename. Refer to Chapter 5 for more information on pathnames.

Your computer's name and workgroup

To see, set, or change your computer's name and to which workgroup it
belongs, you must visit *another* place in Windows. (The section heading
"Windows Networking Central, earlier in this chapter, is a joke.) This time,
you need to visit the System Properties dialog box. Follow these steps:

1. **Right-click the My Computer icon on the desktop.**

2. **Choose Properties from the pop-up menu.**

    This step displays the System Properties dialog box.

3. **Click the Computer Name tab.**

   Here, you can set the three names for your networked computer: the computer name, description, and name of the workgroup.

4. **Type a description for your computer in the Computer description text box.**

   For example, the computer named Ming, as shown earlier, in Figure 18-5, is given the description Dan Writes Here. Eniac is called Internet Slave. The computer Vishnu lacks a name (in that figure).

5. **To change the computer name, click the Change button.**

   The Computer Name Changes dialog box appears.

6. **Enter a new computer name.**

   Note that changing your PC's name disrupts the paths and connections for other computers on the network that are accessing files or printers on your PC. If you rename, go around to each other computer and check or reset the connections.

7. **Enter a new workgroup name.**

   I use single names, all caps. The name must be the same in order for all computers in a workgroup to see each other. Changing this name also affects other computers on the network that are connected to your PC.

8. **Click OK to set the new names in the Computer Name Changes dialog box.**

9. **Click OK to close the System Properties dialog box.**

For a small network, names are just for show. Even so, it helps to know which computer you're dealing with on a network. That's why I gave my computer's names rather than silly numbers or cryptic things only I would understand.

- ✔ The computer's network name cannot be the same as another computer on the network.
- ✔ Do not bother messing with multiple workgroup names if you're networking PCs only in your house or small office. Trust me — it's too much of a hassle.

Doing Net Things

Here's a list of fun things you can do on a PC network. Keep in mind the basic network mantra as you review these sections: "Networking is about sharing."

Logging in to the network

Windows XP forces you to log in. Because of this, you have no further need for identification in order to use the network; you log in to the network when you log in to Windows.

However, I recommend that you password-protect your account — even if you're the only one using the computer. Individual password-protected accounts become even more vital when your computer is networked.

Sharing a folder on the network

If you want others on the network to have access to a folder on your computer, you *share* the folder. This makes the folder — and its contents (all files and subfolders) — available to all other computers on the network. Here's how to share a folder:

1. **Select the folder you want to share.**

   Click the folder's icon once to select it.

2. **Choose File➪Sharing and Security.**

   The folder's Properties dialog box Sharing tab appears, similar to what you see in Figure 18-7.

3. **Click to put a check mark by the option labeled Share This Folder on the Network.**

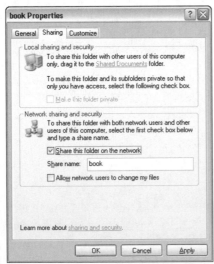

Figure 18-7:
A disk drive's Properties dialog box.

4. **Optionally, click the item Allow network users to change my files.**

   Checking this item allows full access to the folder and its files. If you don't check this item, the folder appears as Read-Only to the other users on the network.

5. **Optionally, change the share name.**

   The share name is the same as the folder's name, but remember that it can be vague; I have many folders named book on my computer. In this case (refer to Figure 18-7), I would change the share name from book to the specific name of the book its contents represent.

6. **Click OK.**

   The folder is now shared.

 Icons for shared folders appear with the graphical "sharing hand" beneath them, as shown in the margin. On other computers on the network, the shared folder appears in the My Network Places dialog box or can be seen by opening your computer's icon inside the workbook folder.

- ✔ Do not share an entire disk drive. This is a security risk; Windows warns you if you try to do so.

- ✔ If you're unable to share a folder, it may be protected. You see a check mark by the option Make this folder private in the folder's Properties dialog box (refer to Figure 18-7). Remove that check mark to share the folder.

- ✔ If you cannot remove the Make This Folder Private check mark (it's dimmed), check the parent folder's Properties dialog box, and so on and so on, until you find the main folder that was originally marked as private. Removing that private status allows the subfolder(s) to be shared.

- ✔ Windows XP uses the Shared Documents folder for things that really need to be shared on the network. My advice is to merely share that folder and then copy into it things you want shared on the network. To share the Shared Documents folder, open the My Computer icon on the desktop. The Shared Documents folder can be found inside.

Sharing a printer

Sharing a printer connected to your PC works just like sharing a folder:

1. **Open the Printers and Faxes folder.**

   It's inside the Control Panel.

2. **Click to highlight the printer you want to share.**

3. **Choose File⇨Sharing from the menu.**

   The printer's Properties dialog box appears, with the Sharing tab selected.

4. **Click to select the item labeled Share this printer.**

5. **Optionally, give the printer a name.**

   For example, name it Color Laser to let everyone know that you're finally sharing your darn precious color laser printer.

6. **Click the OK button.**

As with sharing a folder, the printer's icon appears with the sharing hand beneath it. In other Printers and Faxes windows all across your network, that shared printer appears, ready to roll. (Unlike in previous versions, Windows XP automatically locates shared printers and instantly installs their drivers.)

Network printers, or printers with their own networking cards, don't need to be connected directly to any PC. To access the network printer, however, you must have software installed on each computer by using the installation program that came on a CD with the printer. Unlike printers directly connected to Windows XP computers, network printers don't have the brains to announce their presence and share their drivers.

Accessing a network folder

You access a folder elsewhere on the network just as you would access any folder on your PC's disk system. The difference is that you need to browse to the folder, which takes some extra steps.

"Who was that madman using my PC?"

It's difficult to see whether anyone is using network resources on your computer. In fact, the only way you may find out is when you try to turn your PC off or restart and you see a message saying "Others are using your computer on the network; are you sure you want to shut down?" To find out who the culprits are, follow these steps:

1. **Click the Start button.**

2. **Choose Programs⇨Accessories⇨Command Prompt.**

   Yes, this is one of those things you must do at the DOS prompt.

3. **Type NETSTAT and press Enter.**

   The NETSTAT command prints a list of active network connections, listing who is using what on your computer.

4. **Look under the Foreign Address column to find the offender.**

   On my computer, it says that IP address 10.0.0.6 is using the computer. Sometimes, it may list the computer name rather than the IP address. There's your guilty party!

5. **Type EXIT and press Enter to close the DOS window.**

The key to browsing to a network folder is My Network Places. Either open that icon on the desktop or choose it from a drop-down list in a folder window or in the Open or Save As dialog boxes.

After displaying the contents of the My Network Places window, you can then choose any folder window shared on the network. Figure 18-8 shows the window's contents as seen from an Open dialog box. The folders shown there are all shared folders from other computers on the network.

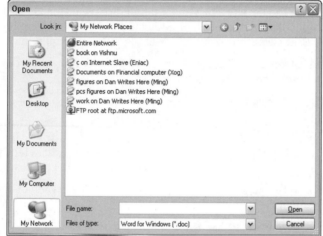

Figure 18-8:
Finding a
shared
folder.

✔ You can also get to the My Network Places window by clicking the icon on the left side of most Open or Save In dialog boxes (refer toFigure 18-8).

✔ After you open a shared folder from the My Network Places window, you see its contents just as you would in a "local" folder on your own hard drive.

Mapping in a network drive

If you find accessing a folder on another computer (as described in the preceding section) tedious, you can opt instead to *map* that folder to your local disk drive system. This choice provides easy, quick, and consistent access to the folder's contents, just as though the folder were another disk drive inside your PC.

To map a folder, follow these steps:

1. **Open the My Computer icon.**

   You can pull this trick in any folder; I chose the My Computer folder because that's where the mapped folder's drive icons show up.

2. **Choose Tools⇨Map Network Drive.**

   The Map Network Drive dialog box shows up, as depicted in Figure 18-9.

3. **Choose a drive letter for the networked drive.**

   You can give the network drive any unused drive letter. Be clever here. For example, if you mapped in a folder full of MP3 files, give it drive letter M. Otherwise, the drive letter choice doesn't really matter.

   The drive letter you assign is personal to your computer. It doesn't affect any other computer on the network.

4. **Select the network folder to map to that letter.**

   If you have recently accessed the folder, you can choose it from the Folder drop-down list. Otherwise, use the Browse button, which opens a special window to My Network Places, where you can select a network folder.

   You can also type a network pathname — if you're in Mensa and can remember a network pathname.

5. **Do you always want to use the network drive?**

   If so, put a check mark by the item labeled Reconnect at Logon. That way, Windows always maps in the folder to that specific drive letter every time you start your computer. Otherwise, the mapping is forgotten when you log out.

6. **Click the Finish button.**

   Windows opens that folder, showing you its contents.

 Back in the My Computer folder, however, you see the mapped folder as a disk drive icon, complete with plumbing (see the margin). Accessing that network folder is as easy, and the same as, using the drive letter on your own PC.

Using a network printer

Because Windows XP automatically spies and loads network printers, all you have to do to use one is choose it from the drop-down list in a Print dialog box.

Figure 18-9:
The Map
Network
Drive
dialog box.

Unsharing a folder

To remove the magical sharing properties from a folder, repeat the steps in the section "Sharing a folder on the network," earlier in this chapter. This time, however, remove the check mark to share the folder on the network. Click OK, and the folder is unshared and the sharing hand vanishes from beneath its icon.

Disconnecting a mapped network drive

To remove a mapped network drive, open the My Computer window and click to select Mr. Disk Drive With Plumbing. From the menu, choose File➪Disconnect. The drive is unmapped.

Unsharing a printer

Unsharing a printer is as simple as sharing one: Repeat the steps in the section "Sharing a printer," a little earlier in this chapter, but click to choose Do not share this printer. The little hand goes away, and the printer is all yours again!

Sharing the Internet Connection

There is no reason that only one person should hog up the only available Internet connection — especially if that connection is broadband. No, as with other resources, you should share Internet connections. It's a resource, after all, and resources are meant to be shared.

Sharing the broadband connection

Broadband modems can plug directly into your network hub, switch, or router, making the modem instantly and equally accessible to all computers on the network. The key to accessing the network is to run the New Connection Wizard (see Chapter 22) and telling it that you have a broadband or high-speed connection accessed via a Local Area Network. That's pretty much it.

Sharing a dial-up

Even though you don't get a high-speed connection, you get advantages from sharing a dial-up connection. For one, you needn't worry about dialing out on a line already used by someone else in your house. If the line is in use, the second computer simply piggybacks onto the modem through the network and accesses the Internet.

To share a dial-up connection, follow these steps on the Windows XP computer with the modem and Internet connection:

1. **Open the Network Connections window. (This step is described earlier in this chapter.)**

2. **Click to select a dial-up connection to share.**

3. **Choose File⇨Properties from the menu.**

4. **Click the Advanced tab in the connection's Properties dialog box.**

5. **Put a check mark by the option labeled Allow Other Network Users to Connect Through This Computer's Internet Connection.**

6. **Put check marks next to the two options below that one.**

   These items together allow other computers on the network to access and control the Internet connection.

7. **Click OK, and the connection is now shared.**

Other Windows computers on the network (not Windows XP systems, but, rather, earlier versions of Windows) need to configure the Internet

Connection Wizard so that they know to use another PC's modem to dial out and connect to the Internet. After that's all set up, whenever another computer tries to access the Internet, it forces the shared modem computer to dial out, make the connection, and then share the connection throughout the network.

Windows XP computers automatically sense a shared Internet connection.

Note that privacy is still enforced with a shared connection. Despite getting information into one computer through another, the first (sharing) computer cannot access or interpret the information flowing through.

To disable sharing, reverse the steps to uncheck the check box. To temporarily disable the connection, you can simply unplug the modem from the phone line.

Chapter 19

Digital Imaging

• •

• •

I believe that photography was developed because people enjoy standing still in a large group with forced smiles and because there just wasn't any other reason for it. Flash photography, for example, was invented by a Latvian scientist who wanted to prove to mankind that after you look at a sudden bright light, you see spots. And then there's that desire to control a group of people standing still with forced smiles: "Back up! A little to the left! More to the right! Sit up, Stacy! And. . . ." Nothing. "But I'm pressing the button?" So Mildred turns the camera toward her face and — poof! — *another* picture of her nose.

In the computer age, everything is digital. Although you still may have an old-fashioned *film* camera, know that you can get those analog prints into the computer's digital world by means of a scanner. But if you're with the times and you have a digital camera, no scanning is involved: Point, shoot, and beam over and soon you have that digital image of your nose up on the screen in no time.

Welcome to the digital imaging chapter.

Digital Imaging Hardware

The hardware part of doing graphics involves getting the image from out there in the real world, where things are alive and colorful and full of life, to inside the computer, where it's dark and filled with pointy electronics, most of which would electrocute you if the lid weren't screwed shut. To make a digital copy of the real world, you need a hardware device called a *scanner*.

Scanners come in two types. The first is the traditional scanner, which looks like a teensy copy machine. The second is a digital camera, which is a portable handheld scanner.

- ✔ Yes, a digital camera is really a portable handheld scanner. Internally, it contains all the electronics that a scanner has, though a lens is used to focus the image as opposed to using a reflected image, as a scanner does.

- ✔ Things inside the computer are digital. Things in the real world are *analog*.

Scan this, Mr. Spock!

Scanners are nifty little devices that work like photocopiers. Rather than copy, the scanner converts the image into a graphics image in your computer. From there, you can modify the image, save it to disk, add it to a document, or send it off as an e-mail attachment. That's the big picture.

Figure 19-1 illustrates the typical computer scanner, not because you may be unfamiliar with what it looks like, but more because I really like that illustration.

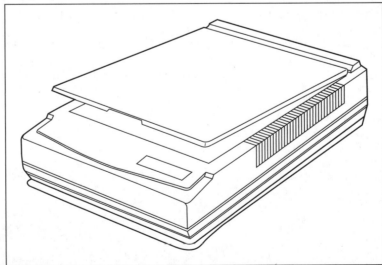

Figure 19-1:
A typical
scanner.

You should consider a few important points when getting a scanner. Here's the short list:

- ✔ How does the scanner connect to the computer? The best and fastest scanners use a Firewire connection. Most scanners, however, use the USB or printer ports.

- ✔ Scanners are judged by their *resolution,* which is measured by the number of dots per inch (dpi) the scanner can read. The higher the dpi resolution, the better the scanned image.

- ✔ Scanners come with software. You usually get three packages. The first is a utility that lets you use the scanner to scan in an image. The second is typically some type of photo-editing program, such as Adobe Photoshop Elements. The third is an OCR program, which is used to translate written documents into editable text.

- ✔ OCR stands for *o*ptical *c*haracter *r*ecognition.

- ✔ Typical scanner prices range from $100 to more than $1,000. You pay more for higher-quality scanners, but those are used mostly by graphics professionals. Also, high-priced scanners contain options such as transparency adapters (for scanning slides or negatives) and sheet feeders (for law offices or other outfits that need to scan in large quantities of text).

- ✔ If your PC has a USB port, get a USB scanner!

- ✔ Don't let anyone fool you into believing that adding a scanner can turn your PC into a photocopier. True, you can scan an image and then print that image. But the process takes more time than it would to drive to the copy store and make a few copies. (Well, maybe not that long, but scanning and printing isn't the fastest thing the PC does.)

Everyone say "megabyte!" (Digital cameras)

The latest PC craze is the digital camera. These wonderful toys not only have come down drastically in price, but the quality of the images they take is also rivaling traditional cameras.

Digital cameras range in price from you-don't-want-it cheap to well over $1,000 for professional setups. The average price for a decent digital camera is between $400 and $800. The prices do come down, but that's because this new technology is continually leaping forward. I don't expect anything to settle any time soon.

Look for three things in a digital camera: resolution, image storage, and how the image gets transferred from the camera to your computer.

Resolution: The ready gauge of a digital camera's resolution is the *MP,* or *megapixel.* For example, a 3MP camera can shoot high-quality images that can be enlarged to the photo-quality 8 x 10 inches. Higher MP values can shoot higher-resolution images that can be enlarged even more. Lower MP values, although they can take good pictures, just don't look good when enlarged.

Image storage: For "digital film," most cameras use a special storage card or memory stick capable of storing many megabytes of pictures. You can remove and replace the card — just like film — allowing the camera to take an infinite number of pictures.

Beaming the image to the computer: The most important thing to consider when selecting a digital camera is how the image is transferred from the camera into the computer. Most cameras use a special cable (such as a USB cable) that you use to send the images to the computer. Or, they may employ a device that reads the memory card, mounting it like a disk drive on your PC.

Here are some other digital camera points to ponder:

✔ Avoid any digital camera with a resolution of less than 3MP.

✔ Most cameras use LCD viewfinders, which means that you must hold them away from your face to get an image — like those camcorders that have LCD viewfinders — same thing.

✔ Beware of digital cameras with too many confusing and poorly labeled dials and buttons.

✔ I prefer using a digital camera that operates using standard batteries. That way, I can find extra batteries easily. Cameras that use special rechargeable batteries don't have such a fast turnaround time (but may save on battery cost in the long run).

✔ If your camera uses storage cards, buy more of them! The more cards you have, the more images your camera can take.

✔ The easiest way to get digital images into your computer is to buy a storage card adapter so that you can plug the storage cards directly into the PC.

Getting the Image from Out There to Inside the Computer

Scanners and digital cameras are merely methods of collecting images. The useful part is getting the images from your scanner or digital camera and into your computer, where you can edit them, save them to disk, print them, e-mail them, or whatever. Thus begins the software side of your digital imaging adventure.

Resolution and image storage

The number of images the camera can store varies depending on the image's resolution. For example, if you're taking all your images at the camera's highest resolution, the memory card may have room for only a few dozen images. But if you take pictures at the lowest resolution (good for e-mail or the Web), the storage card may read that it has room for hundreds of images.

Another way to improve image storage is to delete unwanted images. This strategy is entirely possible in any digital camera; review the images stored on the memory card and delete those you don't like.

The tedious overview of how to scan an image

A scanner can convert anything flat into a graphical image. Oh, I suppose that you could scan the cat if it would hold still long enough, but that's not the device's true design. If it's flat or can fold that way, you can scan it.

Windows doesn't have a scanning program or wizard, so you have to use whatever scanning program came with your scanner. The problem is that they all work differently, plus you need *two* programs to complete the operation: a photo-editing program and the utility that runs the scanner, or the scanning program. Here's a vague, nonspecific overview of how it works:

1. **Activate the scanner.**

   This may be an automatic step. Some scanners pop on when you raise their lids or use the scanning software. Other types must be switched on.

2. **Start your photo-editing software.**

   Most scanners come with photo-editing software, such as Adobe Photoshop Elements. In this program is where your scanned image ends up. But note that it's *not* the program that scans the image. For that, you run an image-scanning program.

3. **Place your image facedown in the scanner.**

   Most scanners scan from back to the front, and they tell you which corner is the *upper right.* Try to place your image snugly against that corner.

4. **Running the image-scanning program from within your photo-editing software.**

   The command you use varies. You may see a Scan button on the toolbar, for example. Or you may have to choose File⇨Acquire or File⇨Scan from the menu. However you get there, this program runs the special scanning utility that controls the scanner. Figure 19-2 shows this type of utility.

5. **Preview the image.**

   Use the scanning software to preview the image — if such a command is available.

6. **Make adjustments.**

   Use whatever options come with the scanning program to fix the image, if necessary. Use a cropping tool to resize the image and select color options, brightness, contrast, and other stuff, as available.

   Some scanning utilities have an Auto Adjust button. Use it to have the computer make its best guess about the settings you need.

7. **Scan the image.**

   In Figure 19-2, in Beginner mode, you click the button associated with the type of image you're scanning. For example, to scan the photograph of Jeremiah, I click the Color Photo button (the one with the lady and the stupid hat on it).

   The scanner may take a few moments to warm up or calibrate itself:

   Scan . . . scan . . . scan. . . .

   (I apologize for not having a better scanner noise to insert here.)

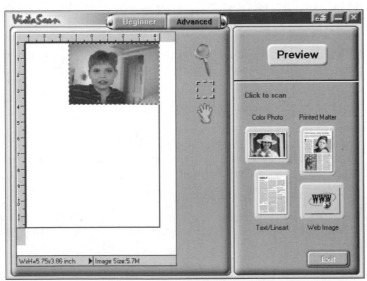

Figure 19-2:
A scanning utility.

8. **Place the image into your application.**

   Some scanner programs have an OK button. If so, click it. The scanning utility closes and you return to the photo-editing program where your image sits, ready for editing, saving, or printing.

9. **Fuss with the image.**

   Back in the photo-editing application, you're ready to edit, print, or save the image.

For more information on editing an image, see the section "Using Photo-Editing Software," at the end of this chapter.

The hardest thing about scanning an image is that you're often working with two different programs, one within another: the scanning program, which operates the scanner, and the photo-editing program, which lets you edit the images scanned into the computer.

✔ You may be able to scan several photographs at once — a gang-scan! Scan the lot and then use the photo-editing software to crop out and save each photograph. This technique takes less time than scanning each image individually.

✔ Wipe the glass clean after you try to scan your face.

✔ Special hardware is needed to scan slides or transparencies. This hardware is either a special slide-scanning device or an attachment to a traditional scanner. You cannot, unfortunately, put your slides of that Bermuda trip into a flatbed scanner and have them appear as anything other than a black rectangle.

✔ TWAIN is an acronym associated with scanning graphics. It stands for Technology Without An Important Name. No, I'm not making that up.

Getting your digital pictures inside the PC

Grabbing an image with a digital camera is another way to soak graphics into the PC. The method of delivery depends on how the camera connects with your computer. In these steps, I assume that a cable is used. Here are the steps to follow:

1. **Connect the cable to the PC and to the camera.**

2. **Set the camera to transmit pictures.**

   The camera needs to start sending pictures so that the software on the PC can recognize it.

3. **Run the picture reading utility on your PC.**

   It can be either a stand-alone program that simply grabs photos from the camera or a command inside a photo-editing program, such as the Photoshop File➪Acquire➪(Your camera) command.

4. **Choose which images to retrieve inside the computer.**

   The program may just eat all the pictures, or it may let you select which ones you want beamed over.

5. **Select a folder into which the images will be saved.**

   This step is important! Organize your prints! I create a folder and name it after the current date, such as `April 9 2004`. Or, if the pictures are from a special event, I use the event name and the date, such as `Disneyland 2004`.

   Be clever! Organize! Use folders!

6. **Send those images over.**

   Activate whichever command sends the images over, where they collect in the folder you have designated.

The next step you most likely want to take is to run a photo-editing program and tidy up the images. You may want to rotate some, resize a few, crop others, or save them in special graphics file formats for sending as e-mail attachments. That's all covered later in this chapter.

✔ The My Pictures folder is the place to start saving your digital photos. That's where you need to create your photo folders.

✔ If your PC can read the camera's storage media directly, you simply plug the media into the computer and use Windows Explorer to copy the images from the camera's media to a suitable place on the hard drive. Cinchy.

✔ After beaming the images into your computer is a good time to erase them from the camera. You're not losing the images because a copy is kept on the computer's hard drive.

✔ Despite the existence of the My Pictures folder, also consider saving images on Zip disks or, over time, stocking the images on a CD-R disk. Remember that graphics images take up acres of disk space. A few rounds with the digital camera, or an event like a wedding or graduation, may fill up your hard drive quicker that you would expect.

Printing your pictures with the Photo Printing Wizard

As long as you have saved your images in a folder within the My Pictures folder, you can easily take advantage of the Photo Printing Wizard in Windows XP to quickly print all your precious digital moments. Here's the scoop:

1. **Get your printer ready to print.**

   There's no need to stock it with high-quality photo paper; just regular inkjet-quality paper does the trick. Consider this "rough draft" printing.

2. **Open the folder containing your digital images.**

3. **Under the Picture Tasks item on the left side of the window, choose Print pictures.**

   This step runs the Photo Printing Wizard for the files in that folder.

4. **Click the Next button.**

5. **Place check marks by the pictures you want to print and then click the Next button.**

6. **Choose the printer to use and then click the Next button.**

7. **Select a layout and picture size option.**

   Figure 19-3 shows a 3½ x 5 picture size selected, along with a print preview. Note that you can also adjust how many copies of each picture to print in the same dialog box.

8. **Click the Next button.**

   The files are printed.

9. **Click the Finish button.**

One of my favorite layout selections is the contact sheet. It allows me to print many tiny images on a single sheet of paper. I can show that to people and then let them pick which images they want. That way, I can print those images individually later, and on higher-quality paper.

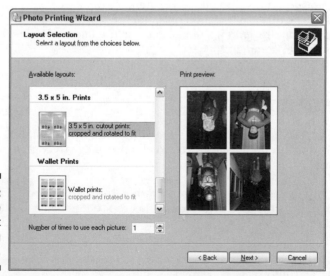

Figure 19-3:
Setting the page layout for printing pictures.

To use the Print pictures command, you must customize a folder. Specifically, you must tell Windows that the folder contains primarily pictures. To do this, right-click in the folder window and choose Properties from the pop-up menu. In the folder's Properties dialog box, click the Customize tab. From the template drop-down list, choose either Pictures or Photo Album, depending on the number of pictures in the folder. Then click OK.

Using Photo-Editing Software

The key to making your photos look good is using photo-editing software. Most scanners and digital cameras come with easy-to-use photo-editing software, such as Adobe Photoshop Elements, which lets you modify or edit the image you have just created.

Entire books have been written about photo-editing software, and I encourage you to check them out if it's something you're into. Otherwise, you probably want to do only a handful of things with the image, some of which I cover in the following sections.

Rotating an image

Not everything is right side up. I often find myself turning the camera sideways to get a "portrait" shot as opposed to the standard "landscape" shot. The problem is that the computer doesn't know the difference. So, after loading the image into the photo-editing software, you must rotate it right side up.

Rotating the image simply turns it a given number of degrees in a certain direction. Because this is a common task, the rotate commands are typically on a toolbar button or right on a menu, such as the Image⇨Rotate 90º CCW (counterclockwise) command.

Cropping an image

Cropping is the same as trimming — what you would do to a photograph with a pair of scissors. Cropping allows you to clip the image to contain only the part you want.

Often, the Crop tool, similar to the one shown in the margin, is used to identify this command. Only the area selected by the crop tool remains in the picture; the rest is discarded.

✔ Note that you can crop only in straight lines with most programs; cropping is a rectangular thing.

✔ In some programs, the Crop command may be called Trim.

Resizing an image

If you're new to photo-editing software, you may assume that scanned images are *huge.* That's not the case. An image's size is measured by its horizontal and vertical resolution — 1024 x 768 pixels, for example. That image may fill your screen (especially if your monitor is set to that same resolution), but when you print it on a 600 dpi printer, the image may end up being only 4 by 6 inches. It's all this crazy resolution stuff. . . .

Fortunately, most image-editing programs have tools that let you calculate exactly how large the printed image will be. (What you have, after all, is a computer, which is good at these things.)

For example, Figure 19-4 shows a Photo Size dialog box, which is used to set an image's size. Note that the image is scanned at 4 x 3-something inches; that's a whopping amount of pixels — 3.96MB, according to the figure.

To change the image size, enter new values in the dialog box. The value can be in inches, centimeters, or pixels. Use inches for the stuff you plan on printing. For Web page and e-mail images, use pixels.

Figure 19-4:
The resizing
dialog box
in Photo-
Deluxe.

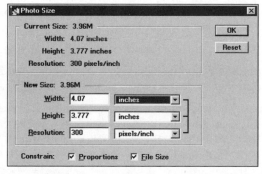

Viewing a huge image

Note the difference between the size of the image on the screen and what is printed — as described in the preceding section. While you're working on the image in your photo-editing program, however, use the Zoom command to adjust its size. The Zoom command is often found on a View menu, though I have seen it also on the Window menu.

You can make the image on the screen larger or the same size or zoom in tight for photo editing, all by using the Zoom command.

Saving an image in a specific format

The one required chore for your scanned image, edited or not, is to save it to disk.

If you choose just to use the Save command — watch out! Most photo-editing programs use their own formats for the images. This strategy is fine if you plan to use that program to edit the image later, but it's not okay for sending the image via e-mail or putting into a word processing document. No, you should select a file format best suited to what you're doing with the image. Here are my suggestions:

- ✔ The best format for sending photographs through e-mail, or saving photos to a Web page, is the JPEG file format.

- ✔ If the image is of artwork, such as an illustration, a kid's drawing, a signature, or anything that isn't a photograph, use the GIF format. GIF images can also be e-mailed or posted to a Web page.

- ✔ For e-mail or the Web, size the image so that the longest edge is between 300 and 400 pixels. Anything larger and the picture is too big and takes too long to send.

- ✔ If you're going to place the image into another program, such as a desktop publishing program, word processor, or other application, save the file as a TIFF image. This format uses a huge amount of disk space, so although it stores the image well, it's impractical for sending via e-mail.

- ✔ For TIFF files, size doesn't matter; make them as large as they need to be.

- ✔ TIFF is the most common graphics file format for images used in documents, spreadsheets, and other professional applications.

- ✔ If you're going to use the image as Windows wallpaper, save the image as a bitmap file, or BMP. That's about the only time you want to mess with bitmap files. (See the nearby sidebar, "Making wallpaper images," for more information about wallpaper.)

To save in these formats, use the proper command, such as File⇨Save As, File⇨Export, or even File⇨Send To.

If you use the Save As command, select the proper file type from the Type drop-down list. (Refer to Chapter 5 for more information on the Save As command.) The Export or Send To commands may also list the file types available for saving the images. Select the proper file type for your image.

TIP

Making wallpaper images

If you're saving the image to be used as your Windows desktop wallpaper, save it to disk as a BMP image in the Windows folder. (Yes, this is one of those rare times when it's okay to save a file in the Windows folder.)

Try to set the image's size to the same size as your desktop. To get the desktop's size, right-

click the desktop and choose Properties from the shortcut menu. On the Settings tab in the Display Properties dialog box, note the size of the Screen area. Resize your image to those exact dimensions.

Refer to Chapter 12 for more information on setting wallpaper.

If you quit after exporting, the program may warn you that the image isn't saved. That's okay! The program means that the image isn't saved in its own, native format. You're not required to do that if the image was saved in another format (and I wish that the program would wake up and realize that, but I'm only a small voice in the wilderness).

Chapter 20

Even More PC Hardware (Peripherals)

· ·

· ·

*O*ne of the things that makes a computer such an interesting device — and endless hobby — is that unlike any other gizmo, the computer can be expanded in an infinite number of directions. Thanks to your PC's expansion slots and the flexibility of its USB port, you can add a virtually endless parade of extra hardware goodies. They all fall under the category of peripherals. And the variety and excitement over peripherals is enough to floor you — if not vacate your entire savings account.

The Wide, Wide World of Peripherals

Peripheral refers to anything outside the main. For example, the *peripheral nervous system* is made up of all the nerves in your body outside your brain (which is called the *central nervous system*). *Peripheral vision* includes things you can see without looking directly at them. And *peripheral nervous vision* is what first-time buyers get when they enter the computer store. On a computer, however, a *peripheral* is any accessory or auxiliary equipment you may buy and connect to the computer.

The variety of peripherals you can buy for your computer is endless. Common peripheral items include scanners, disk drives of all types, digital cameras, videocameras, and numerous other toys you can connect to the typical PC.

- ✔ All peripherals are hardware.

- ✔ Many devices that were once considered peripheral are now considered part of the basic computer system: the mouse and modem, for example, were once optional peripherals.

- ✔ Peripherals enable you to expand your computer system without having to buy a totally new computer. You can add these extra hardware devices yourself or have a guru, computer consultant, or some other overpaid individual do it for you.

- ✔ Although the word *peripheral* refers to things outside a computer, you can also add peripherals *internally* — inside the PC's console. (In a way, peripheral refers to anything beyond what comes standard in the computer.)

Installing a peripheral

The hardware side of adding a peripheral is cinchy. Most peripherals sit outside the PC. All you need to do to connect them is find the proper hole and plug the thing in.

Granted, you need to follow other instructions when adding a peripheral, but plugging the thing into the proper port is usually part of the action.

Because peripherals can also live inside the PC, installing one may involve opening the console and plugging in an expansion card. Again, this process isn't that tough, but it's not the sign of a PC wimp if you pay someone else to do it.

- ✔ Most peripherals plug into standard connectors on the back of every PC. Refer to Chapter 9.

- ✔ Whenever you install hardware inside your PC, you should first turn off the computer. Refer to Chapter 2 for the official turning-off instructions.

- ✔ USB and Firewire peripherals are the easiest by far to install. You don't even need to turn off your PC; just plug in the cable and you're on your way.

- ✔ Sometimes, you must install the peripheral's software *before* you install the peripheral; at other times, the software must be installed afterward. Refer to the manual for the proper sequence of events.

Telling Windows about your new hardware

After the hardware is attached, Windows detects it and adds the device to the Windows secret internal list of hardware. If not, you must manually add the device yourself. Again, the device's manual tells you whether Windows can recognize it.

For example, Windows may not recognize some modems. To finish modem installation, you need to open the Phone and Modem Options icon in the Control Panel and click the Add button to add your modem. Ditto for joysticks: Open the Game Controllers icon in the Control Panel and click the Add button to manually add your joystick.

- ✔ The Windows capability to instantly recognize new peripherals is known as *plug and play:* When you restart your computer after installation, Windows instantly recognizes the new hardware (unless it's a USB or Firewire peripheral, in which case you don't have to turn the PC off in the first place).

- ✔ The software that controls your hardware is a *driver.* When someone says "Windows needs a new driver," he's not insulting you as the computer operator.

- ✔ Plug and play isn't foolproof. For that reason, many people in the industry have dubbed it "plug and pray."

"Windows is stupid and doesn't recognize my new peripheral!"

In some rare cases, Windows may not recognize your new hardware. The problem could be that the hardware isn't plug-and-play compatible, or you could be installing something that doesn't grab the computer's attention directly, such as a modem or joystick.

 When Windows refuses to recognize the new hardware, you should run the Add Hardware Wizard. Open the Control Panel and then double-click the Add Hardware icon to run the wizard.

Follow the steps to load the driver. Read the screen. Click the Next button or select options as necessary. In mere moments, your new hardware should be up and running, and everything is groovy.

The Big Decision point in the Add Hardware Wizard is whether to let Windows look for the new hardware or select it yourself from a list. Sometimes, it's tempting to taunt Windows: "Go ahead! Find that hardware! I dare you to find it! I double-dog dare you!" At other times, plucking the device from a list on your own is easier and quicker.

Some Popular Peripherals

This chapter gets shorter and shorter with each edition of this book. In this book's first edition (1992), modems and CD-ROM drives were considered peripherals. The most popular PC peripheral is now a scanner, though it became so popular that I put it in Chapter 19, along with digital cameras. So that leaves the most popular peripherals as external disk drives (Zip disks and CD-R/RW drives) and videocameras.

External disk drives

You can easily expand your system's storage: Just plug in another disk drive! Adding a CD-R, CD-RW, hard drive, DVD, Zip disk, or multiple combinations of each one is a snap.

The best way to add external storage is via the USB port. (If your PC lacks a USB port, buy a USB expansion card for $20 and you're in business!) With the USB port, you can add as many external storage devices as your VISA card can afford.

The second-best way to add external storage is to use the PC's printer port. Unfortunately, that method allows you to add only one device, so if the printer port is already used for a scanner or some device, you cannot daisy-chain another device.

- External disk drives work better with the USB 2.0 standard. Ensure that your PC has USB 2.0 installed (checking your invoice is the easiest way). If not, don't purchase USB 2.0 peripherals.

- Firewire peripherals are better than USB, though not every type of external storage device comes with a Firewire interface.

- If you have Firewire, buy Firewire devices!

- One major bonus for external storage devices is that they can survive your current computer setup. For example, my external Firewire hard drive may outlive my current computer and end up plugged in to next year's model. That way, I don't have to copy over my software; instead, I just plug in the Firewire drive.

It's live, and it's living on top of your monitor!

An interesting toy to add to your PC is a videocamera. These little mechanical eyeballs perch near your PC, usually on top of the monitor. You can use them to record movies or single images or to send live images over the Internet — it all depends on the software that comes with the camera.

- ✔ If you want one of those cameras that sends pictures to the Web, what you want is a *Webcam*. I have such a device in my office (it's a *wireless* Webcam), which you can view by visiting `www.wambooli.com/fun/live/`.

- ✔ Note that a difference exists between a cheap little monitor-top video-camera and a digital videocamera used to create movies. I'm not sure what the technical differences are, but pricewise, one is about $50 and the other is about $2,000 (and up).

- ✔ Make sure that the software you need is included with the camera. For example, videoconferencing is possible only with the proper software. The camera is just a device; you need software to play with it.

"I Have Some Money, and I Want to Upgrade My Hardware"

Most people don't trade in their cars each year. TVs, VCRs, blenders, and clock radios usually stay put until they break, and then you buy a new one. It's the Bic lighter theory: Why repair something that's cheap when you can just buy a new one? The same thing applies to most pets. For example, why incur a $35 vet bill on a $1.59 mouse? Toss it out and buy the kid a new one! But I digress. . . .

The computer world, bizarre and different as we know it, offers monthly — if not weekly — updates and upgrades. It's technology! Something new and better is available! And you still have $1,500 of credit on your MasterCard!

What to buy first

Instead of buying a new computer, upgrading the old one may be cheaper. Or, rather, have somebody else upgrade your old computer for you. But where do you spend your money first? Too many enticing things can get in the way of a sane decision. Let me help.

Memory: Your first upgrading priority should be memory. It's not that expensive, and installation isn't a major headache. Just about all your software enjoys having more memory available.

- ✔ Increased memory can make these programs work faster and handle larger chunks of information. It also lets the computer handle more graphics and sound.

- ✔ More memory is the best thing you can buy for your PC.

- ✔ For more information about memory stuff, read Chapter 11.

Hard drive: Buy a second hard drive. Make it a big one. Most PCs can handle two hard drives internally (and dozens externally). And, by the time you need another one, you know exactly how many more gigabytes of storage you need.

- ✔ The best way to add hard drives is via the Firewire (preferred) or USB port. You can add dozens of hard drives to your computer this way.

- ✔ Be sure to plug any external hard drives into a UPS. Otherwise, the computer may not be able to save your documents if the power goes out. (Refer to Chapter 2 for more information about a UPS.)

- ✔ By the way, larger hard drives don't take up any extra room in the computer's case, so don't worry about needing a bigger case.

Microprocessor: Upgrading the microprocessor is something I don't recommend. Generally speaking, it's just better to buy a whole new computer. That way, you get *all* new components at a cost cheaper than buying a new PC one bit at a time.

My opinion is that you're better off adding more memory to your system or installing a bigger hard drive. These two upgrades give you instant results, whereas a faster microprocessor may or may not be noticeable right away. Of course, this is my opinion, and if you're dead-set on making an upgrade, go for it.

When to buy a new computer

Plan on it: Every four or five years, replace your PC. By then, the cost of a new system is cheaper than any upgrading you do.

Do it yourself? Don't forget to ground yourself!

If you elect to upgrade your own PC, *be careful.* Ensure that you not only turn it off but also unplug it. That's because you can easily turn the PC on again accidentally while you're working inside it. If your computer is unplugged, the odds of that happening drop considerably.

Also, make sure that you don't accumulate a static charge while you're working inside the PC. You can maintain equal potential by always touching the PC's case as you work on it. Or, you can invest in an antistatic wrist strap. One end of the wrist strap attaches to your wrist (obviously), and the other either clips onto the PC's case or plugs directly into the grounding socket on the power receptacle on the wall. Scary, but it works.

Your PC is essentially out-of-date the moment you purchase it. Somewhere right now in Silicon Valley, they're devising new microprocessors and better motherboards that will cost less money. It may not happen the *minute* you purchase your PC, but sooner or later your leading-edge technology will be yesterday's kitty-litter box.

Do you really need to buy a new computer? Maybe not. Look at the reasons you bought it in the first place. Can the computer still handle those needs? If so, you're doing fine. Upgrade only when you desperately need to. There's no sense in spending more money on the monster.

- Computer technology grows faster than mold in an Alabama hot tub. But, unless your computing needs have changed drastically, your computer can still handle the tasks you bought it for.

- Compare the price of a new computer with the amount of time you will save at a faster processing speed. If you spend lots of time waiting for your computer to catch up with you, an upgrade may be in order.

- Avoid the lure and seduction of those computer magazines that urge you to "Buy! Buy! Buy!" the latest PC. Remember who most of their advertisers are.

Chapter 21

Using Software

*W*hen you use your computer, you're really using software. Even something as hardware-like as ejecting a disk is really software in action. You tell the software to eject the disk and the disk drive hardware obeys the software and (hopefully) ejects the disk. Yea, verily, software hath the power.

There's no need for this book to go into gross detail on how all your computer's software works. I consider *PCs For Dummies* to be a hardware book, for the most part. So I have distilled the essence of software into the most necessary nuggets. The first of them is the chore of installing and updating software, which is something you may not do often but typically leads to trouble.

A Few Words on Buying Software

"Software? Son, you in the wrong place! This here is Big Earl's Ace Hardware Store, and I should know 'cause I am Big Earl. We ain't got no E-Z-Calc here. We have caulk. We got paint. We got power tools — things men 'ud use. Or would you know anything 'bout that? Nope. Didn't think so. Yup. You in the wrong place, son."

Buying software is part of the computer buying process. If you heed my advice in *Buying a Computer For Dummies* (Wiley Publishing, Inc.), you know to pick out your software *first* and then the hardware to match. Even so, you probably don't buy all your software at once. No, eventually you wander into the computer store (not the hardware store) and sift through the selection. When you do, keep these things in mind:

- ✔ If you're utterly unfamiliar with something, try to get recommendations from friends on which programs to use. For example, if you want to get into genealogy, hound someone who's already into genealogy about what they use.

- ✔ Try before you buy software. If the store doesn't let you, find a store that does. They're out there!

- ✔ Don't forget the Internet! Many great software packages are available for free or near free on the Internet. See Part IV of this book for more information on searching for software on the Internet as well as how to get or download software. Also, see the nearby sidebar "Software for (almost) free."

- ✔ Always check out a store's return policy on software. If the store doesn't let you return opened software, it's basically saying that you cannot return the software at all. Watch out for that.

- ✔ Check the software's requirements. They should match your computer's hardware inventory. For example, you don't want to buy the DVD version of a program when your PC has only a CD-ROM drive.

What's That Stuff in the Box?

Surprisingly, many large software boxes contain air or cardboard padding to make the boxes look bigger and more impressive in the stores. I suppose that the idea is to literally push the competition off the shelves — or to justify paying $279 for what ends up being a CD and a pamphlet.

The most vital items inside the software box are the discs. Nearly all software comes on one (or more — many more!) CDs. Some stuff still does come on floppy disks, however. And you occasionally see a DVD disc, especially in packages with multiple CDs.

After you find the disks, you may find one or more of the following items:

The Hideous Manual: Most programs toss in a printed manual, typically the size of a political pamphlet and about as interesting. More than one manual may be included. Look first for the "Getting Started," "Installation," or "Setup" section of the manual. (Gone are the days of finding a thick manual, and never were the days of finding a useful manual.)

Registration card: If you decline to register the product over the Internet, you can fill out the postcard-size registration card. Filling in the blanks and mailing it back supposedly entitles you to special goodies, though most often it just puts you on some damn junk mail list.

Software for (almost) free

Frustrated by the system, some programmers give away their programs for free. Or almost free. Or sometimes, free-with-strings-attached. Here's a breakdown of the several types of this freebie software available, each of which has its own clever name:

Public domain software: This stuff is absolutely free, written for the good of the people. No charge is ever made for the software, and you're free to do whatever you like with it.

Freeware: This software is also free for the taking, but the author retains ownership. You cannot modify the software or repackage it without permission.

Open source: This kind is also a type of freeware, though in addition to using the program, you can examine the programming code. That doesn't mean the programs are difficult — just that the programmer is making his precious code available.

Shareware: You can try this type of software for free. It may have a special startup screen begging for money, or some feature may be disabled. After you pay for the software, you get the full program.

If software is available for free, as all these categories specify, the program clearly states so. If the software doesn't state that it's public domain, freeware, open source, or shareware, it's not free.

Some companies require you to fill out the registration card before they offer technical support over the phone.

Quick reference card: The manual works fine for explaining everything in great detail, but you continually repeat some commands. A quick reference card contains those useful commands; you can prop it up next to your keyboard for quick sideways glances. Not all software comes with these cards, however.

Quick installation card: Computer users thrive on instant gratification: Push a button and watch your work be performed instantly. Nobody wants to bother with slow, thick manuals, especially when installing software. A quick installation card contains an abbreviated version of the manual's installation instructions. By typing the commands that are on the card, you can install the software without cracking open the manual. Victory!

License agreement: This extensive batch of fine print takes an average of 3,346 words of legalese to say four things:

- Don't give away any copies of this program to friends — make them buy their own programs.
- If you accidentally lose any data, it's not the developer's fault.

- If this software doesn't work, it's not the developer's fault, either.

- In fact, you don't even own this software. You merely own a license to use the software. We own the software. We are evil. We will one day own the world. Ha-ha!

Read me first: When the company finds a mistake in its newly printed manual, it doesn't fix it and print a new manual. It prints the corrections on a piece of paper and slaps the headline "Read Me First!" across the top. Staple that piece of paper to the inside cover of your manual for safekeeping.

Unsolicited junk: Finally, some software comes with company catalogs and *free* offers from related companies for their stuff. You can toss all this stuff out.

The days of getting all this stuff with your software are numbered. Most of these items are now included electronically on the disk. For example, you're taunted with the license agreement, which you must click the Yes button to agree to or else you cannot use the software. So much for modern conveniences.

Never toss out the CD-ROMs or floppy disks! And, by all means, keep any CD keys or product activation codes. I keep everything in the original boxes, especially after installation, which makes finding the disks easy in case I ever need them again.

Rating the games

Nothing can be as disappointing as buying what you think is a nice, engaging computer game for your 9-year old, only to find him frothing at the mouth as he controls a character on the screen who's ripping the spine from his electronic opponent. To prevent such shock (to the parent, not to the electronic opponent, who really doesn't feel a thing), two rating systems have evolved to allow parents or any PC game buyer to know what to expect before buying anything.

The Entertainment Software Review Board (ESRB) uses a 5-level scale, similar to movie ratings, for its games (I would show you the graphics, but they're trademarked and I'm too lazy to get permission):

- **EC (Early Childhood):** Designed for young children and would probably bore a teenager to tears

- **E (Everyone):** A G-rated game for kids to adults

- **T (Teen):** Contains some violence and language, but nothing too offensive

- **M (Mature):** For mature audiences only, preferably 17 years old or older — the type of game the teenager *wants*

- **AO (Adults Only):** Contains strong sexual content or gross violence

You can get more information from the ESRB Web site, at www.esrb.org/.

Software Installation Chores

Anyone who has owned a computer for more than a month has had to install some new software. It's a chore we all have to put up with. I'm assuming that you have already experienced the ecstasy of ripping off the shrink-wrap and the thrill of smelling the industrial plastic odor of the box's insides. Sift through the junk and get ready to start:

1. **Read the *Read Me* blurb.**

   When you first open the box, scrounge around for a piece of paper that says "Read Me First!" Follow the first instruction: Read it. Or, at least try to make some sense of it.

   Sometimes, the Read Me First sheet contains a sentence or two left out of the manual's third paragraph on page 127: "Dwobbling your shordlock by three frips." If you don't understand the sheet, don't throw it away. It may come in handy after you have started using the program.

2. **Set the manual(s) aside.**

   Say "There" when you do this.

3. **Put the installation disk into your disk drive.**

   Find the disk marked with the words *Installation* or *Setup* or *Disk 1* (or the only disk if you have just one) and place that disk in the disk drive where it fits.

4. **Start the installation program.**

   If you're lucky, the installation program runs automatically when you insert the CD into the CD-ROM drive.

   If the installation program doesn't start automatically, you need to run it yourself. You can do this by opening the Add/Remove Programs icon in the Control Panel. Use the dialog box that's displayed to help you hunt down your program.

5. **Obey the instructions on the screen.**

   Read the information carefully; sometimes, they slip something important in there. My friend Jerry (his real name) just kept clicking the Next button rather than reading the screen. He missed an important notice saying that an older version of the program would be erased. Uh-oh! Poor Jerry never got his old program back.

6. **Choose various options.**

   The software asks for your name and company name, and maybe for a serial number. Type all that stuff in.

   Don't freak if the program already knows who you are. Windows is kinda clairvoyant in that respect.

When you're asked to make a decision, the option already selected (the *default*) is typically the best option. Only if you know what's going on and *truly care* about it should you change anything.

You can find the serial number inside the manual, on the CD-ROM case, on the first disc, or on a separate card you probably threw away even though I told you to keep everything in the original box. Don't lose that number!

7. Files are copied.

Eventually, the installation program copies the files from the CD-ROM drive to your hard drive for full-time residence.

If asked, replace one CD-ROM disk with another. This process may go on for some time.

8. It's done.

The installation program ends. The computer may reset at this point. That's required sometimes when you're installing special programs that Windows needs to know about. (Windows is pretty dumb after it starts.)

Start using the program!

- The preceding steps are vague and general. Hopefully, your new software comes with more specific instructions.

- You can get software from the World Wide Web on the Internet. This process is known as *downloading,* and Chapter 26 covers it as well as installing programs after you have downloaded them.

- Keep the quick reference card next to your computer immediately after installing the program; the card is more helpful than the manual.

- Some programs require you to disable your antivirus software before installation can begin. This idea is generally a good one; antivirus software, though necessary, tends to slow down and interrupt regular computer processes more than necessary.

- If the software has a serial number, keep it! Write it down in the manual. Don't lose it! With some software, such as Adobe PageMaker, you cannot order the upgrade unless you have a proper serial number.

Uninstalling Software

To remove any newly installed program, you use an uninstall program. This program isn't a feature of Windows. Each software program comes with its own uninstall feature.

Uninstall programs are usually on the Start panel, right by the icon used to start the program.

How do I quit all other programs?

The installation program most likely asks you to quit all other running programs before installing the new program. The reason is that installation is often monitored to make uninstallation easier. Having other programs run "in the background" can disturb this process. Also, because some programs, after installation, require the computer to be reset, if you haven't yet saved your data, you're out of luck.

To make sure that no other programs are running, press the Alt+Tab key. If Windows switches you to another program, close it. If you're switched to another window, close it. Keep pressing Alt+Tab until the only program you see is the installation program. That way, you're assured that all other running programs have closed. (And there's no need to close any background applications or other processes.)

Figure 21-1 shows a submenu for the IconCool Editor program. The command to uninstall that program, Uninstall, is shown right below, on the submenu. This setup is common for most programs.

Figure 21-1:
An uninstall
program on
a submenu
on the
Start panel.

If your software lacks an obvious uninstall program, you can attempt to use Windows to rid yourself of it: Open the Control Panel's Add or Remove Programs icon. This action displays the Add or Remove Programs Properties dialog box, as shown in Figure 21-2.

The list of programs that Windows knows about and can uninstall is listed in the dialog box (refer to Figure 21-2). Click one of those programs, the one you want to uninstall, and then click the Change/Remove button. Continue reading instructions on the screen to uninstall the program.

- ✔ Do not attempt to uninstall any software by deleting it from your hard drive. You should never delete any file you did not create yourself. (You can, however, delete any shortcuts you create.)

- ✔ Some stubborn programs don't fully remove themselves. If you have tried everything, feel free to remove the program by deleting its icon or folder. Do not, however, delete any program or file installed in the Windows folder or any of its subfolders.

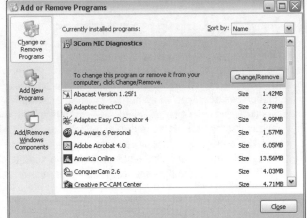

Figure 21-2:
The Add or
Remove
Programs
dialog box.

Updating Your Software

After a novel is written, it's finished. Subsequent reprints correct a few misspellings, but that's about it. Software is never finished. It's too easy to change. Most software packages are updated about once every year or two.

The reason that software is updated used to be to fix problems or to introduce new features. But, honestly, the main reason for new versions of programs appear now is to make more money for the software developer. Upgrading means that everyone who owns the software may buy a new version and generate revenue for the company. Yup, it's greed.

My advice: Order the update only if it has features or makes modifications you desperately need. Otherwise, if the current version is doing the job, don't bother.

- ✔ "Software never gets obsolete." — Bill Gates

- ✔ Consider each upgrade offer on its individual merits: Will you ever use the new features? Do you need a word processor that can print upside-down headlines and bar charts that show your word count? Can you really get any mileage out of the intranet version when you're a sole user sitting at home?

- ✔ Here's something else to keep in mind: If you're still using DoodleWriter 4.2 and everybody else is using DoodleWriter 6.1, you may have difficulty exchanging documents. After a while, newer versions of programs become incompatible with their older models. If so, you need to upgrade.

- ✔ In an office setting, everybody should be using the same software version. (Everybody doesn't have to be using the *latest* version, just the *same* version.)

What about upgrading Windows?

Upgrading Windows is a *big deal*. Why? Because everything else in your computer relies on Windows. Therefore, it's a major change, something to think long and hard about.

Often, the newer version of Windows has many more features than the older version. Do you need those features? If not, don't bother with the update.

One problem you may have if you decide to upgrade is that your software may not work properly. None of my Adobe applications worked with Windows 95 when it first came out. I had to wait months and pay lots of money for upgrades before things got back to normal.

After a time, you may notice newer software packages coming to roost on the newest version of Windows. The new stuff is better than your current stuff, so you need to upgrade if you want to take advantage of it.

Where does this leave you? *Don't bother updating Windows!* Just wait until you buy a new computer, and that PC will have the newest version of Windows, all preinstalled and set up nicely.

What about patching Windows?

Occasionally, Microsoft comes out with patches, security updates, or other fixes to Windows. It makes these fixes available automatically over the Internet, or you may opt to manually select an update by using the Windows Update program.

My advice about patching Windows is the same as upgrading: If the patch affects you directly, consider applying it. Otherwise, it isn't required. This topic can get touchy with the issue of security patches; sometimes, applying the patch can do more damage to your system than any potential security threat.

To run the Windows Update program, click the Start button and choose Programs⇨Windows Update. This command connects you to the Internet, where you can choose which updates you want to apply to your PC.

Automatic updates are handled in the System Properties dialog box: Right-click the My Computer icon on the desktop. Choose Properties from the pop-up menu and then click the Automatic Updates tab. Three update settings are available, as shown in Figure 21-3.

My preferred setting is *not* to have Windows automatically update my PC, as shown in Figure 21-3. The other two settings are self-explanatory.

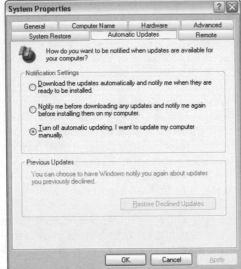

Figure 21-3:
Automatic
update
settings for
patching
Windows XP.

Having the updates downloaded automatically doesn't really consume much time. However, doing so may prevent Windows from automatically disconnecting from the Internet when you're done; in that case, what's happening is that Windows is downloading an update. It's okay to manually break the connection in that situation. (See Chapter 22 for more information on manually breaking an Internet connection.)

Part IV
The Anti-Geek Guide to the Internet

The 5th Wave   By Rich Tennant

Don't get your hopes up, Ted. The other end may not be plugged in.

In this part . . .

At first, no one really understood the Internet. There were cries that it was going to take over all media, that TV viewership would plummet, that no one would ever subscribe to a magazine again, that newspapers would fail — and that was back in 1995. Rather than consume some other portion of the infotainment pie, the Internet has merely made the pie larger and given everyone more choices over how to receive information. Its presence is accepted and welcome. Some folks have even come to accept that the world will not be taken over and human existence dominated by the Internet. (That job is still up to the domesticated robots of 2040.)

I'm happy that the Internet has become such a popular thing. For one, it has made this part of the book easier to explain. When two grandmas can get together over lunch and exchange e-mail addresses, I know that the Internet has finally become something necessary and easy to use.

Chapter 22

Hello, Internet!

- -

- -

*I*t's information! It's communications! It's entertainment! It's shopping! It's research! It's the future! It's a colossal waste of time!

Yes, it's the Internet, and it's practically indescribable. What began as a method for scientists and researchers to exchange information from remote locations has grown into a way for teenage girls to exchange information right next door. Truly, the Internet is one of the most exciting phenomena in human history.

This chapter provides an introduction to the one computer concept that most likely doesn't need an introduction: the Internet. Even if you think that you already know everything, consider giving this chapter a skim. The Internet is ever changing, and there's always a chance that you may learn something new.

What Is the Internet?

The *Internet* is composed of hundreds of thousands of computers all over the world. The computers send information. They receive information. And, most important, they store information. That's the Internet.

Some common misconceptions about the Internet

The Internet is a piece of software or program you buy. Although you use software to access the Internet and you need software to send or retrieve information from the Internet, the Internet itself isn't a software program.

The Internet is a single computer. The Internet consists of all the computers connected to the Internet. Whenever your computer is "on" the Internet, it's part of the Internet.

Bill Gates (or some big corporation) owns the Internet. The Internet began as a military project run by the government. Large corporations and communications companies now supply most of the resources for the Internet. No one person can own the Internet, just as no one person can own the oceans.

The Internet can be turned off. Although your connection to the Internet may "go down" and parts of the Internet do occasionally fail, because of its decentralized organization the Internet can never be turned off or cease to exist. After all, the military originally designed the Internet to survive a nuclear war. It's not going down.

Getting information from the Internet

The information on the Internet is next to useless unless you can access it. So, the whole idea behind getting on the Internet is to access all that information and take advantage of the Internet's communications abilities.

- ✔ The best way to get at the information stored on the Internet is by using a piece of software called a *Web browser*. I cover browsers in the next two chapters.

- ✔ Information is also exchanged via e-mail, which people use more than they use the Web. (Believe it or not, e-mail is number one, and using the Web is a distant second.)

- ✔ Chapter 25 covers e-mail. Chapter 26 does as well. E-mail is a big topic.

How to Get on the Internet

Getting on the Internet is no ordeal. Yet, like many rites of initiation, it takes some time and organization. The good news is that it's tough only the first time. After that, all this stuff is a snap. The bad news is, of course, that it *is* tough the first time.

Five things you need in order to get on the Internet

You need five things to access the Internet, four of which you probably have and one of which you have to go out and get:

- ✔ **A computer**
- ✔ **A modem**

  Rare is the PC without a modem. If yours is one of the rare ones, mull over your modem options, as covered in Chapter 16.

  Note that high-speed modems are available through your ISP (see the last item on this list); don't buy a broadband modem until you have discussed this type of service with your ISP.

- ✔ **Internet software**

  Windows comes with nearly all the software you need.

- ✔ **Money**

  This item is perhaps the toughest thing to come by. Access to the Internet costs money: You subscribe to it, just like with cable TV. Expect to pay anywhere from $5 to more than $100 a month to get on the Internet, depending on which type of service you get. The average cost is less than $20 a month.

- ✔ **An Internet Service Provider, or ISP**

  This item is the thing you need to go out and get. Like the cable company, the *ISP* is the outfit that provides you with Internet access. Obtaining an ISP is a big deal, so it's covered in the next section.

In some situations, you may not need any of these things. For example, if you work for a large company, it may already give you Internet access through the network at your office. Ditto for universities and some government installations. And you can always find free Internet access at a community library near you.

- ✔ Though I hate using acronyms, ISP is becoming popular enough that I feel I must. Not only is it easier to type, but many people also now say "ISP" and don't even know that it stands for Internet Service Provider.

- ✔ Though no one owns the Internet, an ISP is necessary in order to provide access to it. Sure, they could give away access, but that makes for a bad business plan.

- ✔ Though the Internet isn't a program, you need special software to access the Internet and to send or retrieve information.

What to look for in an ISP

Internet Service Providers (ISP) come in sizes large and small, vast and local, big business and mom-'n'-pop. For nearly all Internet users, the ISP is the outfit that provides the direct connection to the Internet.

The most important thing about an ISP is its *S*. The *S* stands for *service*. For the money you pay, the ISP must provide you with service, which includes at least the following items:

- ✔ **Internet access:** Access is the most basic item.

- ✔ **Modem access:** For dial-up modems, the ISP provides a local phone number to dial. For broadband, the ISP provides the modem and the service to install and supports the connection.

- ✔ **An e-mail account:** That's where you pick up your Internet e-mail. Some ISPs offer multiple accounts or mailboxes. Check into family or office plans: Every person needs an e-mail account. Get the login names and passwords too.

- ✔ **Help!** Use a *Getting Started* booklet, classes, special software, or other information to ease you onto the information superhighway. Don't forget a toll-free, 24-hour help line. It's a key element, especially for beginners.

I rave about ISPs that offer those *Getting Started* pamphlets. The pamphlet should contain everything you need to know about connecting to the Internet, all the secret numbers you need, plus the phone number and your passwords and other information. It's a must.

Beyond the basics, try to find an ISP that offers most of the following items:

- ✔ **Unlimited access time:** Some ISPs charge by the hour. Avoid them. If they charge by a block of time, get a plan where you can have 100 or more hours a month. Only the very sturdy can be on the Internet for more than 100 hours in a month.

- ✔ **Web space or disk storage space:** You can use this small amount of the provider's disk storage for whatever. If the provider offers it, you can use the space to create your own Web page at some point.

- ✔ **Web support tools:** These tools include mostly advanced goodies used for Web publishing, such as FTP access, CGI programming, Web page statistics, and even programmers for hire.

- ✔ **Other stuff:** The list of items an ISP can offer is endless, including broadband support, newsgroups, domain registration, support for online businesses, plus even more and even stranger goodies that are way too complex to get into now. The more they offer, the merrier.

How to find an ISP

Most cities and even towns and hamlets have their own ISPs. I highly recommend that you go with a local outfit, not some large, impersonal organization like — well, for legal reasons, I can't mention them. No, service is important in an ISP, and nothing beats the local Ma-and-Pa Internet Shop.

If your area is blessed with more than one ISP, shop around. Find the one that gives you the best deal. Often times, the cheapest ISP lacks lots of features that other ISPs offer (but it doesn't tell you that unless you know what you're missing). Also, paying quarterly or annually (if you can afford it) is cheaper than paying monthly. These places can wheel and deal with you — if you know a bit about what you want.

✔ You can find ISPs in the Yellow Pages, under *Internet*. Some of them even advertise on TV, usually late at night along with the 1-900 psychic hot-tub-babe hotlines.

✔ I might add that ISPs with 24-hour service rank high on my list. If your e-mail dies at 11 p.m. and you need to get online, it's nice to have someone there who can help you.

✔ Don't be afraid to change ISPs if yours doesn't work out. I have done it twice. Please don't put up with crummy service; change ISPs if you need to.

Is AOL an ISP?

AOL has its fans, but I'm not one of them. For the price, I think AOL is a rip-off. Yet, if you enjoy AOL and feel that you're getting your money's worth — great. Before moving on, however, consider some arguments both pro and con for AOL as your ISP:

Pro: AOL is great if you're just starting out. The software is free, and it's easy to set up. Access is available all over, which means that you can get your mail and go online when you travel. AOL is widely supported by many companies, news organizations, and online retailers. If you're happy with AOL, why rock the boat?

Con: Using AOL is *slower* than connecting directly to the Internet through an ISP. You're limited by the AOL software, through which Web pages are funneled, as opposed to viewing them directly with a true Internet Web browser. AOL e-mail is nonstandard, which means that some attachments cannot be received (see Chapter 26). Though the AOL phone lines may not be as busy as in days past, AOL is still subject to outages. The AOL help system is impersonal and bad.

I favor a local ISP because you often get home-town service and the fastest Internet access possible. All your Internet software works, and you're not restricted to certain places or prevented access because the system is busy. Because of that, this book doesn't cover AOL.

Configuring Windows for the Internet

Setting up your PC to access the Internet isn't all that hard, if you have these three things:

- ✔ A silver bowl
- ✔ A ceremonial knife, preferably bejeweled
- ✔ An unblemished goat

No. Wait. You needed those things in the *old days*. Now, all you need is some information from your ISP, and the New Connection Wizard does the rest.

Here's the info from your IPS that you need to run the wizard:

- ✔ For a dial-up modem, the phone number to call
- ✔ For a broadband modem, the modem's IP address, the DNS address, and possibly a gateway address
- ✔ Your ISP's domain name — the `blorf.com` or `yaddi.org` thing
- ✔ Your Internet login ID and password
- ✔ Your Internet e-mail name, address, and password (if it's different from your login ID and password)

Additionally, you may need the following items, so have them handy:

- ✔ The number for your provider's DNS (Domain Name Server). This four-part number is separated by periods, like this: `123.456.789.0`.
- ✔ The name of your ISP's e-mail server, which involves the acronyms POP3 or SMTP.
- ✔ The name of your ISP's news (NNTP) server.

Fortunately, your ISP probably provided you with *all* this information when you signed up. It should be handy on a sheet of paper for you or located inside a booklet. All you need to do is tell the New Connection Wizard about the numbers. It does the rest.

Running the New Connection Wizard

To set up your Internet connection, you need to run the New Connection Wizard. If you see a shortcut icon to that program on your desktop, open it and begin. Otherwise, you can run the New Connection Wizard from its secret place on the Start thing menu: From the Start panel, choose Programs⇨Accessories⇨Communications⇨New Connection Wizard.

Run the wizard, obey its whims, and answer its questions using the information provided by your ISP. *Read the screens!* Click the Next button to move on.

After everything is done and you click the Finish button, your Internet connection is saved in the Network Connections folder. That folder contains the icon representing the settings you have just made, by using either the Local Area Connection icon or a special dial-up connection icon (as shown in the margin).

- Refer to Chapter 18 for more information about the Network Connections folder.
- You need to run the New Connection Wizard only once.
- I lied: If you change or add ISPs or switch from a dial-up to broadband connection, you need to run the New Connection Wizard again.
- Never toss out the booklet or sheet of information your ISP gives you! You need those numbers.
- Your Internet login ID and password are different from the user ID and password you use to get into Windows. You need a different ID and password for each system you access.
- $111,111,111 \times 111,111,111 = 12,345,678,987,654,321$.

Connecting to the Internet

Connecting to the Internet is cinchy: Simply run any Internet program on your computer. Windows is smart enough to connect automatically. Here's how things go most of the time:

1. **Start your Web browser.**

   In Windows, the browser is Internet Explorer. Double-click the Internet Explorer icon on your desktop or choose Programs⇨Internet Explorer from the Start panel.

   For a broadband or always-on connection, such as through a Local Area Network, ta-da! You're on the Internet. That's it. That's all you need to do. As they say at the end of the French movie, *Fin!*

   For dial-up modems, the madness continues:

2. Fill in the connection dialog box (if it appears).

If you see a Connect dialog box, as shown in Figure 22-1, fill it in. Use the information provided by your ISP, though most of the information may already be there. Click the Dial button to connect.

Figure 22-1:
Dialing in to
the Internet.

3. Wait while the modem dials.

Doh-dee-doh.

4. You're connected!

 When a dial-up connection is established, a new, teensy icon appears on the system tray, looking like the graphic shown in the margin. That's your Connected To Whatever teensy icon indicator, telling you that you're online with the Internet and ready to run your Internet software.

✔ For several reasons, you may always have to manually enter your password. The first is that you're using a laptop, which doesn't save your Internet password, for security reasons. The second is that you didn't properly log in to Windows with a password-protected account. The third is that, for some reason, Windows forgets your password and forces you to reenter it (perhaps for security reasons). For the fourth reason, see the next section.

✔ If it bugs you later that Windows connects automatically to the Internet, you can always turn off that option. See the next section for some tricks.

✔ Keep an eye out for the Connected To Whatever teensy icon indicator on the taskbar! It's your reminder that your PC is dialed in to and talking with the Internet.

Customizing the connection

Many juicy options for connecting with a dial-up account can be set in the Network Connections window, where Windows stores information about your Internet connections and dial-up accounts. There, you can gain access to your ISP's or dial-up Internet connection icon and change some vital settings. Here's the down-low:

1. **Open the Control Panel.**

2. **Open the Network Connections icon.**

3. **Click to select your ISP's or dial-up Internet connection icon.**

4. **Choose File⇨Properties.**

5. **Click to select the Options tab in the Properties dialog box.**

   Various dialing and redialing options appear, as shown in Figure 22-2.

Figure 22-2: Internet dial-up settings and options.

If you always want to see the Connect dialog box (refer to Figure 22-1), click to put a check mark by the option labeled Prompt for Name and Password, Certificate, Etc. That's one way to prevent automatic dialing.

6. **Set the options as necessary.**

   Don't forget the Redialing options in the bottom part of the dialog box.

   One setting to note in the Redialing options area is Idle time before hanging up. That's the number of minutes of inactivity after which Windows automatically drops the dial-up connection. Set it to something higher if the connection drops out on you.

7. **Click OK to save the settings and close the dialog box.**

8. **Close the Network Connections window as well.**

Refer to Chapter 18 for more information about the Network Connections window.

Not connecting to the Internet

You don't always have to connect to the Internet. For a broadband connection, you're online all the time anyway, so it isn't such a big deal. But, for dial-up modems, don't feel compelled to connect just because the connection seems to automatically dial itself — especially when the computer starts.

- ✔ To cancel the connection, click the Cancel button when you see it dialing.

- ✔ Also consider the suggestions from the preceding section for forcing the Connect dialog box to appear. In that case, the computer cannot connect to the Internet unless you click the Dial button.

- ✔ Why is your computer connecting to the Internet? Most likely, it's because some program or Windows itself is requesting information. Canceling that request isn't a problem, nor does it mess things up. Programs can wait until *you* want to connect to the Internet to conduct their business. Dammit! You're in charge!

The Importance of a Firewall

A firewall is a safety device. For a building, the firewall is created from special slow-burning material, rated in hours. For example, a 3-hour firewall theoretically takes three hours to burn through — and that helps protect a building from burning down before the fire department gets there.

On a computer with an Internet connection, a *firewall* is designed to restrict Internet access, primarily to keep unwanted guests out. The firewall effectively plugs holes through which bad guys could get in and mess with your PC.

- ✔ The Internet wasn't designed with security in mind. Back in the original days, scientists were open about their systems and didn't feel the need to protect their computers from other Internet users.

- ✔ Now, the Internet is full of bad guys who want to take over your computer and use it to relay pornography or spam e-mail or hijack your computer and use it to attack other computers.

- ✔ Especially if you have a broadband connection, your PC is most vulnerable to attack. You must get a firewall.

Installing the Windows XP firewall

Windows XP comes with limited firewall security, available through your Internet connection. Follow these steps to set it up:

1. **Open the Control Panel's Network Connections icon.**

2. **Right-click your ISP's or dial-up Internet connection icon and choose Properties from the pop-up menu.**

3. **Click the Advanced tab in the Properties dialog box.**

4. **Click to put a check mark by the option Protect My Computer and Network.**

5. **Click OK, and the firewall is set.**

That's pretty much the best Windows can do as far as a firewall is concerned. To allow specific services to access your PC — which is rare — click the Settings button in the Properties dialog box, on the Advanced tab (refer to Step 4). That allows you to let in certain services — if you need them. For most folks, however, the preceding steps are enough.

Third-party firewalls

The advantages of a third-party firewall are that, well, they're far more robust and capable than what Windows offers. For example, Zone Alarm, from Zone Labs, monitors *both* incoming and outgoing requests for the Internet and offers e-mail protection. I highly recommend it: www.zonelabs.com.

Other third-party solutions exist. If you enjoy the Norton stuff, consider getting the Norton Personal Firewall or the Norton Internet Security programs (www.symantec.com). Another fine firewall is available from Kerio Technologies (www.kerio.com).

Your ISP can be a great resource if you want more information or recommendations on this subject.

Doing Something on the Internet (Using Internet Software)

After you have made the connection to your ISP, you're ready to run any or all of your Internet software. Fire up your Web browser, e-mail package, or any of a number of applications designed for fun and folly on the Internet.

✔ As long as you have an Internet connection, you can run any program that accesses information on the Internet.

✔ Yes, you can run more than one Internet program at a time. I typically have three or four of them going. (Because the Internet is slow, I can read one window while waiting for something to appear in another window.)

✔ You can also stay on the Internet while using an application program, like Word or Excel. Just don't forget that you're online.

✔ Close your Internet programs when you're done with them.

Adios, Internet!

To wave bye-bye to the Internet, simply close all Internet programs. That's it!

For a broadband connection, you're done. In fact, you don't even have to close your Internet programs because the connection is active all the time. For dial-up, you want to disconnect. After closing the last open Internet program's window, you see a Disconnect dialog box. Click the Disconnect or Disconnect Now button.

If you don't see the Disconnect dialog box, double-click the wee Connection icon on the system tray. That displays the connection's Status dialog box; click the Disconnect button there to hang up.

✔ Dial-up connections must always disconnect from the Internet. Do not forget!

✔ Sometimes, the connection may drop automatically, especially if you haven't done anything on the Internet for a while. Refer to the section "Customizing the connection," earlier in this chapter, for more information on setting the idle time disconnection value.

✔ Your ISP may sport an idle time disconnection value. After a given amount of time, the ISP may just hang up on you if it thinks that you're not alive.

✔ Keep track of how much time you have spent online by viewing the Status dialog box; double-click the connection icon on the system tray. This information is important when you eventually spend several more hours on the Internet than you intended. View the time. Exclaim "My goodness, that's a long time!" and then click Close.

Chapter 23

Basic Internet Stuff

· ·

· ·

*I*f you're just starting out on the Internet, you should know about and use two basic Internet concepts: The first is the World Wide Web, and the second is e-mail.

The World Wide Web — or "the Web" — is directly responsible for making the Internet as popular as it is today. The Web introduced pretty graphics and formatted text to the Internet, propelling it from its ugly all-text past. And, e-mail is the most compelling reason to use the Internet. Something about the instant nature of electronic communications makes some folks live for e-mail.

This chapter covers the Web and e-mail. They are the two things you waste time, er, spend time doing on the Internet more than anything else.

Welcome to the Web

The chief piece of software used to access information on the Internet is a Web browser, or *browser,* for short. It's used to view information stored on Web sites throughout the Internet.

The most popular Web browser is Internet Explorer, or IE. It comes with Windows, and it's your key to viewing the World Wide Web.

Starting Internet Explorer

 Open the Internet Explorer icon on the desktop to start your Web browser. (Note that the icon is also found in numerous other places in Windows; it's ubiquitous.)

If you're not already connected to the Internet, after starting Internet Explorer, you are (refer to Chapter 22). Soon, Internet Explorer's main window fills with information from the World Wide Web, such as the *Web page* shown in Figure 23-1.

Figure 23-1: The Internet Explorer Web browser program.

The first Web page you see in the Web browser's window is the *home page*. It's merely your starting point on the Web, and it can be changed. (See the section "There's no place like home page," later in this chapter.)

Touring the Internet Explorer window

You should notice a few things in the Web browser window:

Button bar: You find, below the menu bar, a series of buttons. You use these buttons to visit various places on the Web and do basic things with your Web browser. If you don't see this bar, choose View⇔Toolbars⇔Standard Buttons from the menu.

Busy thing: The far right end of the button bar has what I call the *busy thing*. The busy thing becomes animated when your Web browser is busy doing something, which usually means that it's waiting for information to be sent from the farflung parts of the Internet. That's your signal to sit, wait, and be patient; the Web is busy.

Address box: This box holds the address of the pages you visit, and it's also an input box where you can type Web page addresses and other commands. If you don't see this box, choose View⇨Toolbars⇨Address bar from the menu.

Web page: The Web browser displays a page of information on the Web, the Web page. In Figure 23-1, you see the Wambooli page, which is my own Web page (`http://www.wambooli.com`).

The Web browser shows you how simple it is to view information on the Internet. In its window, you see graphics and text — almost like reading a magazine — and more; keep reading.

 ✔ The busy thing is busy a lot. It's often said that the World Wide Web should be World Wide Wait.

 ✔ If you have trouble seeing the text on a Web page, consider changing the text size. Choose View⇨Text Size from the menu and then choose a larger or smaller size from the submenu.

 ✔ Web pages can be wider and often longer than what you see displayed in your browser's window. Don't forget to use the scroll bars! Better still, maximize the browser window to get the full-screen effect.

 ✔ The thing you type in the Address box is officially known as a *URL* ("you are ell"). It's an acronym for Uniform Resource Locator. Essentially, it's a command you give the Web browser to go out and find information on the Internet.

Typing a new Web page address

An estimated three billion pages of information are on the World Wide Web. Why not visit them all? You can start by typing on the Address bar the address of a new place to visit.

Suppose that you want to visit the popular Yahoo Web portal. Its address is written like this:

```
http://www.yahoo.com
```

Use the mouse to select any text already on the Address bar; press the Backspace key to delete that text.

Type **http**, a colon, two forward slashes, **www**, a period, **yahoo**, another period, and **com**. (Don't type a final period at the end of the address.)

Double-check your typing and then press the Enter key. Soon, the Yahoo Web page appears in the browser's window.

If something goes wrong: The most obvious reason for something going wrong is that you mistyped the address. Double-check it! Everything must be *exact*. Upper- and lowercase mean different things. Use the forward slash (/), not the backslash (\). Go ahead and edit the address if you can, or just start over and type it again.

- ✔ If the Web page doesn't load, you may see some type of error message. The first thing you should do is try again! The Web can be busy, and often when it is, you get an error message.

- ✔ If you get a 404 error, you probably didn't type the Web page address properly. Try again!

- ✔ Web page addresses are often listed without the http:// part. Sometimes, the www part is missing as well. Even so, the www part is required for typing an address into a browser.

- ✔ Technically speaking, the http:// part is required if the Web page address doesn't begin with www (and quite a few are like that).

- ✔ If the URL starts with ftp:// or gopher://, you're required to type those commands.

Clicking a Web page link

The automatic way to visit a Web page is to click a Web page link. It appears as underlined text on a Web page, often colored blue (though that's not a hard and fast rule.) But the clear sign that you have found a link is that when you point at it, the mouse pointer changes to a pointing hand, as shown in the margin.

To use the link, click it once with the mouse. The Web browser immediately picks up and moves off to display that Web page — just as though you had typed the address manually.

- ✔ It's called the *Web* because nearly every page has a link to other pages. For example, a Web page about the end of the world may have links to other Web pages about Nostradamus or the guy who walks around with a sandwich board that says "Doom is near."

✔ Not all links are text. Quite a few links are graphical. The only way to know for certain is to point the mouse pointer at what you believe may be a link. If the pointer changes to a pointing hand, you know that it's a link you can click to see something else.

✔ Quite a few Web pages are simply collections of links.

✔ Any good, informative Web page has links relating to other topics.

✔ Links can appear anywhere on a Web page.

✔ Link is short for *hyperlink* — yet another bit of trivia to occupy a few dozen neurons.

Going back, way back, and forward and stopping

Following links can be fun. That's the way most people waste time on the Web. For example, I found a Web page recently about UFOs that was too funny to be true. Yet I don't know how I got there; I just ended up there after clicking a few dozen links. Unlike Hansel and Gretel, I neglected to leave bread crumbs along the information superhighway. Fortunately, the Web browser does that for you.

To return to the Web page you were just ogling, use your browser's Back button. You can continue clicking the Back button to revisit each Web page you have gawked at, all the way back to the first page you saw 18 hours ago.

If you really need to dig deep, click the down arrow by the Back button. A list of the last several Web pages you have visited appears.

If you need to return to where you were after going back, use the Forward button. Back. Forward. It's like playing the game Sorry! with a sadistic 8-year-old.

If you accidentally click a link and change your mind, click the Stop button. The Internet then stops sending you information. (You may need to click the Back button to return to where you were.)

Ah, how refreshing!

The browser's Refresh button serves a useful purpose in the world of ever-changing information. Refresh merely tells the Internet to update the Web page you're viewing.

The reasons for clicking the Refresh button:

Web page not found: Don't give up too easily! The Internet can lie; click the Refresh button and give that Web page another try.

Changing information: Some Web pages have updating information on them. Clicking the Refresh button always gets you the latest version of the Web page.

Missing pictures: Occasionally, a graphical image may not appear. In that case, a *blank* icon shows up, telling you that the image is missing. Often, clicking the Refresh button works some magic that causes the image to reappear.

Accidentally clicking the Stop button: Oops! Click Refresh to unstop and reload the Web page.

There's no place like home page

 To visit your home page, click the Home button. This action takes you back to the first page you saw when you connected with the Internet.

The beauty of the home page is that you can change it. Your *home page* can be any page on the Internet — or even a blank page, if you like.

To set a home page, follow these steps:

1. **Visit the page you want to call home.**

   For example, my Web page is at www.wambooli.com. Type that in the Address box to visit that page.

2. **Choose Tools⇨Internet Options.**

   The Internet Options dialog box appears; click the General tab if necessary so that it looks like Figure 23-2.

3. **In the Home page area (in the top part of the dialog box), click the Use Current button.**

4. **Click OK.**

The new home page is now set. And, you can change it again at any time. After all, it's *your* home page!

Note that you can also set the home page to be blank, if that's what you desire.

Figure 23-2:
The Internet
Options
dialog box.

Closing Internet Explorer

After you're done browsing the World Wide Web — meaning that it's 4 a.m. and you need to get up in 90 minutes to get ready for work — you should close Internet Explorer. This task is easy: Choose File⇨Close from the menu.

Closing Internet Explorer doesn't disconnect you from the Internet. If you're using a modem connection, you must manually disconnect if Windows doesn't automatically prompt you. Refer to Chapter 22 for more information on disconnecting from the Internet.

Mail Call!

Nothing perks up your Internet day like getting fresh e-mail. *Ahhhh, people care enough about me to write! I'm loved!*

The following sections deal with e-mail, which can be an obsession for some folks. In fact, if you're like most people, you probably run both your Web browser and e-mail program at the same time. That way, you don't "miss anything" while you're on the Internet.

- ✔ This book assumes that you have Outlook Express (Version 6), the e-mail package that comes free with Windows.

- ✔ Outlook Express is *not* the same program as Outlook, which is another e-mail program distributed with Microsoft Office.

✔ If you haven't yet set up your e-mail accounts on your computer, the first time you run Outlook Express it starts a wizard that walks you through the necessary steps.

Starting Outlook Express

 Start Outlook Express by opening the Outlook Express icon on the desktop (as shown in the margin). You may also find the icon on the Quick Launch bar.

If you aren't already connected to the Internet, starting Outlook Express connects you. If not, refer to Chapter 22 for information on connecting to the Internet.

 You cannot send or receive e-mail unless you're connected to the Internet.

The main screen

The first thing Outlook does is check for new mail. Refer to the section "Reading e-mail," later in this chapter, if you *really* can't wait to get started. Outlook also sends any mail you have waiting.

Figure 23-3 details the Outlook Express screen. It consists of three parts:

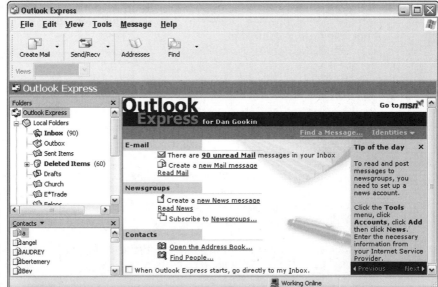

Figure 23-3: Outlook Express, your e-mail program.

Folders list: In the upper-left area of the window is the list of folders where sent, received, trashed, and filed mail goes.

Contact list: In the lower-left area is a list of *contacts,* people with whom you may normally communicate.

Message summary: On the right is a "home page" of sorts for messages, newsgroups, and stuff. You may or may not see this screen. Instead, you may configure Outlook to display your Inbox whenever you switch it on: Click to put a check in the box by the option When Outlook Express Starts, Go Directly to My Inbox.

The inbox

The opening screen for Outlook Express is something you really don't want to see. No, you want to get that mail! Click the Inbox link to see any old or new messages you have received.

When you go to the Inbox (see Figure 23-4), the right side of the screen splits into two parts. The top part shows the queue of e-mail in the Inbox. Bold text indicates unread mail; normal text indicates read mail (and the open/closed envelope icon confirms this information).

The lower-right part of the window shows a preview of the message's contents.

Figure 23-4:
The Outlook
Express
Inbox view.

Between the left and right sides of the window is a separator bar. You can drag that bar with the mouse, making either side larger. My advice is to drag the separator bar to the left, making the Inbox and preview windows larger.

That's it for your introduction! If you have mail waiting, jump forward to the section "Reading e-mail." Otherwise, continue with the next section, on composing a new message.

Sending e-mail

To get e-mail, you must first send it.

To create a new message in Outlook Express, click the Create Mail button. The New Message window appears, as shown in Figure 23-5. Your job is to fill in the blanks.

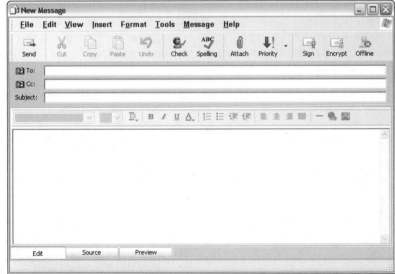

Figure 23-5:
The New Message window.

To: To whom are you sending the message? Type the person's e-mail address in the To field.

✔ To compose an e-mail epistle, you need to know the e-mail address of some other person on the Internet. Your friends and coworkers can give you this information, and it's extremely trendy to put your e-mail address on your business card and résumé.

✔ Don't put spaces in an e-mail address. If you think that it's a space, it's probably an underline or a period.

✔ You must enter the full e-mail address: `zorgon@wambooli.com`. Note the single exception: If you have e-mail nicknames set up, you can type the nickname rather than the full e-mail address in the To field. (See Chapter 25 for information on nicknames.)

✔ You can type more than one address in the To field. If so, separate each with a semicolon, as in

```
president@whitehouse.gov;first.lady@whitehouse.gov
```

✔ If you type the wrong e-mail address, the message *bounces* back to you. It isn't a bad thing; just try again with the proper address.

Cc: The *carbon copy* field contains e-mail addresses of people you want to carbon-copy the message to. Those people receive the message, and they know that the message wasn't directly intended for them.

Subject: Type the message's subject. What is the message about? It helps if the subject is somehow related to the message (because the recipients see the subject in their Inboxes, just like you do).

The message: The last thing to fill in is the contents.

```
Not at all! When we're through with Newfoundland, why,
              they'll never recognize the place!
```

When you're done, check your spelling by clicking the Spelling button. Your message is scanned, and potential misspelled words are flagged. Select the properly spelled word from the dialog box — the same drill you go through with your word processor's spell check feature.

Review your message! Spell checking doesn't check for grammatical errors or potentially offensive outrageous statements. Remember that you can't recall e-mail after it's sent!

Finally, you send the message. Click the Send button, and it's off to the Internet, delivered cheaper and more accurately than by any post office on earth.

If you don't want to send the message, close the New Message window. You're asked whether you want to save the message. Click Yes to save it in the Drafts folder. If you click No, the message is destroyed.

✔ You can start a new message by pressing Ctrl+N or choosing File⇨New⇨ Mail Message from the menu bar.

✔ An e-mail message is sent instantly. I sent a message to a reader in Australia one evening and got a reply from him in fewer than 10 minutes.

✔ Please don't type in ALL CAPS. To most people, all caps reads like YOU'RE SHOUTING AT THEM!

✔ Spell checking in Outlook Express works only if you have Microsoft Word or the entire Microsoft Office package installed. Otherwise, you cannot spell-check in Outlook Express.

✔ Be careful what you write. E-mail messages are often casually written, and they can easily be misinterpreted. Remember to keep them light.

✔ Ignore people who write you nasty messages. It's hard, but you can do it.

✔ Don't expect a quick reply from e-mail, especially from folks in the computer industry (which is ironic).

✔ To send a message you have shoved off to the Drafts folder, open the Drafts folder. Then double-click the message to open it. The original New Message window is then redisplayed. From there, you can edit the message and click the Send button to finally send it off.

Reading e-mail

To read a message, select it from the list in the Inbox. The message text appears in the bottom of the window, as shown earlier, in Figure 23-4. You can read any message on the list like this, in any order; selecting a new message displays its contents in the bottom part of the window.

TIP

Avoiding that hero instinct

People new to Internet e-mail somehow feel emboldened that they are personally responsible for the health, safety, and entertainment of everyone else they know on the Internet. Let me be honest: If you're just starting out, be aware that those of us already on the Internet have seen that joke. We have seen the funny pictures. We know the stories. And everyone has already sent us that e-mail saying that if you send it to seven people you know, somehow Bill Gates will write you a check for $4,000.

Please don't be part of the problem. Telling others about viruses and *real* threats is one thing, but spreading Internet hoaxes is something else. Before you send out a blanket e-mail to everyone you know, confirm that you're sending the truth. Visit a few Web sites, such as www.truthorfiction.com, www.ciac.org/ciac/, and www.vmyths.com. If the message you're spreading is true, please include a few Web page links to verify it.

Thanks for being part of the solution, and not part of the problem!

Of course, you're not stuck viewing the message in the crowded jail of the Outlook Express multiple-window inferno. No, if you like, you can open a message window by double-clicking the message in the Inbox. A special message-reading window opens, similar to the one shown in Figure 23-6.

Because the message has its own window, you can resize or drag around the message anywhere on the screen. And, you can open more than one message-reading window at a time, which helps if you need to refer to more than one message at a time (those he-said-she-said things, for example).

The message-reading window also has two handy buttons: Previous and Next.

 Click the Previous button to read the previous message in the Inbox, the one before the current message.

 Click the Next button to read the next message in your Inbox. If you're reading the last message in the Inbox, clicking the Next button makes an annoying sound.

 As with a Web page, if you have trouble seeing the text in an e-mail message, choose View⇨Text Size from the menu and choose a larger or smaller size from the submenu.

After reading e-mail

After reading a message, you can do one of many things to it:

 To print an e-mail message, choose File⇨Print from the menu. The Print dialog box appears; click OK to print. You can also print a message by clicking the Print button on the toolbar.

 To send an answer or follow-up to an e-mail message, click the Reply button.

Note that Outlook Express does several things for you automatically:

✔ The sender's name is automatically placed in the To field. Your reply goes directly to the sender without your having to retype an address.

✔ The original subject is referenced (Re) on the Subject line.

✔ Finally, the original message is *quoted* for you. This feature is important because some people receive lots of e-mail and may not recall the train of the conversation.

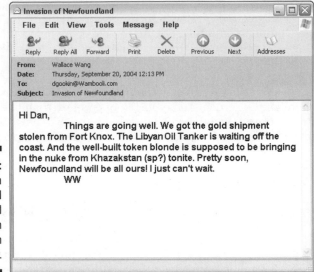

Type your reply and then click the Send button to send it off.

Forwarding a message is the same as remailing it to someone else. To forward a message, click the Forward button. The forwarded message appears *quoted* in the body of the new message. Type any optional comments. Fill in the To field with the address of the person to whom you're forwarding the message. Finally, click the Send button to send it off.

To delete the message you're reading, click the Delete button. Poof! It's gone. (To be accurate, the message is merely moved into the Deleted Items folder on the left side of the Outlook Express window.)

- ✔ You don't have to do anything with a message after reading it; you can just keep it in your Inbox. There's no penalty for that.

- ✔ You can edit the quoted text when replying or forwarding a message. The quoted text isn't "locked" or anything. I typically split up quoted text when I reply to e-mail — even delete chunks — so that I can address topics individually.

- ✔ Use the Reply All button when you reply to a message that was carbon-copied to a number of other people. By clicking Reply All, you create a reply that lists *everyone* the original message was sent to so that they can all read the reply.

- ✔ You can use the Forward button to resend bounced e-mail messages to the proper address. The forwarding keyboard command is Ctrl+F. Just type the proper address, and maybe an explanation of how you goofed or something, and click the Send button to send it off again.

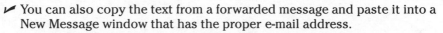
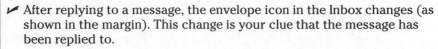

- ✔ You can also copy the text from a forwarded message and paste it into a New Message window that has the proper e-mail address.

- ✔ After replying to a message, the envelope icon in the Inbox changes (as shown in the margin). This change is your clue that the message has been replied to.

- ✔ Deleted mail sits in the Deleted Items folder until you clean out that folder. To clean it out, choose Edit⇨Empty Deleted Items Folder from the menu.

Closing Outlook Express

To close Outlook Express when you're done, close the program's window. Or, choose File⇨Exit from the menu.

If Outlook Express is the last Internet program you close, dial-up connections are prompted to disconnect from the Internet. If you're finished, disconnect!

Chapter 24

General Advice for the Web Weary

· ·

In This Chapter

▶ Searching the Web

▶ Shopping and spending online

▶ Organizing your Favorites

▶ Using the Links bar

▶ Learning from your Web history

▶ Rewriting your Web history

▶ Printing Web pages

▶ Dealing with pop-up windows

▶ Fighting spyware

· ·

*I*t's a worldwide web we weave. . . .

One reason the Web is so successful is that it doesn't really take much to figure out how it works. It may have once, but thanks to well-designed Web pages and a simple point-and-click interface, using the Web isn't tough for anyone. So, rather than give you the Big Web Tour and waste your time reading about how to buy airline tickets online or browse to the Chinese restaurant down the block for take-out, I have decided to dedicate this chapter to various Internet Explorer tips, tricks, and general advice for the Web weary. This advice saves you tons of time and gives you something to read while you wait for your General Tso's chicken.

Finding Things

The Web is like a library without a librarian. It doesn't have a card catalog, either. And forget about finding something on the shelves: Web pages aren't organized in any fashion, nor is the information in them guaranteed to be complete or accurate. Because anyone can post anything on the Web, well, anyone does.

Engines for searching

You find something on the Web by using a *search engine*. It's a Web page that features a huge catalog of other Web pages. You can search through the catalog for whatever you want. Results are displayed, and you can click links to eventually get to the Web page you want. It's all very nifty.

My main search engine these days is Google, located at www.google.com and shown in Figure 24-1.

Type in the text box what you're looking for and click the Google Search button. After a few moments, Google displays a new page full of findings — Web pages on the Internet that more or less match what it is you're looking for in one way or another.

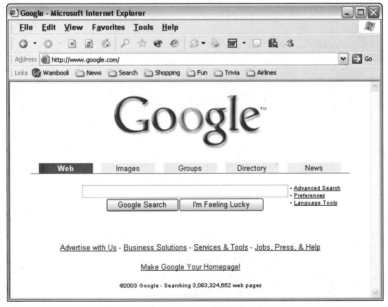

Figure 24-1:
Google.

Google isn't the only search engine, though I believe it's probably the best. I have listed a variety of others in Table 24-1.

Table 24-1	A Smattering of Search Engines
Site	**Address**
Ask Jeeves	www.ask.com
Dogpile	www.dogpile.com
C|NET's Search.com	www.search.com
KartOO	www.kartoo.com
Teoma	www.teoma.com
Vivísimo	www.vivisimo.com
WebCrawler	www.webcrawler.com

✔ If the search engine finds more than one page of information, you see a <u>Next 20 Matches</u> link (or something similar) at the bottom of the page. Click that link to see the next list of Web pages that were found.

✔ To see a map to a specific location, type the address in the Google text box and click the Google Search button.

✔ To get information about someone, type their phone number in the Google search box. If the phone number is unlisted, you see information about whoever owns the number. Hello, *1984!*

✔ For a sample people-finding site, visit people.yahoo.com.

✔ Don't freak out when you find yourself (and your address and phone number) listed. Most people-searching places let you unlist yourself, though it may not be obvious how to do it.

The key to a successful search

The more information you give in the Search text box, the more accurate the Web page results. Avoid using small words (such as *the, of, and, but, with,* and *for*) and put the most important words first.

Suppose that you want to find a MIDI file of the theme from the old "Dragnet" TV show. Type this line:

```
Dragnet Theme MIDI
```

If words *must* be found together, enclose them in double quotes, such as

```
"Gilligan's Island" Theme MIDI
```

or

```
"Toro Riding Lawnmower" repair
```

This search finds only Web pages that list the words *Toro Riding Lawnmower* together in that order.

If the results — the matching or found Web pages — are too numerous, click the link (near the bottom of the page) that says "Search within results." That way, you can further refine your search. For example, if you found several hundred pages on Walt Disney World but you're specifically looking for a map of the Animal Kingdom, you can search for "Animal Kingdom map" within the results found for Walt Disney World.

More than search engines: Portals

More powerful than a mere search engine is the Web portal. In addition to offering searching abilities, a Web *portal* provides other services, such as news, Web-based e-mail, games, chat, and other goodies, all designed to enhance the whole Web experience.

The most popular Web portal is Yahoo at www.yahoo.com, but it's not the only one. Table 24-2 lists the gamut of search engines and Web portals.

Table 24-2	Popular Portal Sites, But Not All of Them
Site	*Address*
C|NET	www.cnet.com
CNN	www.cnn.com
Excite	www.excite.com
Lycos	www.lycos.com
Microsoft	www.msn.com
Yahoo!	www.yahoo.com
ZDNet	www.zdnet.com

A portal is a great thing to have as a home page. That way, you can always quickly return there by clicking the Home button. (Refer to Chapter 23 for information on setting your home page.)

The Web Wants Your Money

The boon of the 1990s was online shopping. It was amazing. You would think that people had never used mail order catalogs, but in any event, Web shopping was *the* thing to do.

Shopping on the Web is still popular, but you can do more things with your money than shop. You can check out online banking, auctions, investing, and . . . gambling. Not all of that is worth discussing, so the sections that follow highlight only the important issues or things that should be of vital concern, in case you ever whip out your wallet while connected to the Internet.

The key to knowing that your information is safe on the Internet is the tiny padlock that appears on the bottom of the Web page window (on the status bar). The padlock means that the site you have accessed is *secure* and no one can spy on you while you're using that site. Also note that the Web page's address begins with https, not http. The *s* stands for *secure*.

Online shopping Q&A

Belay your fears: Shopping online is fast, easy, and "safe." You're just a few clicks away from maxing out your Visa card. . . .

Q: What can I buy online?

A: Anything and everything — even concrete.

Q: Isn't it a little weird that they sell computers online?

A: Not really. When radio first became popular, the commercials all advertised new radios.

Q: How do I shop?

A: You find a Web page that sells something. The most famous is Amazon.com (www.amazon.com), which started as an online bookstore, but now sells other goodies.

Q: How do I pick out something?

A: You pick out a product by adding it to your *virtual shopping cart.* You click a button, which places the item into a *bin* that you can check out later.

Q: How do I pay for it?

A: Just as you pay for items at a store, you open your shopping basket window (usually by clicking a shopping basket link or icon) and review the items listed there. Follow the instructions on the screen for checking out, which usually involve filling in personal and shipping information as well as a credit card number.

Q: Is my credit card information safe?

A: It's very safe. Most shopping sites and Web browsers use special encryption technology to ensure that no one snags your credit card on the way to the store. (This process is much safer than, for example, handing your credit card to a waiter in a restaurant.)

Always pay by credit card. That way, if you don't get what you want, or you get nothing, you can easily cancel the debt. A credit card is a good form of protection in case the online retailer turns out to be a phony.

Q: What about returning things?

A: This is very important: Check the store's return policy. Some places are very good and quick to accept returns. If possible, try to find a place that has a no-questions-asked return policy. But watch out! Some places are secretive and hide return information. Always check!

Some other advice tidbits I couldn't fit into the Q&A format:

- ✔ Check for a real phone number or an address for the online retailers you deal with. A major online scam has never occurred; companies doing business online are legitimate. Those that aren't probably don't have a phone number or address listed.

- ✔ Some online retailers offer payment alternatives if you fear paying online. You may be able to phone in an order or direct the company to phone you for confirmation. Some places may let you print and fax an order.

- ✔ The big online retailers have search engines that search their sites for the stuff you need. So, you can either browse for that perfect hammock or type **night vision goggles** in the Search box and see what comes up.

- ✔ Many online retailers have lists of best-selling products. Check them out! Also, refer to comments from other users on the products sold, if available. Don't forget the specials! I buy *Web-only* specials all the time. Save money!

Auctions without the auctioneer

Two types of auctioneers exist. First, there's the rapid-fire auctioneer, who spews out numbers like a machine gun: *budda-budda-budda-budda.* Then there's the Sotheby's or Christy's type of auctioneer — very polite: "I'm bidding $35-point-2 million for the Van Gogh. Do I hear 35-point-3? Mr. Gates?"

Online auctions don't have auctioneers, per se. In most cases, the auctioneer is the Web page itself. It works like a combination search engine and online retailer.

The most popular online auction site is eBay (www.ebay.com). It lets you buy or sell just about anything. You can browse the crap, er junk, er stuff on eBay just as you would browse a search engine. To buy or sell, however, you have to register. Then — let the bidding begin!

- ✔ An online auction site makes its money off commissions collected from the seller.
- ✔ One key to bidding is to bid late and quickly, right before the auction times out.
- ✔ Set a bid limit and don't go over it.
- ✔ If you hold the winning bid, you and the seller decide on payment and shipping terms (or they may be dictated in advance).
- ✔ To avoid being ripped off, many of the better online auction sites offer information about the seller, including comments from other buyers. You can also vie to use an online escrow service if you want to hold your payment until you receive the merchandise.

We All Have Our Favorites

Often, you find some Web place you love and want to visit again. If so, drop a *bookmark* on that page. That way, you can visit it at any time by selecting the bookmark from a list.

To drop a bookmark, use the Ctrl+D command — D for drop.

This command places the bookmark on the Favorites menu in Internet Explorer. That way, you can revisit the Web page by plucking it from the Favorites menu. It's a walk in the park, minus the bunions.

- ✔ Never fear to add a Web page to your Favorites! It's better to add it now and delete it later than to regret not adding it in the first place.

✔ If you forget to drop a bookmark, use the drop-down list on the Address bar's Back button to locate a Web site you have visited recently. Or, you can use the History list; see the section "History 101," later in this chapter.

✔ I really wish that Microsoft would call *favorites* by their proper name: bookmarks. Every other Web browser uses bookmarks instead. That name is just so much more descriptive than *favorites*.

Organizing your Favorites

The Favorites menu can get messy quickly. The solution to that, or to any mess on the computer, is to *organize*. You can organize your Favorites menu by deleting unwanted bookmarks or by creating submenus and sub-sub-menus full of Web pages you have visited. It's all quite easy.

To organize the Favorites menu in Internet Explorer, choose Favorites⇨ Organize Favorites. The Organize Favorites dialog box appears, as shown in Figure 24-2.

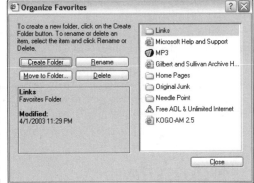

Figure 24-2: The Organize Favorites dialog box.

To move a selected bookmark into a folder, you can drag and drop the bookmark with the mouse or use the Move to Folder button.

To create a new folder, click the Create Folder button. The New folder appears, named New Folder, though you can type a new name for it at that time.

Rename a bookmark by selecting the bookmark and then clicking the Rename button. This is a good idea, especially for long bookmark names, which make the Favorites menu very wide. For example, I changed the quite long name of my 235-character local weather Web page to read only Weather, which is all I need to know when choosing that site from the Favorites menu.

And, of course, to delete unwanted bookmarks, select them with the mouse and click the Delete button.

- ✔ I try to keep on the Favorites menu only as many bookmarks as will fit on the screen. If I open the Favorites menu and it starts to scroll off the screen, I know I need to go in and do some organizing.

- ✔ Create folders for specific categories of bookmarks: News, Weather, Sports, Music, Movies, Fun Stuff, Computer Reference, or whatever you're into.

- ✔ You can use submenus to further organize your topics.

- ✔ Feel free to delete any favorites that Microsoft preinstalled on the Favorites menu. Those bookmarks are from companies that paid money to have their products advertised there.

Using the Links folder and Links toolbar

One special folder that comes already set up inside the Internet Explorer Favorites menu is the Links folder. The items that appear in that folder also appear on the Links toolbar in Internet Explorer, which makes those links even handier to get at.

To make the Links toolbar appear, choose View⇨Toolbar⇨Links from the menu. The toolbar displays whatever links are saved in the Favorites\Links folder. That's where I put my most favorite Web pages: news, weather, Wambooli, and shopping, for example. They appear right on the Links toolbar, as shown in Figure 24-3.

Figure 24-3:
The Links
toolbar
shows
bookmarks
saved in the
Links folder.

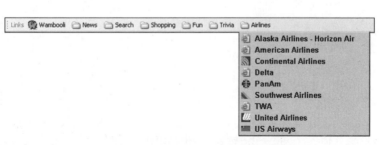

Subfolders in the Links folder appear as menus on the Links toolbar. In Figure 24-3, you see the Airlines menu displayed on the Links toolbar. That menu is really the Airlines subfolder located inside the Links folder on the Favorites menu. Each menu item you see is really a bookmark. Handy.

History 101

Internet Explorer remembers every Web page you have visited today, yesterday, and sometimes for the past several weeks. Many people like this feature; it lets them review where they have been and revisit those places. Many more people despise this feature because it lets anyone else snoop on where they have been on the Internet.

Looking at the History list

To see the History list, click the History button on the Internet Explorer toolbar. The History panel appears on the left side of the Internet Explorer window. The panel is divided into areas by date: Today, Last Week, 2 Weeks Ago, and 3 Weeks Ago, similar to what's shown in Figure 24-4.

Figure 24-4:
The Internet
Explorer
History
panel.

Beneath each date are folders representing the Web sites you have been to. Open a folder to view the list of individual pages.

Close the History list when you're done with it: Click the X (close) button in the History panel, or just click the History button on the toolbar.

✔ To revisit a page, simply choose it from the History list. For example, open the Last Week item, choose the Scandinavian Puns Web site, and choose an individual page from the site you visited last week.

✔ The keyboard shortcut for the History list is Ctrl+H.

Clearing the History list

Often, history doesn't reflect kindly on you. Fortunately, Internet Explorer offers several ways to delete, if not rewrite, your history:

✔ To remove a page or Web site from the list, right-click that item. Choose Delete from the pop-up shortcut menu.

✔ To clear all items from the History list, choose Tools➪Internet Options. In the Internet Options dialog box, on the General tab, click the Clear History button. Click OK.

✔ To disable the History list, choose Tools➪Internet Options to display the Internet Options dialog box. On the General tab, locate the History area. Reset the Days to Keep Pages in History option to zero, which disables the Internet Explorer History feature. Click OK.

Really, really clearing the History list

Even though the History list may be empty, you may still see some poor choices in the sites you have visited, which appear when you type a Web page on the Address bar. What you're witnessing is the AutoComplete function in action.

AutoComplete is a quick way to not have to fully type old Web page addresses; just type part of an address and use the down-arrow key or the mouse to pluck the full address from the drop-down list that appears.

If you would rather not see the AutoComplete list, disable it:

1. **In Internet Explorer, choose <u>T</u>ools➪Internet <u>O</u>ptions from the menu.**

   The Internet Options dialog box appears.

2. **Click to select the Content tab.**

3. **Click the AutoComplete button.**

4. **Remove the check mark by the Web Addresses option.**

5. **Click OK.**

6. **To remove those Web page addresses stored in your AutoComplete repertoire, click the General tab.**

7. **Click the Clear History button.**

   The evidence is gone.

8. **Click OK.**

Don't enable the Content Advisor!

Internet Explorer comes with a feature named the Content Advisor. It's designed to control the Internet content you view by preventing certain sites from being display on the screen. This idea sounds good because I know of no one who really wants to be surprised or shocked by suddenly seeing some porn they weren't expecting.

Alas, the Content Advisor isn't the best way to protect your eyes from seeing porn on the Internet. In fact, it can really mess up your Web browsing. So I recommend that, rather than use it, you consider some of the other antiporn or safe-surfing programs available, such as Net Nanny (www.netnanny.com) or Cybersitter (www.cybersitter.com). They offer better service and do a far superior job than the silly Internet Explorer Content Advisor.

Printing Web Pages

To print any Web page, choose File⇨Print from the menu. No tricks.

Some Web pages, unfortunately, don't print right. Some are too wide. Some are white text on a black background, which doesn't print well. My advice is to always use the Print Preview command to look at what's printing before you print it. If you still have trouble, consider one of these solutions:

- ✔ Consider saving the Web page to disk; choose File⇨Save As. Ensure that you choose from the Save As Type drop-down list the option labeled Web Page, Complete. Then you can open the Web page file in Microsoft Word or Excel, or any Web page editing program, and edit or print it from there.

- ✔ Use the File⇨Page Setup program to select landscape orientation for printing wider-than-normal Web pages.

- ✔ Use the Properties button in the Print dialog box to adjust the printer. These settings depend on the printer itself, but I have seen printers that can reduce the output to 75 or 50 percent, which ensures that the entire Web page prints on a single sheet of paper. Other options may let you print in shades of gray or black and white.

Oh, Those Annoying Pop-Up Windows!

Pop-ups are special windows that appear while you're browsing the Web. They show up in addition to the main window you're viewing, with some pop-ups appearing on top of the page and others beneath or behind the page.

The annoying part? You didn't ask for them. In fact, they're advertising, and their presence is unwanted by most Web users.

To deal with pop-ups, you need anti-pop-up software. These programs work with Internet Explorer to help you prevent windows from popping up. Table 24-3 lists some anti-pop-up programs I recommend.

Table 24-3	Pop-Up Solutions
Program	*Address*
Pop-Up Stopper	www.panicware.com
Pop-Up Killer	http://software.xfx.net/utilities/ popupkiller/index.php
Pop-Up Popper	www.bayden.com/popper

✔ Pop-ups appear because *they work*. People respond to them. If you don't like pop-ups, don't click them or use products from people who advertise using pop-ups.

✔ Check out my anti-pop-up Web page:

www.wambooli.com/help/internet/pop-ups/

✔ Another anti-pop-up solution is to use another Web browser, one that specifically contains tools to prevent pop-ups. Two that I can mention are Mozilla (www.mozilla.org) and Opera (www.opera.com). Yes, you can run more than one Web browser in Windows; it's just another Internet program.

The Horrors of Spyware

The latest bad thing to hit the Web is *spyware*. These secret programs — they're not exactly viruses —infiltrate your computer. They monitor where you have been on the Web and report that information to a central computer, which then sends you piles of advertising appropriate to where you have been.

The problem with spyware is that it's unwelcome and unwanted. Amazingly, programs can automatically invade your computer without your permission.

Internet Explorer has no practical tools to abate spyware. Antivirus software doesn't protect against it either. Instead, I recommend that you get specific and potent antispyware software and use it on your computer. Antispyware programs cull your system for signs of spyware and then remove those signs.

Two antispyware programs I can recommend are Ad-aware (`www.lavasoft.de`) and Spybot (`http://security.kolla.de/`). Between them, Ad-aware is easier to use; Spybot is a heavy-duty program, designed for more experienced PC users.

- ✔ Often, you *invite* spyware into your PC. If you sign up for Internet tools, companions, or toolbar extras, you're often signing up for programs that are spyware. *Read the agreement before you click OK!*

- ✔ Some spyware programs are next to impossible to remove by themselves. Bonzi Buddy, Gator, and Xupiter require the muscle of antispyware software to pry them loose from your system.

- ✔ If you notice that your PC continually wants to connect to the Internet, it could be a spyware program in action.

- ✔ Antivirus software doesn't scan for spyware. So, even if you're using an antivirus utility, don't think that you're completely safe from the bad guys on the Internet.

Chapter 25

E-Mail and Beyond

In This Chapter

▶ Creating custom e-mail

▶ Adding a signature

▶ Working with mail folders

▶ Using the Deleted Items folder

▶ Creating address book entries

▶ Using nicknames

▶ Making mail groups

▶ Fighting spam

E-mail has many layers. You can use it on the surface and only send and receive messages. Yet, most e-mail programs — Outlook Express included — have many more features than just the basic sending and receiving of e-mail. These features can help you organize your e-mail, keep track of who you send e-mail to, and even deal with unwanted e-mail. The features are all there. You paid for them! Why not read this quick chapter on how to use them?

✔ Basic e-mail is covered in Chapter 23.

✔ Also see Chapter 26, which covers e-mail file attachments.

Personalizing Your E-Mail

All e-mail is text. All of it! Letters, numbers, punctuation symbols — that's the basis of all the e-mail sent all over the world. Despite that, you have ways of sprucing up and individualizing your e-mail beyond boring text, which are covered in the next two sections.

Composing messages in style

Outlook Express can let you compose prettymail. I call it prettymail because the mail looks better than plain old boring text.

To make prettymail, start a new message by clicking the down arrow next to the Create Mail button. A list of stationery appears, as shown in Figure 25-1. Select a type from the list and Outlook Express displays a new message window with a special background pattern, picture, or design. You then proceed to create your new message, inspired by floral beauty or motivated by glacial determination.

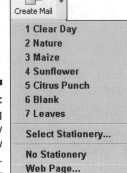

Figure 25-1: Selecting stationery for a new message.

Use the buttons on the formatting toolbar to change the message's font, size, color, and other formatting attributes. The buttons on the toolbar are similar to buttons you find in your word processor, and they have the same effect on your text.

Click the Send button to send your heavily formatted e-mail epistle.

✔ You can create your own stationery. Choose the Select Stationery command from the New Mail drop-down menu (refer to Figure 25-1). In the Select Stationery dialog box, click the Create New button to run the Stationery Setup Wizard.

✔ Not every e-mail program receives the message formatted the way you see it. If you get a reply claiming that the message looks like jumbled text, consider composing messages *without* the fancy formatting and stationery.

✔ The easiest way to ensure that you send a nonformatted e-mail message is to choose Format⇨Plain Text from the menu.

Creating a signature

Another way to personalize your messages is to create a *signature*. It's a bit of text that gets appended to every message you send. For example, my signature is

```
Cheers!
DAN
```

That text is automatically appended to each e-mail message I compose or reply to. Setting up your own signature is a snap in Outlook Express:

1. **Choose Tools⇨Options.**

   The Options dialog box is displayed.

2. **Click the Signatures tab.**

3. **Click the New button to create a new signature.**

4. **Enter the text you want to appear in the bottom of the dialog box.**

   Figure 25-2 shows how I created my signature. You can type multiple lines in the Text box, just as though you were typing those lines at the end of an e-mail message.

   Another option is to use a file on disk as your signature, in which case you click File and use the Browse button to locate the signature file. That can be any plain-text file, the contents of which are appended to each e-mail message you send.

Figure 25-2:
You create a
signature in
the Options
dialog box.

5. **Click to put a check mark by the option Add signatures to all outgoing messages.**

   You want Outlook Express to append your signature to the messages. Optionally, uncheck the Don't Add Signatures to Replies and Forwards box if you want your signature to go out all the time.

6. **Click OK.**

   The signature is ready for use.

The next time you create a new message, you see your signature appear in the message area. Ta-da! — automatic typing.

- ✔ You can have several signatures. To set the one you prefer to use, select it in the Options dialog box and click the Set as Default button.

- ✔ To switch signatures in a new message, choose Insert⇨Signature and then choose the proper signature from the submenu that appears.

- ✔ Use the Notepad program to create a signature file and save it to disk. Or, you can use your word processor if you want to spell-check the signature — just remember to save the file as a plain-text file. Remember where you put it!

- ✔ Be mindful if you select a text file for your signature. If you delete that text file, Outlook Express complains each time you create a new message when the signature file cannot be found.

Managing Your Messages

Vinton Cerf — the Father of the Internet and the creator of the @ (at-sign) in all your e-mail messages — said that e-mail can be like barnyard manure: It accumulates if you don't take care of it.

To help you take care of your e-mail, Outlook Express has the Folders window (refer to Figure 23-3, in Chapter 23). It has five standard folders:

Inbox: Where all your unread mail messages sit and also where read mail sits until you delete those messages or move them elsewhere.

Outbox: Contains messages waiting to be sent. If you're online, this folder is empty most of the time.

Sent Items: Stores a copy of all messages and replies you have ever sent.

Deleted Items: Keeps messages you have deleted.

Drafts: Stores any messages you decide not to send.

In addition to these folders, you can create your own folders for storing and organizing your messages. The following sections detail the process:

- ✒ Folders with blue numbers in parentheses by them contain unread mail. The number indicates how many messages are unread.

- ✒ As with the Recycle Bin in Windows, messages in the Deleted Items folder aren't deleted until you "empty the trash." To do so, choose Edit➪Empty Deleted Items Folder from the menu.

- ✒ To remove a message from the Drafts folder, open it. After it's open, you can view or edit the message and click the Send button to send it off. Or, you can drag a message from the Drafts folder to any other folder on the list.

Creating a mail folder

To create your own mail folder, a place for specific types of messages, follow these steps:

1. **Choose File➪New➪Folder from the menu.**

   The Create Folder dialog box appears, as shown in Figure 25-3.

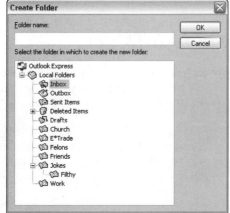

Figure 25-3:
The Create
Folder
dialog box.

2. **Enter a name for the new folder.**

   Type the name in the Folder Name box.

   For example, create a folder named Online Orders for e-mail receipts you get when you order things online. Another good folder to create is a Jokes folder for humorous things people send you.

3. **Select where you want the folder created.**

Click the folder in which you want the new folder to be placed. If you select the Local Folders item, Outlook places the folder on the *main level.* Selecting another folder creates a subfolder.

I keep my folders on the main level, so I select the Local Folders item from the bottom of the Create Folder dialog box.

4. **Click OK.**

The new folder is created, appearing on the Folder list on the left side of the window.

You manage the folders you create by right-clicking them. A pop-up menu materializes with commands for renaming or deleting the selected folder(s).

To view the contents of a folder, select it from the Folders list. Click once to highlight the folder and any messages stored there are listed on the left side of the window.

The folders Outlook Express uses for mail are *not* the same as the folders you use in Windows to store files. Technically, each folder is a text file on disk, a file that Outlook Express indexes and chops up to reflect the individual mail messages within that huge text file. Using Outlook Express to manage those folder and text files is easier than trying to hunt them down in Windows and manage them yourself.

Moving a message to a folder

I try to keep my Inbox empty of all read mail. After reading a message, I simply drag it off to the proper folder. This process works just like dragging any icon in Windows. Or, you can use the Edit⇨Move to Folder command, which does the same thing but via a dialog box.

From the Inbox, for example, you can drag a message over to the Jokes folder: Click the envelope icon next to the message and drag it to the proper folder on the left side of the window.

Note that you can delete messages from any folder by dragging them to the Deleted Items folder.

Deleting (and undeleting) messages

Generally speaking, I don't recommend that you delete any of your valued e-mail. Instead, consider moving those messages to a folder. I do that with all my worthy e-mail; a copy of it goes to a related folder: friends, family, business, fan mail, and hate mail, for example. I delete only mail messages not specifically directed to me, such as junk e-mail, which is known in the Internet universe as *spam.*

If you do delete e-mail, it goes into the Deleted Items folder. And there it sits until you empty the Deleted Items folder. Or, you can undelete a message by dragging it from the Deleted Items folder back to your Inbox or some other, custom folder.

To empty the Deleted Items folder, choose Edit➪Empty Deleted Items Folder from the menu.

Note that deleting messages from the Deleted Items folder *permanently* erases messages. You cannot recover them after they have been deleted from the Deleted Items folder.

The Valued Address Book

Whenever you get e-mail from someone new, or whenever you learn a friend's new online address, you should note it in the Outlook Express Address Book. Not only does the Address Book let you keep the addresses in one spot, but you can also easily recall an address for sending mail later.

Adding a name to the Address Book

You can add an e-mail name to the Address Book in one of two ways: manually or automatically.

Manually adding names: To manually add a name to your Address Book, choose File➪New➪Contact from the menu. Outlook then creates a new Address Book entry (as shown in Figure 25-4), which you fill in.

The dialog box has many tabs and gizmos for you to work, but you need to fill in only four items on the Name tab: First, Last, Nickname, and E-Mail Addresses.

The Nickname item is optional, though it can be handy. For example, you can type **goober** rather than your brother's full e-mail address in the To field of a new message. Outlook Express recognizes the shortcut and replaces it with the proper, full e-mail address.

After filling in the four fields (or more, if you're entirely bored), click the Add button and then click OK.

Figure 25-4:
Filling in
a new
Address
Book entry.

Automatically adding names: To automatically add a name to the Address book, display an e-mail message from someone whose name you want to add. Choose Tools⇨Add to Address Book⇨Sender from the menu. Outlook instantly adds the name to the Address Book.

Click the Addresses button on the toolbar to display the Address Book window. From there, you can edit or manage the entries in your Address Book.

Using the Address Book when sending a message

The Address Book really comes in handy when you're creating a new message. With the New Message window on the screen, click the To field's button, as shown in the margin. A special Address Book window appears, as shown in Figure 25-5.

To add someone to the To field, select that person's name and click the To button. Likewise for the Cc or Bcc fields. To select more than one e-mail address at a time, press the Ctrl key and then Ctrl+click to select the names.

When you're done, click OK and the message's To, Cc, and Bcc fields are already filled in for you.

Figure 25-5:
Select
people here
to send
e-mail to.

Creating a group

Often, you want to send out e-mail to more than one person — for example, all the folks on your Jokes, Sappy Stories, Family, or whatever lists. By creating a group, you can save yourself some time spent typing all those addresses over and over.

To create a group, follow these steps:

1. **Choose Tools⇨Address Book to open the Address Book.**

2. **Choose File⇨New Group.**

   A dialog box appears, where you can create the group.

3. **Type a name for the group.**

   Be clever and descriptive. The Jokes group can be named Jokes. The people you send messages to regarding your nude quilting group can be named Nude Quilters.

4. **Add members to the group.**

   Use the Select Members button to pick whom you want to be in the group. This action displays another dialog box, from which you can cull your list of e-mail contacts and add them to the group: Select the name and address from the left side of the window and use the Select button to add them to the group on the right side.

5. **Click OK when you're done adding members.**

6. **Click OK to close the group's Properties window.**

7. **Close the Address Book window.**

You're ready to use the group.

To send a message to the group, type the group's name in the To, Cc, or Bcc field. The message is then sent to that group of people automatically.

You can also click the To button, as described in the preceding section, to choose a group from the list in your Address Book.

Remember that you must always have a name in the To field; if you don't want to put anyone specific there, just use your own e-mail address.

By the way, putting the group in the Bcc field is a wonderful idea; see the nearby sidebar "Putting Bcc to work" for more information.

Spam, Spam, Spam, Spam

Junk e-mail is known as *spam*. It's prolific, almost worse than regular junk mail because laced throughout e-mail spam are pornography and truly shocking things.

Spam proliferates because it's profitable. Everyone is affected by it, and everyone has to put up with it — unless you use some of the antispam tricks covered in the sections that follow.

- ✔ Spam is in a reference to an old *Monty Python* comedy sketch about a restaurant that served lots of spam for breakfast. Computer geeks in years past applied the term to junk e-mail.

- ✔ SPAM is a spiced meat product from the Hormel company.

- ✔ Never respond to spam, either to buy the product or to protest or request to be removed from its e-mail lists. If anything, responding to spam often makes the situation worse; the spammers identify your reply as a "live" e-mail address, which results in even more spam in the future.

Blocking messages

The easiest way to deal with spam is simply to block the address of the person sending it to you. Whenever you receive an unwanted e-mail, choose Message➪Block Sender from the menu. Click Yes and Outlook Express removes all e-mail from that person and automatically deletes any incoming and future e-mail.

Putting Bcc to work

The sneaky Bcc field is used to *blind carbon-copy* a message, which involves sending a copy of a message to someone and having that person's name *not* appear in any copy of the e-mail. That way, you can clue people in to a message without having its true recipients know the names of everyone else who received the message.

To access the Bcc field, choose View⇨All Headers from the New Message window's menu. The people in the Bcc field receive a copy of the e-mail message just like everyone else; however, the people in the To or Cc fields don't see the Bcc field names listed.

A great way to use Bcc is when you send out a message to several people. For example, when sending out That Latest Joke, just put everyone's name in the Bcc field and put your own name in the To field. That way, everyone gets the joke (or not, as the case may be), and they don't see the huge stack-o-names at the start of the e-mail message.

The only problem here is that spammers often change e-mail addresses, so you end up blocking lots of people.

Unblocking innocent folks

You can too easily get into a message-blocking frenzy and accidentally block someone you didn't intend to block. To remove that person from your list of bad guys, follow these steps:

1. **Choose Tools⇨Message Rules⇨Blocked Senders List.**

   The Message Rules dialog box appears.

2. **Click to select the person you want to unblock.**

3. **Click the Remove button.**

   The person is back in.

4. **Click OK.**

Other ways to deal with spam

Spam is such a pervasive problem that you can use many available tools to help stem the tide of unwanted e-mail.

Within Outlook Express, for example, you can study how to create Message Rules. The downside to this strategy is that Message Rules are complex and, well, written backward, so it takes a while to understand how to create them and make them work.

Better solutions, as usual, happen out on the Internet. One program I whole-heartedly recommend is MailWasher (`www.mailwasher.net`). The program has a simple interface and easy-to-follow instructions. It previews your e-mail before it's sent to Outlook Express, which means that you can filter many obnoxious messages without them ever even arriving on your computer.

The joys of an alternative e-mail account

Here's a good way to deal with spam that doesn't cost anything or involve using programs or figuring out how to filter e-mail: Get a second e-mail account. I recommend that everyone get one.

First, keep your ISP's e-mail account a secret. Give it out to only a few trusted friends. Tell them never to send you online greeting cards or click any links on any Web pages that involve entering your e-mail address. Or, heck, if you don't trust 'em with that information, don't give them the e-mail account address; keep it a secret. Shhhh!

Second, sign up for a free, Web-based e-mail account at `mail.yahoo.com`, Hotmail, MyWay.com, or any of a number of free, Web-based e-mail services.

Third, use that Web-based e-mail account as your public presence on the Internet. That's the account you use to sign up for mailing lists, for shopping, for sending e-mail greeting cards, and everything else you do.

Eventually, that public account starts getting spam. It's inevitable; the mere process of submitting your e-mail address anywhere on the Internet subjects you to spam attacks. Finally, when the spam gets to be too much, bail on the free Web e-mail account. Close it, or just stop using it. Sign up for a new Web-based e-mail account, repeating the second and third steps. Then you can start afresh, away from the spammers. Tell everyone you know about your new account.

All the while you're doing this, the real ISP account you have remains secret and untouched. Those few who know about it send you e-mail — and that's all the e-mail you get. No spam ever shows up as long as you keep the e-mail address a secret and your trusted friends don't let it out either.

Chapter 26

Files to Here, Files from There!

• •

• •

*T*he Internet was borne of the need to fling files far and wide between the steam-powered computers of the early 1970s. Thank goodness, it's much easier to do today. You can send a file to anyone by adding an attachment to your e-mail. You can fetch files either through an e-mail message or by grabbing them from a Web page. This chapter tells you all the details.

Grabbing Stuff from a Web Page

The Internet is brimming with files and programs just waiting for you to grab a copy. Work some magic and the file is piped into your PC just as though you had copied it from a CD-ROM or floppy disk (though not as fast). You can grab files, programs, fonts, graphics — just about anything and everything you want. And, it's as cinchy as clicking your mouse.

- ✔ Copying a file to your computer is known as *downloading*. When some-one sends you a file over the Internet, you *download* it. (Think of the other computer as being on top of a hill; it may not be, but it helps to think of it that way.)

- ✔ Sending a file to another computer is known as *uploading*.

- ✔ Complaining to your best friend is known as *unloading*.

Saving an entire Web page to disk

To save an entire Web page to disk, choose File➪Save As in Internet Explorer. A Save Web Page dialog box appears, similar to the Save As dialog box in any other application. Use the dialog box to save the Web page to disk.

- Saving a Web page saves an *HTML file* to disk. That file contains the formatting instructions for the Web page. (It's basically a text file, though not that readable.)

- You can view the Web page offline by using Internet Explorer; the saved Web page opens up and is displayed just as though you were connected to the Internet.

- You can also view saved Web pages by using a Web page editor, such as FrontPage. Business applications, such as Microsoft Word and Excel, can also be used to view Web pages.

- I know many people who save Web pages for reading later, offline. In fact, saving a fun Web page for reading during a long airplane flight is a great way to spend your time.

Saving an image from a Web page

To save an image from a Web page to your PC's hard drive, right-click the image and choose Save Picture As from the pop-up menu. Use the Save As dialog box to find a happy home for the picture on your hard drive.

- Nearly all images on the Web are copyrighted. Although you're free to save a copy to your hard drive, you're not free to duplicate, sell, or distribute the image without the consent of the copyright holder.

- To set the image as your desktop wallpaper, choose Set as Background from the pop-up menu after right-clicking the image.

- If you point the mouse at a picture long enough, an image toolbar appears. The buttons are, from left to right, Save the image to disk, Print the image, Send the image as an e-mail attachment, and Open the My Pictures folder.

Saving text from a Web page to disk

Most Web pages display plain text. You can copy that text and save it to disk just as you would copy text from one application and paste it into another. Here's how:

1. **Select the text you want to copy.**

Drag the mouse over the text, which highlights it on the screen. The text is now selected.

2. **Choose Edit⇨Copy.**

3. **Start any word processor.**

   You can start Notepad, WordPad, or your word processor, such as Microsoft Word.

4. **Paste the text into your word processor.**

5. **Print. Save. Whatever.**

   Use the proper menu commands to save or print or edit the text you copied from the Web page.

I have used this technique a number of times, mostly to copy quotes from famous people and paste them into my books. I then attribute the quote to myself and become very famous for it — for example, "When Bill told me about Monica, I was furious." I made that one up.

Getting Software from the Internet

The Internet is a great repository of software, various programs for free or nearly free, which you can *download* to your computer for use, tryout, or just because. The following sections cover downloading software from the Internet.

Searching for programs

The first step to getting software from the Internet is to find it. Many companies have a direct Internet presence, so by merely finding their Web pages, you can visit the download area and see which files they have up for grabs.

You can also use a search engine to locate files, or, specifically, you can use file-searching engines to find things. Two examples are the C|NET Shareware. com (www.shareware.com) and IT Pro Downloads (http://itprodownloads. com) sites. Use these sites just like search engines; you can search for files of a specific type, or you can browse by the categories to see what's available.

Creating a Downloads folder

Because downloads need a place to be saved on your computer, I recommend creating a special Downloads folder for them. That way, you can always keep your downloaded programs and files together and quickly locate a downloaded file if you ever need to reinstall it.

Follow these steps to create a special Downloads folder:

1. **Open the My Documents icon on the desktop.**

2. **Choose File⇨New⇨Folder.**

3. **Name the folder My Downloads.**

Whenever you download a file, use the Save As dialog box to browse to the My Downloads folder and save your downloaded file there.

✔ Keep a copy of the program's registration number in the Downloads folder, in case you eventually buy the software. Most registration numbers are e-mailed. When you receive that e-mail, use the File⇨Save As command to save a copy of the message in the Downloads folder.

✔ Another folder, found in the Windows folder, is named Downloaded Program Files. This folder is used for updates to Internet Explorer, and its contents aren't for you to play with.

Downloading a file from the Internet

To download a file, simply click the proper link. This instruction is apparent whether you're using a file search engine or downloading a program from a developer's Web site; clicking the link starts the downloading process.

After clicking the link, you see a File Download dialog box, as shown in Figure 26-1. Click the Save button. Do not click the Open button! Never, never, never; Save is the button you want.

Figure 26-1: The File Download dialog box.

Clicking the Save button displays the Save As dialog box. Use it to browse to the Downloads folder (which you may have created in the preceding section).

Rename the file. In the Save As dialog box's File name box, type a new, more descriptive name for the file. Be sure *not* to rename the EXE or ZIP filename extension (if it's visible).

How long does it take to download a file?

Honestly, the progress meter you see when a file is being downloaded is for entertainment value only; no one really knows how long it takes to download a file. If the Internet is busy, it may take longer than estimated — even for a fast modem. Consider the time displayed as only a rough estimate.

For example, rename the file DSLST45.ZIP to DSL Speed Test 45.ZIP. That's a much more memorable name than the original name. There's nothing wrong with renaming a file you're saving on your computer.

Click the Save button and the file is sent.

While the file is downloading, feel free to go off and do something else on the Web; you don't have to sit and watch the file download — but you must stay connected to the Internet. If the connection drops, you have to start over and redo everything.

To find out what to do after the file is downloaded, see the next section.

Installing and using downloaded software

Two things need to happen after you successfully download a file. These two things depend on the type of file you have downloaded.

If you just saved to disk a regular EXE or program file, you should run it: Double-click its icon in the Downloads folder, which should start the Setup program and get you going. Follow the instructions in the Setup program.

If the file is a ZIP file, you have more work to do. ZIP files open as compressed folders in Windows XP, so your first step is to open the compressed folder and see what lies inside. Hopefully, you see a README document that you can open and view to see what to do next.

If you see no README document, your job is to extract all the files from the compressed folder archive into their own folder on the hard drive. Right-click the Compressed Folder icon and choose Extract All from the pop-up menu. Then use the Extraction Wizard to set a folder in which the files are extracted.

For example, create a new folder in the C:\Program Files folder for a program or utility you just downloaded.

After extracting the files from the ZIP archive, check to see whether it has a Setup or Install program you then have to run to complete installation.

✔ Downloading the file is free. If the file is shareware, however, you're expected to pay for it if you use it.

✔ Even though the file was downloaded, if you don't want it, you have to uninstall it as you would uninstall any program (refer to Chapter 21).

Downloading an MP3 file

MP3, which stands for something, is a file format used to store audio. The quality of the format makes the music, when it's played back, sound nearly perfect. And, the file sizes are small, relatively speaking — about 1MB of disk space for every minute of music. That's pretty good; five minutes of audio on a CD occupies only 5MB of disk space in MP3 format, as opposed to 100MB or more for other, similar sound files.

To find MP3 music, visit the MP3 Web page at www.mp3.com. Note that other sources are available; use Google to help you find them (see Chapter 24).

After you find the music you want, click the download link with the mouse. The file is then sent to your computer.

If clicking the download link causes the Windows Media Player to pop up, stop! You want to save the file to disk and not just hear Media Player play it. (You have no way to save a file in Media Player.) Close the Media Player and, instead, right-click the download link. A pop-up menu appears, as shown in Figure 26-2.

Figure 26-2:
Choose
Save Target
As to
download
any link.

Choose Save Target As from the menu. Doing so produces a Save As dialog box, which you can use to save the file to a specific spot on disk. (Say! How about an MP3 folder in your Audio folder in your My Documents folder?)

After the file is on disk, you can play it: Double-click its icon to open it and away it goes — if you have an MP3 player. The latest version of Windows Media Player works okay. For other, snazzier players, refer to the same MP3 Web page for some great software to download.

- ✔ Note that some MP3 files are play-only; you can listen to them on the Web only by using a program like Windows Media Player. This type of file cannot be saved to disk, unless you obtain specific software that saves, rather than plays, the file. You can find this type of software on the www.mp3.com/ Web site.

- ✔ MP3 files aren't zipped; you can play them right away after downloading.

Look, Ma! It's an E-Mail Attachment!

E-mail attachments are fun. They're a convenient way to send files back and forth on the Internet. For example, use your vast scanner knowledge to scan in an image of your kids, save it to disk as a JPEG file, and then attach it to an e-mail message to Grandma! If Grandma has read this book, she'll be gazing at her beautiful grandkids in mere Internet moments.

- ✔ Refer to Chapter 23 for more basic information on e-mail.

- ✔ At some point, you may receive a file that your PC cannot digest — a file of an unknown format. If so, the dreaded Open With dialog box appears. Quickly, ignore it! Choose Cancel. Then respond to the e-mail and tell the person that you can't open the file and need to have it re-sent in another format.

- ✔ Beware of surprise attachments because they can contain viruses or other harmful programs. See the section "Fighting the Viral Plague," later in this chapter.

- ✔ You can send more than one file at a time — just keep attaching files.

- ✔ Or, instead of sending several small files, consider putting them all in a compressed folder and just sending the single compressed folder instead.

- ✔ Don't send file shortcuts; send only the originals. If you send a shortcut, the people receiving the file don't get the original. Instead, they get the 296-byte shortcut, which doesn't help.

- ✔ Try not to move or delete any files you attach to e-mail messages until *after* you send the message. I know that this sounds dumb, but too often, as I wait for my e-mail to be sent out (while I'm not busy), I start cleaning files. Oops!

Grabbing an attachment with Outlook Express

 The secret of Outlook Express attachments is the paper clip icon. When you see the paper clip icon next to the message subject in the Inbox, it indicates that the e-mail message has one or more files attached to it.

When you read the message, you see an Attach header line appear in the regular list of From, Date, To, and Subject. That header appears by the file(s) attached to the message.

Attachments aren't anything until you open them. To open the attachment, double-click its icon by the Attach heading. A warning dialog box may appear; my advice is to always save the attachment to disk; choose that option and click OK. Then use the Save Attachment As dialog box to save the file to a memorable place on your computer's hard drive.

An exception for attached files is graphics files. They appear as images below the message body itself. You don't have to do anything; the images just show up. (If not, the images sent aren't JPEG or GIF files.)

With the attachment saved, you can reply to or delete the message as you normally would.

- ✔ I save my attachments in the My Documents folder. After looking at them or examining their contents, I then shuffle them off to the proper folder.

- ✔ To save multiple attachments at one time, choose File➪Save Attachments. You can then use the Save Attachments dialog box to save them all at once to a folder on the hard drive.

- ✔ Even if Outlook Express displays graphics files directly in your message, you may still want to choose File➪Save Attachments to save them to disk.

- ✔ Do not open attachments you weren't expecting, especially program files — even if they're from people you know. Refer to the section "Fighting the Viral Plague" later in this chapter.

Sending an attachment in Outlook Express

 You attach a file in Outlook Express by — can you guess? — clicking the big paper clip Attach button in the New Message window. Yup, it's that easy.

Start by creating a new message or replying to a message. (Refer to Chapter 23 for the details.) When you're ready to attach a file, click the Attach button or choose Insert⇨File Attachment from the menu.

Use the Insert Attachment dialog box to find the file you want to attach. It works exactly like an Open or Browse dialog box. After finding and selecting the file, click the Attach button.

The file you attach appears on a new line in the New Message window, right below the Subject line.

To send the message and the file, click the Send button. And it's off on its merry way. . . .

- ✔ Sending a message with a file attached takes longer than sending a regular, text-only message.

- ✔ You should ensure that the recipient of a message can read the type of file you're sending. For example, sending a Word file to a WordPerfect user may not meet with the results you want.

- ✔ Note that some folks cannot receive large files. Sometimes, the limit is 5MB, but I have seen it as low as 1MB. The alternative? Burn a CD-R and send the file(s) through the regular mail. (Refer to Chapter 7 for information on burning CD-Rs.)

- ✔ Send JPEG or GIF pictures. Any other picture format is usually too large and makes the recipient wait a long time to receive the message.

Fighting the Viral Plague

Viruses and worms are nasty program you can get in your PC. They wreak havoc, often destroying data or an entire hard drive. Some merely proliferate by sending out e-mail that looks like you wrote it, but contains more copies of the virus and sends it to everyone in your Address Book. What a nightmare!

I could go on and on about viruses, but the key is to prevent them. You do that with third-party antivirus software. (No, Windows doesn't come with any antivirus software.) The program just about everyone uses is Norton AntiVirus (NAV), available from www.symantec.com. Other antivirus products are out there as well, such as McAfee VirusScan (www.mcafee.com), AVG (www.grisoft.com), and Kaspersky (www.kaspersky.com).

- ✔ A *virus* is a program that infects your computer, causing it to do harmful or unwanted things.

- ✔ A *worm* is a type of virus that infects your computer and then replicates itself, often by sending out copies of itself using your e-mail program.

- A *Trojan horse* program pretends to do one thing, but in fact is disguised as something else. For example, a program may claim to increase Internet speed when it really sends your accounting information to a computer in Albania.

- Most viruses come in the form of e-mail attachments. Do not open e-mail attachments you weren't expecting — even from people you know. Sometimes, the From part of the message is forged. Don't be tempted and open the message's attachment.

- E-mail viruses come in attachments with the filename extensions EXE, VBS, HTM, SCR, WSH, PIF, COM, and BAT.

- In addition to antivirus software, consider running antispyware software on your PC (refer to Chapter 24).

Part V
The Part of Tens

The 5th Wave   By Rich Tennant

"This is amazing. You can stop looking for Derek. According to a web search I did, he's hiding behind the dryer in the basement."

In this part . . .

Mankind just loves to make lists. It happens when kids discover that there is such a thing as a *favorite*. They first ask "Dad, what is your favorite movie?" Then they ask "Dad, what are your top 100 movies of all time?" Then they realize the importance of keeping the count to 10. Humans can easily make up 10 of anything. I suppose that that's thanks to our having 10 fingers. But, until we meet a species with 8 fingers and they rattle off things in lists of 8, we'll never know for certain.

Welcome to the traditional The Part of Tens, which caps every good *For Dummies* book. Here is where you'll find my list of tens for all sorts of helpful things to do, tips to remember, or stuff to avoid — in no particular order.

Chapter 27

Ten Common Beginner Mistakes

Sure, you can make a gazillion mistakes with a computer, whether it's deleting the wrong file or dropping the printer on your foot. But I have narrowed the list to ten. These are the day-to-day operating mistakes that people tend to repeat until they're told not to.

Not Properly Closing Windows

When you're done with Windows, shut it down. Choose the Turn Off Computer command from the Start panel, click the Turn Off button, and wait until your PC turns itself off.

✔ Don't just flip the power switch when you're done.

✔ Refer to Chapter 2 for detailed PC shutdown instructions.

Buying Too Much Software

Your PC probably came out of the box with dozens of programs preinstalled. (No, you're not required to use them; refer to Chapter 21, the section about uninstalling software.) Even with all that software preinstalled, don't overwhelm yourself by getting *more* software right away.

Buying too much software isn't really the sin here. The sin is buying too much software and trying to learn it all at once. The buy-it-all-at-once habit probably comes from buying music, where it's okay to lug home a whole stack of CDs from the store. You can listen to several CDs over the course of a few days. They're enjoyable the first time, and they age well. Software, on the other hand, is gruesome the first day and can take months to come to grips with.

Have mercy on yourself at the checkout counter and buy software at a moderate rate. Buy one package and figure out how to use it. Then move on and buy something else. You learn faster that way.

Buying Incompatible Hardware

Whoops! Did you forget to notice that the new keyboard you bought was for a Macintosh? Or maybe you thought that you were getting a deal on that USB modem, and, lo, your PC doesn't have a USB port. The biggest disappointment: You buy a new AGP expansion card, and all you have available are PCI slots.

Always check your hardware before you buy it! Especially if you're shopping online — if you're not sure that the hardware is compatible, phone the dealer and ask those folks specifically.

Not Buying Enough Supplies

Buy printer paper in those big boxes. You *will* run out. Buy extra floppy disks, Zip disks, CD-Rs, and whatever type of disks your PC's disk drives eat.

Not Saving Your Work

Whenever you're creating something blazingly original, choose the Save command and save your document to the hard disk. When you write something dumb that you're going to patch up later, choose the Save command too.

The idea is to choose Save whenever you think about it — hopefully, every few minutes or sooner.

You never know when your computer will meander off to watch television while you're hoping to finish the last few paragraphs of that report. Save your work as often as possible. And, always save it whenever you get up from your computer — even if it's just to grab a Fig Newton from the kitchen.

Not Backing Up Files

Saving work on a computer is a many-tiered process. First, save the work to your hard drive as you create it. Then, at the end of the day, back up your work to floppy or Zip disks. Always keep a safety copy somewhere because you never know.

At the end of the week (or monthly), run a backup program. I know that this process is a pain, but it's much more automated and easier to do than in years past. You can back up to Zip discs, but that's expensive; backing up to floppy disks is crazy; so use software such as Dantz Retrospect Backup to back up to your CD-R drive. You'll be thankful!

Opening or Deleting Unknown Things

Computers have both hardware and software rules about opening or deleting unknown items. On the software side, I have a rule:

If you didn't create the file, don't delete it.

Windows is brimming with unusual and unknown files. Don't mess with 'em. Don't delete them. Don't move them. Don't rename them. And, especially, don't open them to see what they are. Sometimes opening an unknown icon can lead to trouble.

On the hardware side, don't open anything attached to your PC unless you absolutely know what you're doing. Some hardware is meant to open. New console cases have pop-off and flip-top lids for easy access. They make upgrading things a snap. If you do open a console, remember to unplug it! It's okay to open your printer to undo a jam or install new ink or a toner cartridge. Even so, don't open the ink or toner cartridges.

Other hardware items have Do Not Open written all over them: the monitor, keyboard, and modem.

Booting from an Alien Disk

The number-one way to get a computer virus is to start your computer from a strange floppy disk. I'm not talking about starting the PC using a boot disk that you create or one that comes in a hermetically sealed software box. I'm talking about that — wink, wink — *game* Bob slipped you last week. You know the one. (Heh, heh.) Boot from that disk and you're inviting who-knows-what into your PC. Don't.

Replying to Spam E-Mail

Don't reply to any spam e-mail unless you want more spam. A popular trick is for spammers to put some text that says "Reply to this message if you do not want to receive any further messages." Don't! Replying to spam signals the spammers that they have a "live one," and you then get even more spam. Never, ever, reply to spam!

Opening a Program Attached to an E-Mail Message

You can receive photos via e-mail. You can receive sound files. You can receive any type of document. You can even receive zip file archives or compressed folders. These files are all okay to receive. But if you receive a program (EXE or COM) file or a Visual Basic Script (VBS) file, do not open it!

The only way to get a virus on a PC is to *run* an infected program file. You can receive the file okay. But if you open it, you're dead. My rule is "Don't open any EXE file you're sent through e-mail."

- Zip files (compressed folders) are okay to receive. You can open them and see what's in them. If they contain programs you're unsure of, just delete the whole deal. You're safe.

- If you have to send a program file through e-mail, write or phone the recipient in advance to let that person know it's coming.

- When in doubt, run antivirus software on the file before you run it.

- Some types of viruses can come in Microsoft Word documents. Antivirus software may catch these viruses, but in any case, confirm that the sender meant to send you the file before you open it.

Chapter 28

Ten Things Worth Buying
for Your PC

I'm not trying to sell you anything, and I'm pretty sure that you're not ready to burst out and spend, spend, spend on something like a new computer (unless it's someone else's money). But you may want to consider buying some nifty little things for Mr. Computer. Like ten things worth buying for a dog (a leash, cat-shaped squeeze toys, and a pooper scooper, for example), these ten things make working with the beast more enjoyable.

Software

Never neglect software. Jillions of different types of software programs are available, each of them designed to perform a specific task for a certain type of user. If you ever find yourself frustrated by the way your computer does something, consider looking for a piece of software that does it better.

Mouse Pad and Wrist Pad

If you have a mechanical (not optical) mouse, then you'll need a mouse pad upon which to roll it. Get one; the varieties are endless, plus the mouse pad ensures that there will be at least one tiny place on your desktop free of clutter for rolling the mouse around.

A *wrist pad* fits right below your keyboard and enables you to comfortably rest your wrists while you type. This product may help alleviate some repetitive-motion injuries that are common to keyboard users. And wrist pads come in many exciting colors, some of which may match your drapery.

Antiglare Screen

Tawdry as it may sound, an *antiglare screen* is nothing more than a nylon stocking stretched over the front of your monitor. Okay, they're *professional* nylons in fancy holders that adhere themselves to your screen. The result is no garish glare from the lights in the room or outside. An antiglare screen is such a good idea that some monitors come with them built-in.

Glare is the number-one cause of eyestrain while you're using a computer. Lights usually reflect in the glass, either from above or from a window. An antiglare screen cuts down on the reflections and makes the stuff on your monitor easier to see.

Some antiglare screens also incorporate antiradiation shielding. I'm serious: They provide protection from the harmful electromagnetic rays spewing out of your monitor even as you read this page! Is this necessary? No.

Keyboard Cover

If you're klutzy with a coffee cup or have small children or others with peanut-butter-smudged fingers using your keyboard, a keyboard cover is a great idea. You may have even seen one used in a department store: It covers the keyboard snugly, but still enables you to type. It's a great idea because, without a keyboard cover, all that disgusting gunk falls between the keys. Yech!

In the same vein, you can also buy a generic dust cover for your computer. This item preserves your computer's appearance, but has no other true value. Use a computer cover only when your computer is turned off (and

I don't recommend turning it off). If you put the cover on your PC while the PC is turned on, you create a minigreenhouse, and the computer — sometimes — melts. Nasty. This result doesn't happen to the keyboard, which is a cool character anyway.

More Memory

Any PC works better with more memory installed. The upper limit on some computers is well over 1GB of RAM, which seems ridiculous now, but who knows about five years from now? Still, upgrading your system to 512MB or 768MB of RAM is a good idea. Almost immediately, you notice the improvement in Windows and various graphics applications and games. Make someone else do the upgrading for you; you just buy the memory.

Larger, Faster Hard Drive

Hard drives fill up quickly. The first time, it's because you have kept lots of junk on your hard drive: games, things people give you, old files, and old programs you don't use any more. You can delete those or copy them to Zip discs for long-term storage. Then, after a time, your hard drive fills up again. The second time, it has stuff you really use. Argh! What can you delete?

The answer is to buy a larger hard drive. If you can, install a second hard drive and start filling it up. Otherwise, replace your first hard drive with a larger, faster model. Buying a faster model is a great way to improve the performance of any older PC without throwing it out entirely.

Ergonomic Keyboard

The traditional computer keyboard is based on the old typewriter keyboard (the IBM Selectric, by the way). Why? It doesn't have to be. No mechanics inside the keyboard require the keys to be laid out in a staggered or cascading style. Repetitive typing on this type of keyboard can lead to various ugly motion disorders (VUMDs).

To help you type more comfortably, you can get an ergonomic keyboard, such as the Microsoft Natural Keyboard. This type of keyboard arranges the keys in a manner that's comfortable for your hands, keeping everything lined up and not tweaked out, like on a regular computer keyboard.

Larger or LCD Monitor

Ever see a 19-inch computer monitor? How about the 21-inch model? They're *wonderful*. The 17-inch monitor you have was probably a good choice when you bought your computer. But check out the screen real estate on that larger monitor.

The nifty thing about Windows and buying a new monitor is that you don't have to toss out the old one. You can use *both* monitors at once. You need a second video adapter to drive the second monitor, but it's absolutely wonderful.

Refer to Chapter 12 for more information on dueling monitors.

USB Expansion Card

USB is the *thing* to have for expanding your PC. If your computer lacks a USB port, you can buy a USB expansion card.

My advice: Get a two-port USB PCI card. (Sorry about all the acronyms and jargon.) Two ports are enough to start. If you get more than two USB devices, you can either swap them out or just buy a USB hub to continue expanding your system. Refer to Chapter 9 for more USB information.

Scanner or Digital Camera

If you want the latest PC toy, buy a scanner or digital camera.

Scanners are wonderful if you enjoy graphics and want to send pictures over the Internet. Digital cameras are great toys, but they're expensive. And, they take some getting used to.

My advice: If you already have a nice camera and take lots of pictures, get a scanner. Wait for digital cameras to drop a bit in price before you make the investment. (Refer to Chapter 19 for more information on scanners and digital cameras.)

Chapter 29
Ten Tips from a PC Guru

I don't consider myself a computer expert or genius or guru, though many have called me all those names. I'm just a guy who understands how computers work. Or, better than that, I understand how computer people think. They may not be able to express an idea, but I can see what they mean and translate it into English for you. Given that, here are some final tips and suggestions before you and your PC go off on your merry way.

Remember That You Control the Computer

You bought the computer. You clean up after its messes. You feed it floppy disks when it asks for them. You control the computer, simple as that. Don't let that computer try to boss you around with its bizarre conversations and funny idiosyncrasies. It's really pretty dopey; the computer is an idiot.

If somebody shoved a flattened can of motor oil in your mouth, would you try to taste it? Of course not. But stick a flattened can of motor oil into a disk drive, and the computer will try to read information from it, thinking that it's a floppy disk. See? It's dumb.

You control that mindless computer just like you control an infant. You must treat it the same way, with respect and caring attention. Don't feel that the computer is bossing you around any more than you feel that a baby is bossing you around during 3 a.m. feedings. They're both helpless creatures, subject to your every whim. Be gentle. But be in charge.

Realize That Most Computer Nerds Love to Help Beginners

It's sad, but almost all computer nerds spend most of their waking hours in front of a computer. They know that it's kind of an oddball thing to do, but they can't help it.

Their guilty consciences are what usually make them happy to help beginners. By passing on knowledge, they can legitimize the hours they while away on their computer stools. Plus, it gives them a chance to brush up on a social skill that's slowly slipping away: the art of *talking* to a person.

- ✔ Always be grateful when you're given help.
- ✔ Beware of False Nerds. These people don't love computers, but went to some sort of school to learn a few by-rote tricks. They may not be helpful or know anything about computers other than what they're told. You can detect False Nerds because they lack the enthusiasm of the True Nerd, the one who helps you.

Get a UPS

The *Uninterruptible Power Supply (UPS)* is a boon to computing anywhere in the world where the power is less than reliable. Plug your console into the UPS. Plug your monitor into the UPS. If it has extra battery-backed-up sockets, plug your modem into the UPS as well.

- ✔ Refer to Chapter 2 for information on using a UPS as well as using a power strip.
- ✔ Using a UPS doesn't affect the performance of your PC. The computer couldn't care less whether it's plugged into the wall or a UPS.

Understand That Upgrading Software Isn't an Absolute Necessity

Just as the models on the cover of *Vogue* change their clothes each season (or maybe I should say "change their *fashions*" each season), software companies issue perpetual upgrades. Should you automatically buy the upgrade?

Of course not! If you're comfortable with your old software, you have no reason to buy the new version. None!

The software upgrade probably has a few new features in it (although you still haven't had a chance to check out all the features in the current version). And the upgrade probably has some new bugs in it too, making it crash in new and different ways. Feel free to look at the box, just as you stare at the ladies on the cover of *Vogue*. But don't feel obliged to buy something you don't need. (I apologize for all the parentheses.)

Don't Ever Reinstall Windows

A myth floating around the tech support sites says that the solution to all your ills is to reinstall Windows. Some suspect tech support people even claim that it's common for most Windows users to reinstall at least once a year. This is rubbish.

You *never* need to reinstall Windows. All problems are fixable. It's just that the so-called tech support people are lazy and resort to a drastic solution as opposed to trying to discover what the true problem is. If you press them, they *will* tell you what's wrong and how to fix it.

In all my years of using a computer, I have never reinstalled Windows or had to reformat my hard drive. Everything is fixable. Anyone who tells you otherwise is full of horse poop.

Refer to my book *Troubleshooting Your PC For Dummies* (Wiley Publishing, Inc.) for all the various solutions you can try instead of reformatting your hard dive or reinstalling Windows.

Perfectly Adjust Your Monitor

I don't have much explaining to do here. Keeping the monitor turned up too brightly is bad for your eyes, and it wears out your monitor more quickly.

To adjust a CRT monitor to pink perfection, turn the brightness (the button with the little sun) all the way up and adjust the contrast (the button with the half moon) until the display looks pleasing. Then turn the brightness down until you like what you see. That's it!

Unplug Your PC When You Upgrade Hardware

Newer PCs don't have a flippable on–off switch, like the older models do. When you open the case to upgrade or add an expansion card, your belly (if it's like my belly) may punch the power-on button, and, lo, you're working in a hazardous electrical environment. To prevent that, unplug the console before you open it for upgrading.

You don't need to unplug the console or even turn off the PC when you add a USB or Firewire device. (You do need to unplug it if you add a USB expansion card, however.)

Subscribe to a Computer Magazine

Oh, why not? Browse the stacks at your local coffeehouse-slash-music-store-slash-bookstore. Try to find a computer magazine that matches your tastes.

✔ One magazine that seems to be worthy for a computer beginner is *SmartComputing*. Look for it in a magazine stand near you.

✔ What sells me on a magazine are the columns and the *newsy* stuff they put up front.

✔ Some magazines are all ads. That can be great if you like ads, or it can be boring.

✔ Avoid the nerdier magazines, but I probably didn't need to tell you that.

Shun the Hype

The computer industry is rife with hype. Even if you subscribe to a family-oriented computer magazine, you still read about the latest this or the next-biggest-trend that. Ignore it!

My gauge for hype is whether the thing that's hyped is shipping as a standard part of a PC. I check the ads. If they're shipping the item, I write about it. Otherwise, it's a myth and may not happen. Avoid being lured by the hype.

- ✔ When hype becomes reality, you read about it in this book.

- ✔ Former hype I have successfully ignored: Pen Windows, push technology, Web channels, Shockwave, Microsoft Bob, Windows CE, and the tablet PC.

- ✔ Hype that eventually became reality: USB, CD-R, Zip drives, shopping on the Web (or *e-commerce*), DVD drives, digital cameras, and home networking.

Don't Take It So Seriously

Hey, simmer down. Computers aren't part of life. They're nothing more than mineral deposits and petroleum products. Close your eyes and take a few deep breaths. Listen to the ocean spray against the deck on the patio; listen to the gurgle of the marble Jacuzzi tub in the master bedroom.

Pretend that you're driving a convertible through a grove of sequoias on a sunny day with the wind whipping through your hair and curling over your ears. Pretend that you're lying on the deck under the sun as the Pacific Princess chugs south toward the islands with friendly, wide-eyed monkeys that eat coconut chunks from the palm of your hand.

You're up in a hot air balloon, swirling the first sip of champagne and feeling the bubbles explode atop your tongue. Ahead, to the far left, the castle's spire rises through the clouds, and you can smell Chef Meisterbrau's awaiting banquet.

Then slowly open your eyes. It's just a dumb computer. Really. Don't take it too seriously.

Index

Notes

Notes

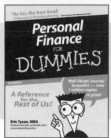

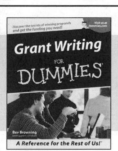

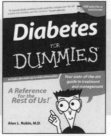

FOR DUMMIES®

A world of resources to help you grow

HOME, GARDEN & HOBBIES

0-7645-5295-3

0-7645-5130-2

0-7645-5106-X

Also available:

Auto Repair For Dummies
(0-7645-5089-6)

Chess For Dummies
(0-7645-5003-9)

Home Maintenance For
Dummies
(0-7645-5215-5)

Organizing For Dummies
(0-7645-5300-3)

Piano For Dummies
(0-7645-5105-1)

Poker For Dummies
(0-7645-5232-5)

Quilting For Dummies
(0-7645-5118-3)

Rock Guitar For Dummies
(0-7645-5356-9)

Roses For Dummies
(0-7645-5202-3)

Sewing For Dummies
(0-7645-5137-X)

FOOD & WINE

0-7645-5250-3

0-7645-5390-9

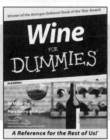

0-7645-5114-0

Also available:

Bartending For Dummies
(0-7645-5051-9)

Chinese Cooking For
Dummies
(0-7645-5247-3)

Christmas Cooking For
Dummies
(0-7645-5407-7)

Diabetes Cookbook For
Dummies
(0-7645-5230-9)

Grilling For Dummies
(0-7645-5076-4)

Low-Fat Cooking For
Dummies
(0-7645-5035-7)

Slow Cookers For Dummies
(0-7645-5240-6)

TRAVEL

0-7645-5453-0

0-7645-5438-7

0-7645-5448-4

Also available:

America's National Parks For
Dummies
(0-7645-6204-5)

Caribbean For Dummies
(0-7645-5445-X)

Cruise Vacations For
Dummies 2003
(0-7645-5459-X)

Europe For Dummies
(0-7645-5456-5)

Ireland For Dummies
(0-7645-6199-5)

France For Dummies
(0-7645-6292-4)

London For Dummies
(0-7645-5416-6)

Mexico's Beach Resorts For
Dummies
(0-7645-6262-2)

Paris For Dummies
(0-7645-5494-8)

RV Vacations For Dummies
(0-7645-5443-3)

Walt Disney World & Orlando
For Dummies
(0-7645-5444-1)

Available wherever books are sold. Go to www.dummies.com or call 1-877-762-2974 to order direct.

FOR DUMMIES®

Helping you expand your horizons and realize your potential

INTERNET

0-7645-0894-6

0-7645-1659-0

0-7645-1642-6

Also available:

America Online 7.0 For Dummies
(0-7645-1624-8)

Genealogy Online For Dummies
(0-7645-0807-5)

The Internet All-in-One Desk Reference For Dummies
(0-7645-1659-0)

Internet Explorer 6 For Dummies
(0-7645-1344-3)

The Internet For Dummies Quick Reference
(0-7645-1645-0)

Internet Privacy For Dummies
(0-7645-0846-6)

Researching Online For Dummies
(0-7645-0546-7)

Starting an Online Business For Dummies
(0-7645-1655-8)

DIGITAL MEDIA

0-7645-1664-7

0-7645-1675-2

0-7645-0806-7

Also available:

CD and DVD Recording For Dummies
(0-7645-1627-2)

Digital Photography All-in-One Desk Reference For Dummies
(0-7645-1800-3)

Digital Photography For Dummies Quick Reference
(0-7645-0750-8)

Home Recording for Musicians For Dummies
(0-7645-1634-5)

MP3 For Dummies
(0-7645-0858-X)

Paint Shop Pro "X" For Dummies
(0-7645-2440-2)

Photo Retouching & Restoration For Dummies
(0-7645-1662-0)

Scanners For Dummies
(0-7645-0783-4)

GRAPHICS

0-7645-0817-2

0-7645-1651-5

0-7645-0895-4

Also available:

Adobe Acrobat 5 PDF For Dummies
(0-7645-1652-3)

Fireworks 4 For Dummies
(0-7645-0804-0)

Illustrator 10 For Dummies
(0-7645-3636-2)

QuarkXPress 5 For Dummies
(0-7645-0643-9)

Visio 2000 For Dummies
(0-7645-0635-8)

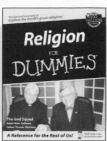
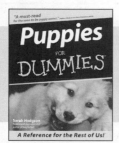

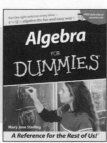

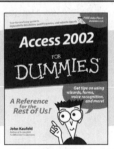